THE WISE ELDER:

Harvesting the Wisdom of Our Fathers and Grandfathers

Barry K. Weinhold, PhD

The Wise Elder:
Harvesting the Wisdom of Our Fathers and Grandfathers

CICRCL Press

4820 Topaz Drive
Colorado Springs, CO 80918
719445-0565
www.weinholds.org

Copyright © 2019
Barry K. Weinhold, PhD.

ISBN: 978-1-882056-29-3

CONTENTS

DEDICATION

TO BILL HENDERSON (1926–2016)

I am dedicating this book to the memory of Bill Henderson, one of the wisest elders I have ever met. Some years ago, I met Bill at a talk he gave at the Earth Fare Market in Asheville, North Carolinas. When I saw in the newspaper that Bill was going to speak about alternative cancer cures, it piqued my interest. I had a cancer scare earlier in my life and I had used alternative methods to rid myself of cancer. I was curious to find out if other alternative cures had been found since that time.

Bill spoke of his book *"Cancer-Free: Your Guide to Gentle, Non-toxic Healing"* that at that time contained over 100 alternative cancer cures all of which had research to prove that they had been effective. He told the audience why he wrote this book. He said, *"my wife died from the treatment of ovarian cancer not the disease itself."* He said that motivated him to do research on alternative cures for cancer that were gentle and non-toxic and led to the publication of his book. I ordered his book and read it with treat interest.

It was several years later when I next spoke with Bill. My 92-year-old Dad had been diagnosed with Stage-4 cancer of the esophagus and was given 3-6 months to live. The doctors convinced him to get radiation and chemo, but after just two doses, he got deathly sick from the treatment. He decided to stop all treatment, so I approached him to see if he was willing to do an alternative treatment that would be gentle and non-toxic.

He agreed and so I called Bill and told him the situation with my Dad. I asked him what alternative treatments he would recommend. He told me a he was not a physician and therefore could not recommend any treatments. However, he said, *"If I were 92 years old and had Stage-4 cancer of the esophagus, here is what I would do to treat my cancer."* He recommended Dr. Budwig's diet and a drink of cottage cheese and flax seed oil, as well as a protocol that involved an immune booster and several over-the-counter herbal remedies designed to keep the cancer from spreading.

My sister who lived around the corner from my widowed father, helped monitor the protocol he ended up using. After just several weeks on this alternative treatment, my father began to feel better. Because of the size of the tumor, he had been unable to eat solid food. He remarked to me that he loved liver and onions and it saddened him to not be able to eat his favorite meal.

After being on this alternative treatment protocol for about 8 weeks he felt well enough to fly down to North Carolina for a visit from Pennsylvania where he lived. The first thing I did was take him out to dinner for liver and onions. He was thrilled. During his visit we went to see Bill Henderson who told him that he was the oldest person Bill had worked with. We had a great visit with Bill and he told my Dad to keep using the protocol as a preventative measure.

After returning to Pennsylvania, my Dad went to see his cancer doctor who, using a scope, looked down his esophagus to see how big the tumor was. What he found was that the tumor was gone. He was shocked and did not know what had happened, so he told my Dad, *"It must have been the effects of the radiation and chemo we gave you."* My Dad tried to explain to the doctor about the alternative treatment he had been doing, but the doctor quickly dismissed that as the reason for his cure.

About 4 months later the doctor was still not convinced of this miraculous cure, that apparently he had never seen before, so he requested that my Dad get some additional tests at the local hospital. They kept him overnight and placed him in a double room with someone who was being treated for pneumonia. Well, my Dad caught pneumonia at the hospital and eventually died from the complications of pneumonia, not from cancer.

Sadly, Bill Henderson died at age 90 in 2016 from a combination of a heart attack, stroke and a pulmonary embolism, not cancer. Shortly before his death, Bill received a *"Lifetime Achievement Award"* as a *"Cancer Coach"* from The Truth About Cancer organization in Nashville, Tennessee. Since his death, his widow, Terry, has been carrying on his work and I get emails from her almost every day with some news of a new alternative cancer treatment that has been proven effective. You can get on her mailing list by contacting her at bill@beating-cancer-gently.com. I highly recommend that you connect with her and get regular up-to-date information about beating cancer gently.

I am deeply grateful to Bill Henderson for his wisdom and the help he provided for my Dad and perhaps thousands of others like him who found the traditional cancer industry lacking in gentle, non-toxic cures for cancer. He is missed, but not forgotten.

ACKNOWLEDGMENTS

Below is the biographical sketch of the wise elder contributors to this book. They are a very diverse group of men. I thank each and every one of you. I could not have written this book without your wise thoughts and ideas.

Robert F. Brown, 86. I was born in Bismarck, North Dakota; a Graduate of Notre Dame, sum laude; Master's degree, Notre Dame University; Graduate Ass't. Band Director Notre Dame 1960; I served as band director at six high schools and one college and was Principal of a Jr. High School. I retired in 2010, living in Colorado Springs with my son-in-law and daughter.

George Butte, 71. I am Professor of English & film studies at Colorado College, I live at 14. E. Cache la Poudre St., Colorado Springs 80903. Author of two books on narrative theory (Ohio State University Press 2004 and 2017); married, father of two. A Rhodes Scholar with advanced degrees from Oxford and Johns Hopkins.

Raphael Peter Engel, 75. Address: 3078 Turner Mtn. Wood Rd. - Charlottesville, VA 22903. I live in gratitude. I co-founded Asheville Playback Theater, playing back real life stories and co-founded Spirit in the Smokies story-magazine. I have trained in numerous life affirming relationship collaborations and produced numerous theatrical (*Global Playback Theatre*) and community events (*Unity in Diversity*). I value the quiet within.

Rafa Flores, 54. I was born and raised in South Texas. While in high school I worked in a hospital and saw death every day. This gave me insights into life that others don't have. I have done wildlife research in the U. S., Central America, South America and South Africa. Visiting many cultures has shaped my life.

Michael A. Harder, 59. I am a computer and legal professional with 40 years of experience holding advanced degrees in Computer Science, Law, International Taxation, Financial Services, and Electronic Commerce. I apply non-dualistic spiritual principles in corporate environments and lead several study groups including *A Course in Miracles*, *A Course of Love* and *Way of Mastery*.

Michael E. Holtby, LCSW, 73. Address: 2665 Xanthia Street, Denver, CO 80238. I was a licensed clinical social worker for 42 years. I had a parallel career as a commercial photographer after attending the Colorado Institute of Art in 1981-82. In my retirement from private practice 4 years ago my energies have shifted to international travel photography.

Byron Johnson, 85. I am a farm boy; Korean War Veteran; forty years' computer systems experience. Married & divorced three times, I am blessed with four children and two grandchildren. I have struggled my entire life to understand my relationship to God and others. I concluded *"We Are One"* and I continue to struggle to understand this.

Mark Joyous, 60. I am an author, entrepreneur and owner of Real Estate businesses; a Visionary Leader & Networker in Conscious Co-Evolutionary Movements including the *"Higher Vibes Tribes"*; lived & traveled worldwide. Current book is *"Flying the Earth Flag."* I am a Shaman-Sage aka the Cosmic Comedy Commando Clown & Scout for the Global Wagon Train.

Howard Kirstel, 74. I am a musician, song writer and composer of musicals. In addition to doing vocals, I play piano and guitar. I occasionally perform in plays & musicals. I am the owner of Red's Music, where I teach budding musicians. I am widowed and dealing with various health issues.

Larry M. Lawn, LPC, 66. Lakewood, Colorado. I am committed to showing spiritually minded, high achieving, professional employees feeling hopelessly stuck in their career, and desperately looking for deeper meaning, how to move forward with clarity and confidence. I have explored both eastern and western approaches to self-discovery, since age 20.

Troy Lee, MSW, 50. I was born in Colorado Springs; still live here with my wife and four children. BA from Colorado State University & MSW from Denver University. Spent 21 years counseling young men in the criminal justice system and in private practice. I enjoy lifting weights, reading, pondering life's deep mysteries, & medieval sword-fighting.

Michael Lightweaver, 70. Address: PO Box 18909 Asheville, North Carolina, 28814, USA. I am a clinical hypnotist and in 1980, I founded the Human Potential Institute in Nashville, TN. I created the Planetary Awakening Network and in 1995, I bought land adjacent to the national forest and created the Mountain Light Sanctuary where I currently host retreats and various events.

Aric Rohner, 56. So far in my life, I have been a US Air Force Officer, a long time Information Security Architect, and a business owner. I've been in long-term relationships with two wonderful people, and best of all, I'm finally learning what it means to be self-actualized.

Franz Schlink, 63. I was born in Bensheim, Germany; studied vocational counseling in Mannheim, Germany; since 1979, a vocational counselor for the German labor office; studied and trained in systemic family therapy and counseling; worldwide international consulting representing the German vocational counseling organization. Married to Cosima Schlink, with two daughters (Elisa, Celia) and one son (Martin).

Gary A. Scott. 61. I began writing about international investing in 1969, almost 50 years ago. I appeared on numerous TV and radio shows, including *"Market Rap"* and was a columnist for *"On Wall Street"*, a magazine for stock brokers. My daily newsletter (www.garyascott.com) looks at how to live with less stress in business and investing.

Richard Shulman, 67. I am a composer, keyboardist and recording artist. I create meditative, jazz and classical music to uplift listeners. I have performed at Carnegie Hall's Weil Recital Hall, the United Nations, numerous venues in North America and Europe, and I have created hundreds of Musical Soul Portraits. My 26 albums are available at RichHeartMusic.com.

Dean Tollefson, 86. Currently, I live in Colorado Springs, CO; and I previously lived in Manitou Springs, CO and Portland, OR. I am a retired university administrator and professor. I currently serve as a community chaplain with Community Ministers and I am free thinker.

Dave Wheeler, 60. Address: 3657 Temple St., Colorado Springs, CO 80910. I grew up in Colombia, South America with my missionary parents among the Siona people in southern Colombia. I have a Master's degree in Electrical Engineering from the University of Colorado at Colorado Springs, play the violin, love flying, reading, writing, public speaking, and am a lifelong student in the Rosicrucian Order, AMORC.

Lloyd G. Wright, 71. My address is 2218 East 25th Street, Tulsa, OK 74114. I am the Political/Policy Strategist and Press Secretary for the Mayor of Tulsa; former Network Affiliate News Director & Station Manager; Emmy Award winning Journalist; Oklahoma State University, BS, Journalism/Marketing; Cardiff University, UK, MA, International Journalism, Media and Cultural Studies. My career includes Real Estate Ownership & Management, Multi-Family Development, and teaching Journalism in MBA programs.

INTRODUCTION

I wrote this book partly because of my own family history. My parents were married young although neither of them finished high school and they had been out working for at least 5 years before they were married. They were neighbors. Their two families lived only a block apart. I was the first born male in the extended family on either side. This meant in the tradition of primogenitor from my German/Lutheran roots that I was to be the chosen one in the family. I was expected to shine, so the rest of the family would have status. I was also supposed to inherit the family fortune. Since there was no family fortune to inherit, I inherited the family dysfunctions instead.

When I was born, my 19-year-old mother freaked out when they showed me to her shortly after my birth. Apparently, they had not cleaned me up and I had dark hair all over my body, which is normal for some babies and they lose it in the first few months. She exclaimed, *"There must be some mistake, this is not my baby. He looks like a monkey."* I know this story is true because every time a family friend was pregnant, my mother would repeat this story with me standing by her side. She had no awareness of the deep impact this had on me and how I saw myself. I thought I was ugly.

Next, she was unable to produce milk and apparently felt like a failure, so she found a full-time baby sitter for me and went back to work a week after I was born. This led to a series of baby sitters and I was not doing well. I weighed 6 pounds at birth and at six weeks I weighed only five pounds. Today, I would have been regarded as a *"failure to thrive"* baby. According to what I learned later, my mother was checked out most of the time after I was born and my Dad was worried about her. I believe she was suffering from an undiagnosed post-partum depression or psychosis.

One night when I was about six weeks old, she was giving me a bath in our bathtub. She held my head above water with her hand behind my head. What happened next changed my life completely. Apparently, she may not have been paying close attention and she let my head go under water. She apparently was so checked out she didn't even notice what happened at first. My Dad who was watching her closely, intervened and probably saved my

1

life. In order to prevent anything like this from happening again, I was sent to live with my Dad's parents. I stayed there during the week when both my parents were working and they came and got me on weekends. In retrospect, this move probably saved my life. My grandmother and my Dad's younger siblings, my aunt and uncle, still lived at home and everybody took very good care of me.

This arrangement worked out okay, I guess, until I was about nine months old. One weekend, while staying at my parent's second floor apartment I was scooting round in my *"walker."* There was a gate at the top of a long steep set of stairs. However, this day my mother forgot to latch the gate and it was left wide open. So I fell down the whole flight of stairs in my walker and landed at the bottom with no apparent injuries. They did not even take me to a doctor to see if there were internal injuries that were not immediately visible.

I believe there were internal injuries and this is how I developed scoliosis in my lumber spine, a condition that has caused enormous discomfort all my life. Shortly after that, my grandmother, who owned a house that she rented out, allowed my parents to move there with me. The thought was it would be a safer place for me to be. I lived in that house until I left for college. My mother continued to work full time and hired a young Mennonite girl to take care of me full time. My first words were not *"momma,"* they were *"Emma"* the name of my nanny. I was likely more bonded to her than to my mother.

I have very fond memories of being at my grandparents' house many times while growing up. My grandfather, grandmother, aunt and uncle lived there and they played with me and gave me a lot of attention and some gifts from time to time as well. When I returned home and showed my mother the gifts I received, she usually got very angry at me. At the time this seemed so devastating to me and so after a while, I asked by relatives not to give me any gifts so I wouldn't have to deal with my mother's anger.

The good news in all this is that because of the great care I received from my extended family, I thrived despite my mother's dysfunction. I am eternally grateful that I had an extended family who could rescue me from a bad parenting situation. I consider it a divine blessing that I was able to spend so much time at my grandparent's house and get so much love and attention.

In addition to all the loving contact I had with my paternal grandmother, my paternal grandfather spent lots of time with me as a kid. When I was really little, he came over to our house every Sunday morning and held me on his lap while he read the *"funny papers"* to me. I remember we laughed and often I didn't understand the meaning of what he was reading, but when he laughed so did I. Later when I was older, he would come over on Sunday mornings and take me and my dog, Rex (an English Shepard) on a hike up Wenger's Hill in back of our house. When we reached the top, I could see all over the town where I grew up. It was the highlight of my week to be able to go for a hike with Grandpa Weinhold, which is what I called him.

Many children today are geographically separated from their grandparents or extended family and don't have the opportunities that I had to interact with their grandparents. Because of this very unique experience, I have always been interested in the role of grandparent in the lives on their grandchildren.

Because of these early childhood experiences with my grandparents, as an adult I wanted to *"give back,"* so I helped create a home visitation program for new parents in my community to help struggling families cope with the responsibilities of their first child. It is called the First Visitor Program and it involves trained volunteer home visitors helping these new families in any way possible to prevent child abuse and neglect. It has been in effect for over 20 years and has served the needs of thousands of young families.

WHAT IS THE REAL MEN SERIES?

This book is the third book in a series of four books that I call the *Real Men Series* to shine a light on hidden and underutilized parts of our modern world, particularly related to men. The first book in the series, *The Male Mother: The Missing Skill Set For Fathers,*[1] looks at the under-appreciated role of fathers in raising responsible children. The second book, *The Servant Leader: What the World Needs Now,*[2] presents a radically new approach to leadership at all levels.

Now The Wise Elder: Harvesting the Wisdom of Fathers and Grandfathers book looks at the over 114 million Americans age 50 or older, whose wisdom has largely have been ignored. As we become an even older population, this oversight will become even more critical to our future as a democratic republic.

The fourth book in the series that is still on the drawing board is tentatively titled, *The Open-Hearted Lover: Love Is All You Need.* It looks closely at how men and women and parents and children give and receive unconditional love. In this book, I look at the confusion people have about the topic of *"love,"* and how to better understand the role of love in mature relationships.

3

In all these books, I describe both the immature and mature feminine and masculine archetypes that are part of the personalities of both men and women. Mostly because the feminine archetypes have been largely ignored in men by our mainstream culture, these books focus on the more hidden mature feminine archetypes in men. Carl Jung discovered archetypes and defined them as collectively unconscious ideas, patterns of thought, images, etc., universally present in individual personalities. There are four main immature and mature archetypes in the personalities of both men and women. Below is a comparison of the mature and immature masculine and feminine archetypes in men:[3]

Table 0-1. The Mature and Immature Masculine Archetypes

Mature Masculine Archetypes	Immature Masculine Archetypes
The King (the energy of just and creative ordering)	The Tyrant & The Weakling
The Divine Child (the emerging mature archetype)	The High Chair Tyrant & The Weakling Prince
The Warrior (the energy of self-disciplined, aggressive action)	The Sadist & The Masochist
The Hero (the emerging mature archetype)	The Grandstander, The Bully & The Coward
The Magician (the energy of initiation and transformation)	The Detached Manipulator &
The Denying Innocent One	Affects speech areas of the brain, blocking the ability to talk about a traumatic state while in it. Because the connections between the amygdala and the language areas of the pre-frontal cortex are not well developed it is difficult to use talk therapy to heal developmental traumas.
The Precocious Child (the emerging mature archetype)	The Know-It-All, The Trickster & The Dummy
The Lover (the energy that connects men to others and to the world)	The Addicted Lover & The Impotent Lover
The Oedipal Child (the emerging mature archetype)	Mama's Boy & The Peter Pan Complex

Table 0-2. The Mature and Immature Feminine Archetypes

Mature Feminine Archetypes	Immature Feminine Archetypes
The Servant Leader	The Controlling Boss, Micromanager, The Bureaucrat
The Male Mother	The Consuming Mother, The Rejecting Father, The Martyr
The Wise Elder	The Narcissist, The Rescuer, The Embezzler
The Open-Hearted Lover	Pick-Up-Artist, Pedophile, the Impotent Lover

From this list is easy to see that the immature masculine and feminine archetypes are the most visible and predominate ones in our modern society. These books look at what would our modern society look like if we had more men and women who had balanced and integrated their inner masculine and feminine archetypes. What would our country look like if we had more *"male mothers," "servant leaders," "wise elders"* or *"open-hearted lovers.?"* In that regard, this book like the other books in this series, is a visionary book that describes a future that is significantly different from one we presently have. I believe if we can vision a different future, then we are halfway there.

Yes, there are a few wise elders present today. I think of some of the people who I consider as my wise elders. They are people like Robert Bly, James Hillman, Michael Meade, Bill McKibben, Lester Brown, Amory Lovins, Robert Redford, Robert Kennedy, Jr., Michael Moore, Ralph Nader, Jimmy Carter, Noam Chomsky, Richard Wolff, Ervin Laslo, Bill Moyers, John Lewis, and Paul Krugman. However, I contend that in addition to these highly visible wise elders, there are millions of invisible wise elders that have important wisdom to pass on.

Early in the book, I describe the contributions of some of the greatest wise elders in our recorded history. I also look at the nine cultures that still celebrate their elders and what effects that has on their culture. This also raises questions about how and why we came to not honor our elders.

WHAT ABOUT THE BABY BOOMERS?

We have an aging population with the Baby Boomers all now being considered elders (50 and over). Here are some statistics that tell us what Boomers contribute to our country:[4]

- 65 percent of plan to work beyond age 65.
- 67 percent say that adult children have a responsibility to provide financial help to elderly parents in need while 84 percent of millennials also believe this.
- 90 percent are married.
- They are most likely to hold the highest paying jobs.
- 65 percent of Boomers feel they suffer from age discrimination.
- 53 percent of Boomers say that men make better leaders than women.
- Boomers are twice as likely to start a new business compared to millennials.
- 45 percent of Boomers consider themselves as entrepreneurs.
- Boomers represent 44 percent of the US population and in the next five years are projected to hold 70 percent of the disposal income in the US and purchase 49 percent of the total consumer products.
- Over the next 20 years, spending by Boomers is expected to increase by 58 percent to $4.74 trillion.
- Boomers will inherit $15 trillion in the next 20 years.
- Boomers own 80 percent of all the money in savings and loan associations.
- 66 percent of Boomers say that preserving Social Security and Medicare is more important than reducing the deficit.

WHAT ARE THE CORE VALUES OF BABY BOOMERS?

The core values of Baby Boomers tell you even more about their potential as wise elders:[5]

- They have a strong work ethic. They are not afraid on putting in a hard day of work.
- They are self-assured. They are independent thinkers and doers.
- They are highly competitive. They like and are used to competition.
- They respond more to intrinsic rather than extrinsic motivation. Self-improvement and personal growth are very important to them.
- They are goal-centric. They like challenges and to set goals and achieve them.
- They are resourceful. They know how to get things done.
- They are mentally focused. They have amazingly long attention spans that enables them to stay on track.

- They are team oriented. They carry a strong value of community and thrive in team environments in person or online.
- They are disciplined. They like structure. Give them the instructions to follow and turn them loose on a project. They will find a way to get it done.

These are qualities that are very important in a wise elder. Boomers make excellent wise elders, if given the chance. The biggest challenge is to help them discover what they can contribute to the next generation. When I contacted men I considered to be wise elders to ask them to contribute to my book, many of them mentioned that they didn't see themselves as wise elders. Several said, *"I am too busy to even consider whether or not I am a wise elder."* Others seemed to be very humble and didn't see themselves as wise.

WHY ARE BABY BOOMERS UNIQUELY QUALIFIED TO BE WISE ELDERS?

Here are some other reasons why Baby Boomers make good wise elders:[6] They are the main consumers in our country and they also volunteer more than any other age group. Many organizations would be hard pressed to function without their older volunteers. They have a *"service to others"* orientation.

- They give generously. They make more charitable donations per capita than any other age group.
- They baby sit and often are primary caregivers for their grandchildren.
- They also care for spouses and friends.

This book contains the wisdom of 18 of these men. You can judge for yourself, whether or not what they have contributed is important wisdom. I believe it is or I would not have included their contributions in this book. I asked these contributors to respond to three different scenarios:

1. Write a short description how you have taken some deliberate action in your life related to one or more of the 17 items on the attached list of *"What Wise Elders Want"* (1-2 pages max). Ex: *"I volunteered at the Domestic Violence Center and here is what I learned."*

2. Write a short narrative about a meaningful mentoring experiences you had with a younger man. It can be one of your children, a friend, a stranger, or someone who you worked with as a volunteer (1-2 pages max).

3. Based on your life experiences, what words of wisdom would you like to pass on to younger men. Maybe this is the advice you wished you had gotten at age 25.

Aging in itself brings challenges to everyone. If you are lucky enough to live beyond retirement age and are still vital, you are faced with the question: *"What I am I going to do with the rest of my life?"*[7]

WHAT ARE SOME OF THE NEGATIVE STEREOTYPES ABOUT OLDER PEOPLE?

Most people are often too busy to plan for this part of their life and wait until it arrives to think about what they want to do next. Some envision doing lots of leisurely and recreational things and after a while they may get bored. Many people don't plan their retirement ahead of time. They wait to see what pulls them and often it is a struggle to make plans at this time of life. Added to that are the negative stereotypes that people carry around about old people.

Granted, the negative stereotypes are much more common than positive images. Researchers have concluded that *"Our negative attitudes towards aging blind us to the fact that millions of people in their 60's, 70's 80's and beyond are robust, active, functional, experienced, capable and talented and they want to remain engaged and contributing. However, we have not created the social structures, roles and institutions to capitalize on that harness these capabilities to the overall benefit of our culture."* The only encouraging thing that I have noticed is the number of commercials lately that show a father with his infant or young child or children. This is the counter to the negative stereotypes of men not being part of raising their children. Some even show grandfathers playing with their grandchildren.

There was a landmark study done in the 1970s that looked at what was the best form of motivation for nursing home residents. One group pf residents were told that they could arrange their room furnishings any way they wanted, to choose what nights they wanted to attend a movie and which house plants they wanted in their room.

The second group of residents were told that the staff was there to do *"everything we can to you help you."* They had their furniture arranged for them, were informed which movie nights were assigned to them and were give a house plant to be cared for by a nurse. After three weeks, the first group of residents experienced significant improvement in physical and mental well-being whereas the members of the second group declined or remained the same. They conducted a follow-up study 18 months later and found that members of the disempowered group were twice as likely to die when compared to the empowered group.

There is scientific evidence that the key to successful aging is to feel that you have contributed to leaving the world a better place than you found it. Many aging volunteers are given meaningless tasks to perform, like licking stamps. They get very little satisfaction from volunteering in these situations.

A recent story in *The New York Times* highlighted the invisibility and marginalization older people experience. They concluded that *"such indignities seem to happen to almost everyone with grey hair or a few wrinkles and at every sort of place. Store clerks, bank tellers, government workers, pharmacists, hairdressers, nurses, receptionists and doctors alike ignore the older person and pay attention exclusively to a younger companion, regardless of who is the actual customer or patient."*[8]

It is hard under this daily barrage of negative experiences to feel good about yourself as an aging person. In a study at Yale they found that older adults who held more positive age beliefs lived 7.5 years longer than peers who held negative age-related beliefs. Recent research shows, however, the positive plasticity of our brain means that aging uses biology, behavior and culture, to constantly reshape the development of our lives into our oldest ages.

WHAT IS THE DIFFERENCE BETWEEN A WISE ELDER AND AN OLD MAN?

Good question, *"What is the difference between as wise elder and an old man?"* My definition of a wise elder is someone who lives an authentic life, shows up and knows what they want and how to get it. They are wise because they have been able to connect the dots in their lives and learn from all their life experiences. They are self-aware and able to self-correct. They also have spent some quality time considering their mortality.

By contrast, an old man is basically just waiting to die. They are not very self-aware and most of what they do is try to stay in their comfort zone. They do not like change or uncertainty. They silently worry about their future and often worry about their children and other loved ones. Henry David Thoreau summed up this picture in his famous quote, *"The mass of men lead lives of quiet desperation."* Thoreau believed that misplaced values was the cause of this condition: people feel a void in their lives, and they attempt to fill it with things like money, possessions, and accolades. Then when they get old they have regrets about how they spent their time. I never heard anyone on their death bed complain that they didn't spend more time at the office.

Currently, we have way too many *"old men"* and too few wise elders. That is the main purpose why I am writing this book. I want to inspire old men to become wise elders and I want to challenge our society to reach out to our elderly men and do things with them that help them develop their wise elder archetype and cast aside their old man archetype. I also believe that men have to take charge of their lives and create more purposeful activities in their twilight years. They can't just wait for society to change and instead they have to help it change.

Michael Meade defines an elder as follows: *"Elders, by tribal imagination, and by more recent definition, are those who have learned from their own lives, those who have extracted a knowledge of themselves and the world from their own lives. We know that a person can age and still be very infantile. This happens if a person doesn't open and understand the nature of his or her own life and the kind of surprising spirit that inhabits him or her."*[9]

WHAT DO WISE ELDERS WANT?

Here is my list that I compiled from various sources:

1. End fighting wars. We are tired of fighting and competing with everyone.
2. Come home to love, to be with family, friends, and community.
3. We want to help others.
4. We want to share our lives with others. We want to tell our stories and offer our wisdom, humor and experiences for the sheer joy of sharing this great adventure of life.
5. We want forgiveness. We know we have made mistakes and may have hurt others. We deeply regret these things we caused and now ask for forgiveness. We also have to forgive ourselves.
6. We want to matter to others. We want to know we are needed and included, not just looked after.
7. We want to stay involved. We love life and now have time to truly enjoy the things that enrich our lives.
8. We want passion. Filled with love and meaningful work. We know our gifts are born from passions still inside ourselves and we want to express them.
9. We want to have fun.

10. We want to be seen as unique individuals. We are not all alike and resist labels.
11. We want to keep learning new things.
12. We want to find meaning in life.
13. We want physical connections and experiences. Hugs, making love, exercise, sports and being in nature are as important as ever.
14. We want to stay as independent as possible.
15. We want to prepare for death in a conscious manner.
16. We want to awaken our spiritual comprehension of life.
17. We want our culture to wake up from the incessant drumbeat of fear, competition and war.

By default, an old man is someone who has not taken good care of himself and lacks self-reflection and self-understanding. These men may have bought the myth of the American dream and fail to achieve it as they had hoped for and now as they look back on their life are left with broken dreams and a cynical view of themselves other people and the world they see. They are often lost souls who don't see any opportunity to improve their lives and can only wait to die.

In Chapter Four of the book, I expand on the things that wise elders want and include the wisdom of the contributors to this book. In Chapter Six I discuss the challenges that men have to face if they want to be considered as wise elders. Here is a list of some of these challenges:

THE CHALLENGES THAT MEN FACE IF THEY WANT TO BE A WISE ELDER.

Again, here is a list of challenges that I compiled from various sources.

1. Don't repeat the past. Look at how the past is influencing the present and determining the future.
2. Don't go to sleep. Be aware of what is happening to you and learn something new every day.
3. Get in touch w/ your true self w/o judgment.
4. Remember, being self-sufficient is not necessarily growth.
5. Eliminate all self-hatred.
6. Open yourself to love however it appears in your life.
7. Strive to understand the meaning and purpose of living, dying and death.
8. Resist all illusions and addictions that help you stay in denial.

9. Face any fears and depressions related to these illusions or addictions.
10. Prepare to let go of your attachments to material security.
11. Surrender the need to be perfect.
12. Maintain a healthy sense of humor and a Positive Mental Attitude.
13. Be humble, perceptive and plan well.
14. Give up your warrior motives and actions. Become an inner warrior.
15. Be patient with yourself and others.
16. Understand and be open to receive the many gifts of aging.
17. Find peace and forgiveness with your family and community.
18. Experience the sacred nature of all life.

Another important task of wise elders is to mentor young men so that these young men can learn life's lessons without undue stress. Chapter Five contains stories of how the wise elder contributors to this book have mentored young men.

I also considered the physical and mental health of wise elders. It is hard to reach out to others if you are suffering from a degenerative disease or a mental health problem that often comes with aging, like depression and dementia. In Chapter Seven, I describe some ways that wise elders can maintain high quality wellness rather than low-level sickness.

The rest of the book describes the personal/psychological and social/cultural barriers to becoming a wise elder that exist in our modern world and the strategies on how to overcome these barriers. One of my wise elder contributors (**Aric Rohner**) who is into marketing, said that the main reason wise elders are not seen or heard is a *"marketing problem."*

Aric wrote the following: *"Popular opinion suggests that the fate of our Elders is to be isolated and lonely victims of circumstances — doomed to declining health, poor mental capacity, and irrelevance — who will finally die alone, forgotten, and meaningless. But I'd like to suggest that what we actually have here is faulty expectations, a failure of responsibility and imagination, and a marketing problem.*

"We are the ones who know what we know. It's silly to expect other people to know what they don't know. And it's even sillier to expect them first to value what they don't know about us and then expect them to take action to search for it, particularly since they would have a massive "needle in a haystack" problem. There are millions of elders. Which of them would be willing, available, and be a good match?

"If we want to be useful, it is our own responsibility to become useful. If we want not to be lonely, it is our responsibility to connect. In our wisdom, let's band together and figure out how to do this. There are even some working examples out there. For example, there are institutions like the Service Corps of Retired Executives (SCORE), whose members counsel business owners and aspiring entrepreneurs.

"And then, once we've figured out some value we can provide, it is up to us to get the word out. If nobody knows about the value we can provide, then they can't find us to get it. That's where good old internet marketing techniques come into play. And even if we don't have the skills to do the marketing ourselves, we can certainly find people (perhaps other elders) who do have these skills. Let's not play the victim here. It's not pretty and it doesn't work."

Finally, the last chapter of the book presents a vision of what I and others believe our world would look like if we honored and valued the wisdom of our elders. I believe as our population grows older, this vison will have to become a reality.

I hope by reading this book, regardless of what age you are, you are inspired to do something to help recognize the contributions of the wise elders in your life. They are everywhere and I am sure you have either encountered some in your life, can claim to be one of them, or both.

WHAT IS THE STORY OF THE IDIOT AND THE WISE MAN?[10]

The following story illustrates how a wise man used his wisdom to help a young man who others in his village labelled as *"an idiot."* *"In a village a man, a young man, is called an idiot by everybody. From his very childhood he has heard that, that he is an idiot. And when so many people are saying it — his father, his mother, his uncles, the neighbors, and everybody — of course he starts believing that he must be an idiot. How can so many people be wrong? — and they are all important people. But when he becomes older and this continues, he becomes an absolutely sealed idiot; there is no way to get out of it. He tried hard but whatsoever he did was thought to be idiotic.*

"That is very human. Once a man goes mad he may become normal again, but nobody is going to take him as normal. He may do something normal but you will suspect that there must be something insane about it. And your suspicion will make him hesitant and his hesitancy will make you suspicion stronger; then there is a vicious circle. So that man tried in every possible way to

look wise, to do wise things, but whatsoever he did people would always say it was idiotic.

"A wise old man was passing by. He went to the wise old man in the night when there was nobody about and asked him, "Just help me to get out of this locked state. I am sealed in. They don't let me out; they have not left any window or door open so that I can jump out. And whatsoever I do, even if it is exactly the same as they do, still I am called an idiot. What should I do?"

"The wise elder says, 'You idiot, prove it! What is beautiful there? I don't see any beauty. You prove it.' If somebody says, 'Look at that beautiful rose flower,' catch hold of him and say to him, 'Prove it! What grounds have you to call this ordinary flower beautiful? There have been millions of rose flowers. There are millions, there will be millions in the future; what special thing has this rose flower got? And what are your fundamental reasons which prove logically that this rose flower is beautiful?'

"If somebody says, 'This book of Leo Tolstoy is very beautiful,' just catch hold of him and ask him, 'Prove where it is beautiful; what is beautiful in it? It is just an ordinary story — just the same story which has been told millions of times, just the same triangle in every story: either two men and one woman or two women and one man, but the same triangle. All love stories are triangles. So what is new in it?' The man said, 'That's right.'

"The wise man said, 'Don't miss any chance, because nobody can prove these things; they are unprovable. And when they cannot prove it, they will look idiotic and they will stop calling you an idiot. Next time, when I return, just give me the information how things are going.'

"And the next time, when the wise old man came back, even before he could meet the old idiot, people of the village informed him that, 'A miracle has happened. We had an idiot in our town; and now he has become the wisest man. We would like you to meet him.'

"And the Wise elder knew who that 'wisest man' was. He said, 'I would certainly love to see him. In fact, I was hoping to meet him.'

"The wise man was taken to the idiot and the idiot said, 'You are a miracle-worker, a miracle man. The trick worked! I simply started calling everyone an idiot, stupid. Somebody would be talking of love, somebody would be talking of beauty, somebody would be talking of art, painting, sculpture, and my standpoint was the same: 'Prove it!' And because they could not prove it, they looked idiotic.

"And it is a strange thing. I was never hoping to gain this much out of it. All that I wanted was to be able to get out of that confined idiocy. It is strange that

now I am no longer considered an idiot, I have become the wisest man, and yet I know I am the same person— and you know it too.

"But the wise elder said, 'Never tell this secret to anybody else. Keep the secret to yourself. Do you think I am wise? Yes, the secret is between us. This is how I became a wise man. This is how you have become a wise man.' This is how things go on in the world. Once you ask, 'What is the meaning of life?' you have asked the wrong question. And obviously somebody will say, 'this is the meaning of life' — and it cannot be proved."

FOR WHOM IS THIS BOOK WRITTEN?

This book is written primarily for men of any age and women who are interested in relating to men. There is a parallel process that exists for women, but since thus book is part of a four book series called the Real Men Series, I decided to focus on male Wise Elders. I believe that young men who hunger for the wisdom of wise elders in their life will learn much from reading this book. In addition, older men who have not yet decided to consciously become wise elders, will receive much encouragement by reading this book.

I may at a later date write a similar book primarily for women. The equivalent mature masculine and feminine archetypes in women to the Wise Elder is often called the Crone or the Earth Healer.

CHAPTER ONE

WHAT ARE SOME OF THE CONTRIBUTIONS OF WISE ELDERS THROUGHOUT HISTORY?

Genetically speaking, we are no smarter or heartier than our relatives were 10,000 years ago. Nonetheless, in practical terms, we are more biologically fit than our great-grandparents.

—Laura L. Carstensen

How have wise elders been treated throughout our history? The short answer is *"much better"* than they are today. From a biological perspective, before the 20th century the life expectancy rates were usually below 60 years. Although a few people lived into their 70s, most people died in their 40s. Nobody expected the rapid increase in life expectancy that we are seeing today. But, it may not even be close to our potential, that is documented in many ancient texts and by biological markers. Throughout history, old age was either seen as a source of wisdom and prestige or as a stage of life were most people lost many of their normal mental and physical functions and suffered a lot.

WHAT HAPPENED IN ANCIENT TIMES?

There are reports from ancient times of people living for hundreds of years. We learned in the Old Testament that Adam supposedly lived to be 960 years old. However, in the Bible, we see a progressive decline over the generations after Adam's 930-year life span, to Noah's 500 years, to Abraham's 175 years.

In ancient China, super-centenarians were apparently commonplace, according to many texts. Joseph P. Hou, Ph.D., a Chinese acupuncturist, wrote in his book *Healthy Longevity Techniques*. He writes, *"According to Chinese medical records, a doctor named Cuie Wenze of the Qin dynasty lived to be 300 years old. Gee Yule of the later Han dynasty lived to be 280 years old. A high ranking Taoist master monk, Hui Zhao, lived to be 290 years old and Lo Zichange lived to be 180 years old. As recorded in The Chinese Encyclopedia of Materia Medica, He Nengci of the Tang dynasty lived to be 168 years old. A Taoist master, Li Qingyuan, lived to be 250 years old. In modern times, a traditional Chinese medicine doctor, Lo Mingshan of Sichuan province, lived to be 124 years old."*[11]

Dr. Hou in his book, said that the Eastern key to longevity is *"nourishing life,"* including not only physical nourishment, but also mental and spiritual nourishment. The mentions the Shahnameh or Shahnama (*"The Book of Kings"*) a Persian epic poem written by Ferdowsi around the end of the 10th century A.D. It tells of kings reigning 1,000 years, several hundred years, down to 150 years, and so on.

WHAT ARE SOME MODERN CLAIMS OF LONGEVITY?

Even today, people report lifespans of some 150 or more years. These reports often come from rural areas, however, where documentation is scant. Documentation was probably even less valued in rural communities more than a century ago, making it harder to prove any of these claims.

One example is that of Bir Narayan Chaudhary in Nepal. In 1996, Vijay Jung Thapa visited Chaudhary in Tharu village of Aamjhoki in the Tarai region. Chaudhary told him he was 141 years old, Thapa wrote in an article for *India Today*. If this claim was true, Chaudhary trumped the Guinness World Record holder for the longest life ever recorded by almost 20 years.

But Chaudhary didn't have the papers to prove it. He did, however, have collective village memory. *"Almost all the elders around remember their youth when Chaudhary (already an elder) would talk about working in the first Nepal survey of 1888,"* Thapa wrote. *"Village logic goes that he must have been more than 21 then, since the survey was a responsible job. Chaudhary claims to have been 33 and still a stubborn bachelor."*[12]

Many people in the Caucasus region of Russia similarly claim ages reaching even over 170 years without the documentation to back their claims.

Dr. Hou wrote: *"These exceptionally long-lived people have invariably lived humble lives, doing hard physical work or exercise, often outdoors, from youth well into old age. Their diet is simple, as is their social life involving families. One example is Shisali Mislinlow who lived to be 170 years old and gardened in the Azerbaijan region in Russia. Mislinlow's life was never hurried.*

He said, 'I am never in a hurry, so don't be in a hurry to live, this is the main idea. I have been doing physical labor for 150 years.'" [13]

IS IT A MATTER OF FAITH?

The issue of longevity in ancient times has long been connected to Taoist practices in China of internal alchemy, or mind-body cultivation. In that culture longevity was connected with virtue.

Mendez quoted first century Roman-Jewish historian Titus Flavius Josephus who wrote: *"Now when Noah had lived three hundred and fifty years after the Flood ... But let no one, upon comparing the lives of the ancients with our lives, and with the few years which we now live, think that what we have said of them is false; or make the shortness of our lives at present an argument, that neither did they attain to so long a duration of life, for those ancients were beloved of God, and [lately] made by God himself; and because their food was then fitter for the prolongation of life, might well live so great a number of years and besides, God afforded them a longer time of life on account of their virtue, and the good use they made of it."*

For now, modern scientists are left either to believe what ancient records and village memory have to say about seemingly unbelievable lifespans, or to consider the accounts just exaggerations, symbolism, or misunderstandings. For many, it's simply a matter of faith. Some say it's due to misunderstandings in the translation process, or that the numbers have symbolic meaning— but against the many explanations are also counterarguments that leave the historian wondering whether the human lifespan has actually decreased so significantly over thousands of years.

For example, one explanation is that in the ancient Near East the understanding of a year was different from our concept of a year today. They speculated that a year meant an orbit of the moon (a month) instead of an orbit of the sun (12 months). But if we follow that logic, while it brings the age of the biblical figure Adam down from 930 to a more reasonable 77 at the time of his death, it also means he would have fathered his son Seth at the age of 11. And Enoch would have only been 5 years old when he fathered Methuselah. Similar inconsistencies arise when we adjust the year figures to represent seasons instead of solar orbits. This theory just does not hold up. [14]

HOW DOES OUR BIOLOGICAL CLOCK PREDICT OUR LIFESPAN?

There is a rule in biology that the average life span of a species can be determined by multiplying the time from birth until the species is able to reproduce itself multiplied by 20 times. This would make the average life span of the human species at about 200-250 years. While this ratio applies to all other species, but why does it not apply to the human species? No one knows. Perhaps it is the stress that most human experience in their lives that lowers their life expectancy.

HOW DID OTHER CULTURES THROUGHOUT HISTORY TREAT THE ELDERLY?

Below is a summary of how other cultures regarded the elderly throughout history. As you will learn, it is an uneven matter.[15]

How Did the Classical Greek Culture Treat the Elderly? In the classical Greek culture, old age was regarded as a stage of decline, while beauty, strength and youth were more valued. Particularly, the residents of Athens did not like older people and often rebelled against them.

How Did Older People Fare During Medieval and Renaissance Times? Neither of these time periods held positive views of the elderly. Older people were often depicted as being cruel or weak. There was some mixture, however, between respecting or despising them.

Sir Thomas Moore, who wrote during the 16th century, envisioned a world where old people could actually choose to suffer or die with dignity.

What About Eastern Thought? Many Eastern cultures, particularly those under the influence of Taoism and Confucianism, valued the elderly. As was described above, Taoist teachers taught people ways to extend their lives and live long and vital lives. Japan has traditionally honored it elderly population for hundreds of years.

How Were Elders Treated in Mediterranean and Latin Cultures? The elderly was treated with much respect in these cultures. They also made practical use of the elderly to care for the youngest members of their families. The importance of the extended family was emphasized.

How Have Elders Been Treated in Our Modern World? Unfortunately, elders are not treated very well in our modern world. As people live longer they often become financial burdens to their children, particularly if they can no longer live independently. The most common term for this disrespect of the elderly is *"ageism."* The focus is generally on youth, self-reliance and individualism. However, there is a recent shift in our attitudes toward elders.

For example, there is a growing interest in protecting our elders. In 2011 the U.N. proposed a human rights initiative designed to protect the elderly. As we have a much older population, these attitudes are beginning to change. Their grey hairs and stiff joints do not prevent our elders from being a rock-solid foundation of our society. The vast experience and wisdom that grows out of those experiences can serve as a beacon for younger generations. It is important to note that children from all cultural backgrounds are willing to take care of their elderly parents out of love, respect and a strong sense of duty.

ARE WE MOVING TOWARD AN AGE INCLUSIVE SOCIETY?

While there are still a significant number of the elderly living in poverty in this country, we have made great strides towards reducing poverty among our aging population. Here are some ideas of how that might develop:

- Local, state and federal policies that support older adults living independently as long as they can. Housing and utilities rebates or grants can help reduce the cost of living in place.
- Many organizations such as Silver Key, AARP, Meals On Wheels, Senior Centers and others provide supportive services to the elderly so they can live independently. Restaurants and retail stores also offer discounted meals and products. Even travel has been made less stressful for older travelers by having separate TSA check-through lines for them. They don't even have to take off their shoes to go through the screening.
- Reduced fees for public transportation can help to keep living costs down.
- Senior Extended Care facilities are increasing and enabling those who can afford it to live in place there.
- Nursing homes have also have recognized the need to mobilize their patients and not treat them like disabled people.

WHAT ARE THE EFFECTS OF PARENTS LIVING WITH THEIR CHILDREN?

Another part of the creation of an *Age Inclusive Society* is the fact that many aging parents are living with their children. A recent survey found that over 20 percent to adult children wanted their parent to live with them. Also, they found that one in four adult caregivers live with an elderly or disabled parent. This arrangement can produce problems and it can produce opportunities for important and regular contact between grandparents and grandchildren.

Interestingly, in my father's family and my mother's family it was considered an obligation for children to bring their aged parents into their home rather than sending them to an assisted living home or a nursing home. In my father's family, his sister was the one was *"selected"* for that role. My aunt, even after she was married, took care for her aging mother and father. That was actually true in the previous generation as well. My great grandmother lived with her daughter until she died at the age of 101. I have fond memories of Grandma Kern, who was a little girl during the Civil War living near Gettysburg and would tell stories of how Lee's army came to her parent's farm and would have burned their crops, but her mother had just baked some pies. Because she offered these pies to the soldiers, they spared their crops.

My maternal grandmother lived with us for much of the time in was growing up. We lived in a duplex and my parents bought the other side and converted it into a home for my grandmother with a doorway cut in to join the two houses. I saw her every day and became very close to her. She was always very kind to me and tried to guide me.

I remember her saying to me when I started school, *"Be a good boy and don't cause any problems for your parents while you are at school, because they have enough problems of their own."* In order to reinforce my attempts to be a *"good boy,"* she would give me a dime for every *"A"* in Deportment that I received on my report card. This wasn't exactly the best advice I ever got. However, it did keep me in line at school until 4th Grade when I got in trouble for stealing the teacher's paddle to use it as a baseball bat on the playground. The paddle broke when I hit a long fly ball and I was put on detention and not allowed to go out at recess. I secretly enjoyed being caught and also enjoyed all the positive attention I got from my peers. They all were overjoyed to learn that the feared teacher's paddle was now broken.

With all these rich experiences involving my grandparents, I highly recommend that children consider caring for their aging parents in their home. There are a few factors to consider, however.

THINGS TO CONSIDER WHEN PLANNING TO HAVE YOUR PARENTS MOVE IN WITH YOU

Here is a list of things to pay attention to if you are planning to have your aging parents come to live with you:[16]

1. **What kind of care will the person need?** What is the person's physical and mental condition and what chronic illness does he or she have? These are the first questions you need to answer. If they are still relatively healthy and independent, this may be the ideal time to move them in. They can become accustomed to their new surroundings and will initially require little care from you or other family members. Your kids will get to know them while they are still healthy.

2. **How much assistance and supervision can you provide?** Caring for an aging relative is a great way to give back some of the love, care, and nurturing he gave to you. When you take care of someone, you provide a model for your children that shows

3. **Know your limits.** If the person needs help with bathing, dressing, or going to the bathroom, are you comfortable helping? If he's incontinent and the idea of changing a diaper makes you uncomfortable, you may need to find an in-home aide. On the other hand, maybe he's just becoming more forgetful, and you're really good at organizing his medications and helping him make sure to take them. However, keep the following in mind as you consider how much assistance your relative needs: Be realistic about what you can and can't do. Realize, too, that the level of assistance needed will most likely increase over time. Consider your schedule. If you have a full-time job and young kids at home, consider the impact of taking in someone who needs a lot of assistance. If, for example, he needs help getting to the bathroom several times every night, you could soon be suffering from a major case of sleep deprivation.

4. **Is your home older-adult-friendly, and if not, can you make it so?** Ideally, place an older adult on the first floor so he doesn't have to climb any stairs. If that's impossible, and he can't handle stairs, you can consider putting in an automatic stair lift. Similarly, if you have steps leading up to your front door, you may have to put in a ramp that enables adaptive access ($400 and up, plus installation).

5. **Will your family member contribute financially?** Moving someone into your home can be a financial drain, but it can also have financial benefits. If you move someone in, it will probably cost you, both in dol-

lars and lifestyle. A recent study by the National Alliance for Caregiving (NAC) and Evercare found that caregivers spend on average about $5,500 a year out of pocket to care for an aging relative. If they can afford it, you can ask them to contribute to basics like food and utilities.

6. **How do your spouse and children feel about the move-in?** This may be a great opportunity for your children to form close ties with their grandparent or other family member. The United States today is such a mobile society that children often don't get much chance to be around older members of the family. Some children barely know their grandparents, especially if they live far away. If the grandparent is still relatively healthy, your children could benefit from the stories Grandpa or Grandma can tell, the oral history and life lessons they can pass down, the arts and crafts they may be able to teach your children, not to mention the babysitting services that benefit everyone.

7. **Will your family member be able to live by the rules of your house?** When someone moves in with you, it creates a sea change in your relationship. You're now the primary caretaker and decision-maker, not your older relative. It's an opportunity for your entire family to reassess current rules, decide which ones work, and make new ones where necessary. If everyone is willing to adapt and compromise, you can create household rules that work for the entire family and give your older relative a chance to adjust gracefully to his new dependent role.

8. **Will you and your family be able to adjust to the lifestyle changes involved in having an older adult in the house?** Think about meals, noise levels in the house, what's on the stereo. Will everyone's preferences and styles be compatible? This may be an opportunity to try some new foods that everyone can enjoy. If your older relative needs to eat bland food and your family likes spicy food, you can put the extra salt and spices on the table to add individually to plates.

9. **Do you have the time to take this on?** If you're working full time, seriously consider the time it takes to have a dependent older adult at home. An independent elderly adult can make his own arrangements, but otherwise the burden of making phone calls for services and medical appointments will fall on you. You may have to fill out medical forms and deal with insurance companies. If he doesn't drive, then a family member has to take him to appointments and meetings. Can you do that given your current work schedule?

10. **Will your elderly relative have a social network available?** If your parents are moving a long distance to live with you, they are leaving their social network and friends. Most caregivers drastically underestimate how hard it is and how long it takes for someone to adjust to a new environment in a new town. They're going to look to you for their socialization at first. How are you going to either integrate them into your life or help them create a new life for themselves?

WHAT ARE THE NINE CULTURES THAT STILL HOLD THE ELDERLY IN HIGHEST REGARD?[17]

The modern Greek and Greek-American cultures honor and celebrate their elders. Respect for elders is a central family value in these cultures.

1. In almost all Native American cultures, elders are respected for their wisdom and life experiences. For example, in most tribes you have to be at least 50 years old before you can begin any formal training as a shaman or teacher of wisdom. In native American families the elders are expected to pass down their wisdom to the younger members of the family. In this tradition, an elder had to have the following traits: knowledge, wisdom, counseling skills, a loving heart, compassion, a willingness to teach, even temperedness, patience and a willingness to take on responsibility.

2. Korean culture regards aging as being rooted in the Confucian principle of full piety. This means that one is expected to honor and respect his/her parents. Younger members of the family are socialized to respect and show deference to older individual as well as authority figures. It is customary to have big celebrations to mark an individual's 60th and 70th birthday. The 60th birthday is seen in families as a celebration of parents' passage into old age. Similar celebrations are held for the 70th birthday.

3. Chinese families traditionally respect their elders as a very high virtue. Children are expected to care for their elderly parents. In their culture to abandon one's family members is considered as deeply dishonorable. Children who place their aging parents in a nursing home are labeled as uncaring or a bad son or daughter.

4. In traditional Indian culture the elders are considered the head of the family. They play a big part in raising their grandchildren. Advice is always sought from the elders on any decision made by children or grandchildren from the investment of family money to traditional wedding

rituals and intra-family conflicts. Like in China, sending a parent to an old-age home is considered disrespectful and carries with it a strong social judgment.

5. African-American families treat death as an opportunity to celebrate life. Elders are treated with respect and are often sought out for their advice. Many grandparents are involved in helping to raise their grandchildren.

6. In ancient Roman culture, elders were considered a precious resource. Although the average life span was only about 25, those who lived into their 70's were respected for their wisdom. If a person lived a virtuous life, they earned high status in this culture. The elders taught the young people by example. This was ingrained into Roman society.

7. The Aboriginal culture in Australia held their elders in the highest regard. One common trait amongst Aboriginal Elders is a deep spirituality that influences every aspect of their lives and teachings. They strive to teach by example - by living their lives according to deeply ingrained principles, values and teachings.

8. The Maori culture of New Zealand also hold their elders in the highest regard. Whether a person can be considered a wise elder depends on age, knowledge of tribal history and traditions, and the presence of other potential elders for younger generations to turn to. People aged in their mid-60s or older would be universally accepted as a wise elder in this culture. Some elders may be considered wise purely based on their age, while others, despite their youth, have knowledge and leadership abilities which get them considered wise at an even earlier age.

WHAT ARE SOME QUOTES FROM THE GREATEST WISE ELDERS THROUGHOUT HISTORY?[18]

Below is a list of wise men in history who were recognized as such by their peers. I am going to list some of them along with one of their wisest sayings:

1. Benjamin Disraeli - *"The fool wonders, the wise man asks."*
2. Benjamin Franklin – *"Early to bed and early to rise makes a man healthy, wealthy and wise."*
3. Jim Hendricks – *"Knowledge speaks, but wisdom listens."*
4. Leonardo da Vinci – *"Where there is shouting, there is no true knowledge."*
5. Leo Tolstoy – *"We can know only that we know nothing. And that is the highest degree of human wisdom."*

6. *"Kahlil Gibran – "Wisdom ceases to be wisdom when it becomes too proud to weep, too grave to laugh, and too selfish to seek other than itself."*

7. Mark Twain – *"He gossips habitually; he lacks the common wisdom to keep still that deadly enemy of man, his own tongue."*

8. Lao Tzu – *"Knowing others is wisdom, knowing yourself is enlightenment."*

9. Will Rogers – *"Good judgment comes from experience. Experience is often the result of a lack of wisdom."*

10. Socrates – *"The only true wisdom is in knowing you know nothing."*

11. Emmanuel Kant – *"Science is organized knowledge; Wisdom is organized life."*

12. Albert Einstein – *"Wisdom is not a product of schooling, but of the lifelong attempt to acquire it."*

13. Thomas J. Watson – *"Wisdom is the power to put our time and our knowledge to the proper use."*

14. Horace – "Who then is free? The wise man who can command himself.

15. Oprah Winfrey – *"Turn your wounds into wisdom."*

16. Alfred North Whitehead – *"Knowledge shrinks as wisdom grows."*

17. Plato – *"He was a wise man to have invented beer."*

18. St Francis of Assisi – *"Where there is charity and wisdom, there is neither fear or ignorance."*

19. Robert Frost – *"A poem begins in delight and ends in wisdom."*

20. Carl Sandberg- *"Back of every mistaken venture and defeat is the laughter of wisdom, if you listen."*

21. Samuel Johnson – *"To keep a secret is wisdom; but to expect others to keep it is folly."*

22. Ernest Hemingway – *"Before you react, think. Before you spend, save. Before you criticize, wait. Before you quit, try."*

23. Mahatma Gandhi – *"It is unwise to be too sure of one's own wisdom. It is healthy to be reminded that the strongest might weaken and the wisest might err."*

24. William Blake – *"Innocence dwells with wisdom, but never with ignorance."*

25. Bob Dylan – *"You can't be wise and in love at the same time."*

WHY WOULD SOMEONE WANT TO BE CONSIDERED A WISE ELDER?[19]

What is the motivation for an elderly person to want to become a wise elder? That may vary widely. Most people when they grow old have a desire to leave this planet a better place than what is was when they were born. That intrinsic motivation is strong and is a part of what Eric Erikson labeled *Integrity vs Despair*. He defined it as follows: *"From the mid-60s to the end of life, we are in the period of development known as late adulthood. Erikson wrote that the main task at this stage of late adulthood is to reflect on your life and feel either your sense of satisfaction or your sense of failure. People who feel proud of their accomplishments feel a sense of integrity, and they can look back on their lives with few regrets. However, people who were not successful at this stage may feel as if their life has been wasted. They focus on what 'would have,' 'should have,' and 'could have' been. They face the end of their lives with feelings of bitterness, depression, and despair."[20]*

Even those who made mistakes and have some regrets can become wise elders. Their motivation may be to pass on what they had to learn the hard way. My Dad who didn't finish high school, passed on the regrets he carried all of his life about this decision. He would often say to me, *"Get an education so you won't have to work as hard as I did."* It was part of why I went on for advanced degrees. He hoped to pass on what he learned from his mistakes that might help me not have to make the same mistakes that he did.

This is a common motivation that many people hold by wanting to pass on what they had learned from the mistakes they made. Several of the wise elder contributors to this book shared mistakes they made in their lives. It can be just as important for elders to share as those who want to share the secrets to their successes. Several of the wise elders who contributed to this book wrote about what they learned from their shared mistakes.

I believe we all learn from elders who can help guide us through the complexities of modern life. Unfortunately, we may have lost trust in our elders along the way who we may now regard as no wiser that ourselves. This is common today and many young people are cynical about the role they think their elders played in messing up the world around them. Cynicism is really broken idealism and sadly this can cause these young people to grow bitter and depressed as they grow old.

By choosing to become a wise elder, you are actually repairing and re-establishing a connection with your descendants and our ancestors. This web of relationship is vital to your survival as a species. Becoming a wise elder is a hallowed task that can bring meaning to all aspects of your life, from all your celebrations and victories to all your times of difficulty and defeat. Wise elders often ask themselves, *"What can I learn from this experience that could be of use to me and someone else?"* or they may ask, *"How can I explain how I got through this difficult time in a way that is helpful to my grandchildren?"*

Once you make the commitment to become a wise elder, you begin to honor and cultivate this spark in everyone around you, especially those of your own age. We all have the potential to be our best self. All of us carry to seeds of grace, kindness, compassion, forgiveness, wisdom and love within us. As a wise elder you have committed yourself to doing your part and passing on the torch of your best efforts and your highest hopes to the next generation as they pass the torch to those who follow them. This is the power of connection to the web of relationship across the generations.

HOW DOES ONE BECOME A WISE ELDER?

While there is some variation in what would be considered wise elder behavior and later in the book I discuss psychological things you can do to prepare yourself to be a wise elder. However, here is my list of 25 simple ways to become recognized as a wise elder:

1. **Smile and be friendly**. Sometimes a simple little thing like this can put a smile and warm feeling in someone else's heart, and make their day a little better. They might then pass it on and do the same for others.

2. **Call a charity to volunteer.** You don't have to go to a soup kitchen today. Just look up the number, make the call, and make an appointment to volunteer sometime in the next month. It can be whatever charity you like. Volunteering is one of the most amazing things you can do.

3. **Donate something you don't use.** Or a whole box of *"somethings."* Drop them off at a charity — others can put your clutter to good use.

4. **Make a donation.** There are lots of ways to donate to charities online, or in your local community. Instead of buying yourself a new gadget or outfit, spend that money in a more positive way by donating to your favorite charity

5. **Redirect gifts.** Instead of having people give you birthday or Christmas gifts, ask them to donate gifts or money to your favorite charity.

6. **Stop to help.** The next time you see someone pulled over with a flat tire, or somehow in need of help, stop and ask how you can help. Sometimes all they need is a push, or the use of your cell phone.

7. **Teach.** Take the time to teach someone a skill you know. This could be teaching your grandma to use email, teaching your child to ride a bike, teaching your co-worker a valuable computer skill, teaching your spouse how to clean the darn toilet. OK, that last one doesn't count.

8. **Comfort someone in grief.** Often a hug, a helpful hand, a kind word, a listening ear, will go a long way when someone has lost a loved one or suffered some similar loss or tragedy.

9. **Help someone take action.** If someone in grief seems to be lost and doesn't know what to do, help them do something. It could be making funeral arrangements, it could be making a doctor's appointment, it could be making phone calls. Don't do it all yourself — let them take action too, because it helps them in their healing process.

10. **Buy food for a homeless person.** Cash is often a bad idea if it's going to be used for drugs, but buying a sandwich and chips or something like that is a good gesture. Be respectful and friendly.

11. **Lend your ear.** Often someone who is sad, depressed, angry, or frustrated just needs someone who will listen. Venting and talking through an issue is a huge help.

12. **Help someone on the edge.** If someone is suicidal, urge them to get help. If they don't, call a suicide hotline or a doctor yourself to get advice.

13. **Help someone get active.** A person in your life who wants to get healthy might need a helping hand — offer to go walking or running together, to join a gym together. Once they get started, it can have profound effects.

14. **Do a chore.** Something small or big, like cleaning up or washing a car or doing the dishes or cutting a lawn or shoveling snow for a neighbor.

15. **Give a massage.** Only when appropriate of course. But a massage can go a long way to making someone feel better.

16. **Send a nice email.** Just a quick note telling someone how much you appreciate them, or how proud you are of them, or just saying thank you for something they did.

17. **Show appreciation, publicly.** Praising someone on a blog, in front of coworkers, in front of family, or in some other public way, is a great way to make them feel better about themselves.

18. **Donate food.** Clean out your cupboard of canned goods, or buy a couple bags of groceries, and just donate them to a homeless shelter.

19. **Just be there.** When someone you know is in need, sometimes it's good enough to just be there. Sit with them. Talk. Help out if you can.

20. **Be patient.** Sometimes people can have difficulty understanding things, or learning to do something right. Learn to be patient with them.

21. **Tutor a child.** This might be difficult to do today, but often parents can't afford to hire a tutor for their child in need of help. Call a school and volunteer your tutoring services.

22. **Create a care package.** Soup, reading material, tea, chocolate… anything you think the person might need or enjoy. Military stationed far from home really appreciate a *"care package."* It is also good for someone who is sick or otherwise in need of a pick-me-up.

23. **Lend your voice.** Often the powerless, the homeless, the neglected in our world need someone to speak up for them. You don't have to take on that cause by yourself, but join others in signing a petition, speaking up a city council meeting, writing letters, and otherwise making a need heard.

24. **Offer to babysit.** Sometimes parents need a break. If a friend or other loved one in your life doesn't get that chance very often, call them and offer to babysit sometime. Set up an appointment. It can make a big difference.

25. **Love.** Simply finding ways to express your love to others, whether it be your partner, child, other family member, friend, co-worker, or a complete stranger … just express your love. A hug, a kind word, spending time, showing little kindnesses, being friendly … it all matters more than you know.

HOW DO WISE ELDERS LEARN TO BALANCE THEIR MATURE MASCULINE AND FEMININE ARCHETYPES?

As I discussed earlier in the Introduction, I believe that what distinguishes a wise elder from an old man is someone who has learned how to balance his mature masculine and feminine archetypes. Let's take a closer look at this process. Most young men and women are still living out of both of their immature masculine and feminine archetypes.

For example, younger men usually identify with the hero who saves a victim or captures a great treasure. The more mature masculine archetype is the Warrior who is able to balance his masculine and feminine energies and becomes more of a guide and an advocate rather than a conqueror. The Warrior seeks spirituality and wisdom over glory and fame. The immature King energy is the Tyrant who rules with impunity. The mature masculine King archetype seeks to be a steward to all life and one who directs and protects others.

The immature Magician is a trickster who cannot be trusted. This is the dishonest politician or crooked Wall Street banker. The mature Magician becomes a trusted Wise Elder. He becomes more protective and nurturing. He embodies wisdom and is also able to be rational. He also has an eccentric nature that allows him to stand up to conventional wisdom and seek a deeper form of wisdom.

The immature lover can be seen in his obsession with sex and power. He loves with his penis rather than his heart, and it often gets him in trouble. One of my friends used to put it this way. *"When I let 'Mr. Johnson' (his penis) make my decisions, I frequently end up regretting what I decided to do."* The mature Lover knows how to balance these adolescent urges with discernment. He can still be sexual, but is not obsessed with it. He can be playful and adventurous, but can keep it in balance.

On the feminine side of the ledger there are opposite, but equal, archetypes to balance with the above masculine ones. In our culture, these archetypes are often suppressed in men and women. Instead of the Warrior who is actually wired to be both protective and be life-taking there is the mature feminine archetype of The Male Mother, who is more nurturing and life-giving. In its immature form it shows up in the Devouring Mother, the Martyr or the Rejecting Parent.

Instead of the King or Ruler, there is mature feminine form I call The Servant Leader, who is the counterpart to the mature King or Ruler archetype, but with more compassion and wisdom. In its immature form we see the Controlling Boss, the Micromanager or the Bureaucrat.

The Wise Elder is the mature feminine version of the Magician. In its immature form we see the Narcissist, The Rescuer or the Embezzler. The mature feminine form of the Lover is the Open-Hearted-Lover. The open-heartedness of the mature feminine form leads to more giving and receiving of unconditional love. The immature forms are The Pick-Up-Artist, the Pedophile and The Impotent Lover.

The task of the mature male Wise Elder is to integrate and balance his self-expression with the energy of the mature masculine and the feminine archetype. Both the masculine and feminine energies within him must be balanced, along with the childhood archetypes that predispose him to grow into the maturity and wisdom he is capable of achieving. Being a protector, provider, life-giver, and teacher is how he can meet the needs of people living in the 21st Century. This is the task that faces the Wise Elder of today.

CHAPTER TWO

WHAT DO WE LOSE WITHOUT THE WISDOM OF OUR WISE ELDERS?

You can live to be a hundred if you give up all the things that make you want to live to be a hundred.

—Woody Allen

When you look at the charts in the Introduction you can easily see that most people living in our modern culture are operating out of immature masculine or feminine archetypes. We hardly ever see anyone in leadership positions who operates as a servant leader with mature balanced masculine and feminine archetypes. This is what wise elders can bring to our modern culture. If they have worked on themselves and learned how to integrate and balance their mature masculine and feminine archetypes in their personality, they can provide living examples of how to combine the best of wisdom and love.

Carl Jung believed that the approximate time between the ages of 56 and 83, each of us has the opportunity to make the process of aging a positive and life-enhancing experience. He called it the *"afternoon" of life.* He added, *"A human being would certainly not grow to be 70 or 80 years old if this longevity had no meaning for the species to which he belongs. The afternoon of human life must also have a significance of its own and cannot be merely a pitiful appendage to life's morning."* [21]

For Jung, the aging process was not one of inescapable decline of body, mind and relevancy, but instead a time of progressive refinement of what is essential. He said it is important to focus on self-awareness, individuation and wholeness as we age. Here is what he wrote about the aging process: *"An ever-deepening self-awareness seems to me as probably essential for the continuation of a truly meaningful life in any age, no matter how uncomfortable this self-knowledge may be. Nothing is more ridiculous or unsuitable as older people who act as if they were still young — they lose even their dignity, the only privilege of age. The watch must be the introspection."*

"Everything is revealed in self-knowledge, what is it, what it is intended to, and about what and for what one lives. The wholeness of ourselves is certainly a rationale..." In other words, as we grow older we are all offered the opportunity to find meaning and purpose in becoming whole and wise. Perhaps instead of aging we could call it, *"sageing."*[22]

Instead of glorifying the roles we played in the *"morning"* of our lives, Jung recommends that we let go of what we were and optimistically welcome where we are and where we are going. He said, *"...an old man who cannot bid farewell to life appears as feeble and sickly as a young man who is unable to embrace it. And as a matter of fact, it is in many cases a question of the selfsame childish greediness, the same fear, the same defiance and willfulness, in the one as in the other."* Finally he wrote, *"The privilege of a lifetime is to become who you truly are."*[23]

As Jung suggests above, another term for a Wise Elder is a Sage. A Sage sees through appearances and illusions to find the truth. He values knowledge for its own sake and uses it combined with wisdom to help others. The Wise Old Man archetype, also known as the *"Senex"*, is the Jungian archetype of wisdom. The Senex, or Wise Elder archetype, permeates literature and mythology from the ancient world to modern day. A modern example of the Senex is Obi Wan Kenobi in the Star Wars movies. Obi-Wan Kenobi is old, wise, and helps Luke. And his wisdom helps Luke and Han rescue Leia. Obi-Wan is killed while attempting to protect Luke from Darth Vader; Luke, Han, and Leia are then able to escape. He serves as a more knowledgeable other and teaches Luke about the Force.

People like James Hillman suggest that you cannot become a Wise Elder or Sage until you have integrated what he called the Senex and the Puer. The Puer is the desire to maintain eternal youth and the Senex represents the acceptance of our elder life. He says we have to understand where we came from (the Puer) before we can fully embrace the Senex. He believes the *"soul"* provides the bridge to help you integrate these two seemingly opposite forces. This seems to me to mean that we have to capture the essence of what we learned in our youth and bring it with us into elderhood so we can then harvest all the information we learned and make it part of the realization of the mature Self.[24]

The Wise Elder understands the steps in the journey to self-realization, but may still not have reached this pinnacle of realization personally. The Wise Elder understands the nature of the outer journey of individuating from his family and culture, his outer experience with the collective conscious, the play of his personas and other adaptations and plays of ego, and his illusions of power and fame and success. As a result, the Wise Elder has come to understand that the first half of life has been the foundation upon which to create a spiritual, psychological and embodied container to work on the real questions of life. In addition, the Wise Elder accepts the pain of his losses and the emptying out in the dissolution of the lesser self that obscures his true Self. The Wise Elder has *"raised the child,"* both inner and outer, and has come to understand the wisdom of the Puer-Senex integration with a higher trust required to realize his ability to be of true service to others.

The Wise Elder understands that *"dying ten thousand deaths before you die"* is the way to becoming part of what lives forever. This emptying process makes room for new information and wisdom to emerge. The Elder understands that such emptying of psychic content is not a metaphysical principle, not an active stance, or not a psychological project, but instead it becomes the art of allowing life to move through him. This means that as a Wise Elder he experiences increasing acceptance and equanimity around whatever happens to him, knowing it all is part of the path to the individuated Self.[25]

In this process, the Wise Elder becomes adept at both embracing and letting go. As a result, others around him feel his strength, his vital aliveness beyond aging, his lack of attachment, and they feel they are in the *presence* of someone who is authentic. Marie Louise von Franz summarized this essential developmental process for becoming a Wise Elder: *"If an individual has wrestled seriously and long enough with the anima (or animus) ... The unconscious again changes its dominant character and appears in a new symbolic form...as an initiator, guardian, a guru/teacher, a wise old man..."*[26]

WHAT ARE THE CHARACTERISTICS OF THE WISE ELDER?

In order to better determine where you are in your journey to become a Wise elder, I have created a Self-Quiz that allows you to rate yourself. This will show you some of specific characteristics of Wise Elders.

SELF-QUIZ: WHAT ARE THE CHARACTERISTICS OF A WISE ELDER?[27]

Directions: For each item on the list below indicate in the blank how you would rate yourself from 1-10. A 10 indicates that you feel you have accomplished this and a 1 indicates that you have a long way to go to accomplish this.

_____ 1. **Show up and tell your truth.** Walk your talk and be *"radically present"* in everything you do in your life. Speak your truth and be vulnerable and transparent. Keep no hidden agendas.

_____ 2. **Have fun.** Find ways to enjoy life to its fullest. Don't take yourself or life too seriously and keep your sense of humor.

_____ 3. **Ask directly for what you want & need.** Be direct and straight forward in asking for what you want directly rather than manipulating others into giving it to you. Expect others to do the same.

_____ 4. **Connect the dots.** Identify what happened to you as a child that still impacts your life. Do personal archeology to learn all you can about your childhood and how it has shaped your adult relationships and life.

_____ 5. **Regulate your emotions.** Calm yourself and quickly *"regain your composure"* when something upsets you.

_____ 6. **Know where you end and others begin.** You are able to establish and maintain a clear sense of your boundaries in close relationships.

_____ 7. **Engage in radical self-care.** Make taking good care of your own physical, mental, emotional, energy and spiritual *"selves"* your number one priority. Do not let anything get in the way of this.

_____ 8. **Keep all your agreements with others.** If you need to change an agreement, contact the person(s) with whom you made an agreement and renegotiate it in a way that is acceptable to both of you.

_____ 9. **Resolve your conflicts directly.** Resolve conflicts of wants or needs in a cooperative, partnership way. Use dialogue skills rather than debate for resolving conflicts involving values or beliefs. Don't triangulate.

____ 10. **Live a life of** *"harmony and balance."* Develop all your talents and keep them balanced so that one overshadows the others. Strive for harmony and balance between work and play, and between serving yourself and serving others.

____ 11. **Be patient with yourself and others.** Maintain good feelings about yourself and others when either you or someone else *"screws up."* Avoid harsh judgments and *"splitting"* against yourself or others.

____ 12. **Take responsibility for everything you say or do.** This means *"owning"* what is yours and giving back to others what is not yours. Forgive (give back) to others anything they gave you or you took on from them that no longer serves you. It wasn't yours in the first place.

____ 13. **Heal your traumas and betrayals.** This is probably the most difficult and also most important thing to master. Heal your father and mother wounds and their role in your childhood traumas and betrayals. This is essential for creating satisfying, intimate and sustainable relationships, and reducing undue stress on your immune system.

____ 14. **Feel and express your emotions.** Share your deepest feelings with others, in appropriate ways. Learn the correct function of each of your feelings and use them to effectively to help you solve problems, make decisions.

____ 15. **Commit to taking back your projections.** Learn the signs indicating that you are projecting something about yourself onto another person. Learn to claim (give back or *"re-own"*) any shadow parts of yourself that you have been rejecting by projecting them on others.

____ 16. **Stay centered.** Stay centered in whatever you do. Recognize when you are pulled off-center and quickly return to center. This skill is an indicator of your psychological health.

____ 17. **Listen with an open heart.** Deep listening to others and yourself requires having an open heart and being present to receive them and what they are telling you. This also helps in listening to yourself and becoming more self-reflective.

____ 18. **Come from** *"knowing"* **rather than believing.** Develop your *"inner knowing"* skills in order to access your feelings and the intuitive guidance you need to live more authentically.

___ 19. **Surrender.** Allow other people's truth to penetrate your defenses. *"Receive without resistance"* what others say to you. Open your heart fully and let it guide your responses.

___ 20. **Trust your gut and follow your destiny.** Listen to and trust the voice inside of you. Use it to create the life you want and develop the courage to take the risks this requires.

___ 21. **Balance your internal masculine and feminine parts.** Learn to be strong and tender and use either or both depending what the situation calls for.

___ 22. **Love fearlessly and unconditionally.** Love yourself and others unconditionally. Examine your fears through the lens of love. Remember, love is your best weapon to conquer your fears.

___ 23. **Identify the mythic aspects of your life.** Myths and archetypes will provide you with larger than life ways of learning life's mysteries. By being able to identify the archetypical and mythic elements of your dreams and your waking life, you will have a compass to guide you through the mysteries of your journey.

___ 24. **Cooperate with others to get all your wants and needs met.** Negotiate with others to get your wants and needs met in a cooperative, partnership way without interfering with the needs of others. Refuse to feel *"victimized"* by others.

___ 25. **Participate in regular spiritual practices.** Prayer is asking the big questions, and meditation is listening for the big answers. Cultivate a sustained relationship with a power greater than yourself. Yoga or martial arts are also considered spiritual practices.

___ 26. **Develop and sustain close intimate relationships.** Initiate, develop and sustain close friendships, and an intimate love relationship with a partner without fear of abandonment or engulfment.

___ 27. **Find something bigger than yourself to give your life purpose and meaning.** Initiate or participate in service projects that benefit others, either as a professional or as a volunteer. Identify a well-defined purpose for your life that involves serving others and the forces of human evolution.

____ 28. **Live a self-directed life.** *"Take charge of your life without guilt and shame."* Master being an independent person, while also sustaining intimacy with friends and loved ones.

SCORING AND INTERPRETATION:

If you rate yourself as "5" or under on any item, that would be an item to do some work on to improve your score. Also, look at what might be keeping your score low on those items to see what you might change.

WHAT ARE THE EFFECTS OF HOLDING MISTAKEN BELIEFS ABOUT AGING?

In order to become an effective Wise Elder, you may have to change some of your long-held beliefs. Researchers found that the saying *"You are only as old as you feel,"* is true. Interestingly, what you believe about how you will age has significant effects on how you actually age.

A longitudinal study in Ireland found that negative attitudes about aging have serious effects on both physical and cognition health in your later years. The lead researcher in this study put it this way, *"The way we think about, talk about and write about aging may have direct effects on health. Everyone will grow older and if negative attitudes towards aging are carried throughout life they can have a detrimental, measurable effect on mental, physical and cognitive health."*[28] The summary of their results indicated the following:

- Older adults with negative attitudes towards aging had slower walking speed and worse cognitive abilities two years later, compared to older adults with more positive attitudes towards aging.
- This was true even after participants' medications, mood, their life circumstances and other health changes that had occurred over the same two-year period were accounted for.
- Furthermore, negative attitudes towards aging seemed to affect how different health conditions interacted. Frail older adults are at risk of multiple health problems including worsening cognition.

HOW DO YOUR PERSONAL BELIEFS AFFECT YOUR AGING PROCESS?

Another study uncovered that the mistaken or *"twisted beliefs"* that people hold about aging and suggest that unless these beliefs are changed, they will adversely affect your experience of healthy aging. This matches what I found about how people's *"twisted beliefs"* adversely affect their behavior.[29] Below is a summary of six major twisted beliefs that can affect how we age:

Twisted Belief No. 1: Depression Is More Prevalent in Old Age. Research indicates that emotional well-being improves until the 70s, when it levels off. Even centenarians *"report overall high levels of well-being,"* In another study they found that as participants aged, their moods steadily improved from negative to positive. The lead researcher concluded *"Contrary to the popular view that youth is the best time of life, the peak of emotional life may not occur until well into the seventh decade."*[30]

In a 2003 study, for example, they found that in contrast to younger adults, older adults presented with an array of happy, sad and angry faces directed their gazes more often toward the happy ones. Why the focus on the positive? They concluded that as people age, they tend to prioritize emotional meaning and satisfaction, giving them an incentive to see the good more than the bad.

National data back up these findings. According to the National Institute of Mental Health, 5.5% of adults age 50 and over said they experienced a major depressive episode in 2012. For those 26 to 49, the rate was 7.6%, and for ages 18 to 25 it was 8.9%.

Twisted Belief No. 2: Cognitive Decline Is Inevitable for Older People. Older adults who believe negative stereotypes about aging can also unwittingly undermine their own performance on memory tests. In a study published in 2012, scientists at the Yale School of Public Health and the National Institute on Aging reviewed memory tests administered to 395 older participants in the Baltimore Longitudinal Study of Aging, all of whom—at younger ages—had filled out questionnaires assessing their beliefs in negative stereotypes about aging.

Over a 38-year period, the decline in memory performance for those ages 60 and over with the most negative stereotypes was 30% greater than for those with fewer negative views. This indicates that—barring dementia—older adults perform better in the real world than they do on cognitive tests. Another researcher said the following: *"Typical laboratory tasks may systematically underestimate the true abilities of older adults,"*

In two recent studies, they tested the memories of 239 adults ages 60 to 90, about one-half of whom spent about 16 hours a week over three months learning new skills, including how to quilt, use an iPad and take digital photographs. Compared with peers who performed word puzzles or engaged in social activities and other tasks that required no new skills, those learning new skills *"showed greater improvements in memory, with some also showing improvement in processing speed,"* says the researcher, who believes that older adults who learn challenging new skills tap more diffuse brain circuits and pathways to compensate for age-related deficits. *"Novelty combined with mental challenge is very important,"* she says. *"Get out of your comfort zone."*

Here is a very important finding. Some scientists also believe older adults can make wiser decisions. In a study published in 2010, scientists asked 247 Midwesterners to read stories about conflicts between individuals and social groups and predict the outcomes.

After transcribing their responses, the investigators removed participants' names and ages and asked students who had received training to rate their responses on the basis of *"wisdom"*—defined, in part, as the ability to see problems from multiple perspectives and show sensitivity to social relationships. The researchers then asked outside experts—including clergy and professional counselors—to rank a subset of the responses according to their own definitions of wisdom, a process that largely confirmed the accuracy of the students' ratings. The average age of those with scores in the top 20% was 65, versus age 46 for the remaining 80%.

Twisted Belief No. 3: Older Workers Are Less Productive Than Younger Ones. The conclusion in the vast majority of academic studies shows *"virtually no relationship between age and job performance."* In jobs that require experience, some studies show that older adults actually performed better. They determined that over that four-year period, the older workers committed slightly fewer severe errors, while the younger workers' severe error rates edged up. They concluded that older workers seemed to know better how to avoid severe errors and have a performance edge on younger workers for this reason.

Twisted Belief No. 4: Loneliness Is More Likely with Older People. Even though, as people age, their social circles contract. But that doesn't mean older adults are lonely. In fact, several studies show that friendships tend to improve with age. In one study, they concluded that *"Older adults typically report better marriages, more supportive friendships, less conflict with children and siblings and closer ties with members of their social networks than younger adults."*[31]

In another study the researchers asked 184 people that they followed for more than a decade to put their friends and relatives into three categories: an inner circle, consisting of people they feel so close [to] that it would be hard to imagine life without them; a middle circle they feel a little less close to but who are still very important; and the rest in an outer circle. The researchers also asked the participants every couple of years to rate—on a scale of one to seven—the intensity of the positive and negative emotions they felt for each person in each group. What they found was, until about age 50, most people added to their social networks. After that, they eliminated people they feel less close to and maximized interactions with close partners who are more emotionally satisfying. Over time, the participants also assigned their networks more positive ratings. Their loved ones seem to mean more than ever, and that is protective against loneliness.

Twisted Belief No. 5: Creativity Declines with Age. Creativity has long been seen as the province of the young. But studies that date as far back as the 19th century, pinpoint midlife as the time when artists and scholars become the most prolific. One researcher says creativity tends to peak earlier in fields such as pure mathematics and theoretical physics, where breakthroughs typically hinge on problem-solving skills that are sharpest in one's 20s.

In fields that require accumulated knowledge, creative peaks typically occur later. Historians, writers, artists and philosophers, for example, "may not reach their peak output until they are in their 60s. One study analyzed the ages at which some 300 famous artists, poets and novelists produced their most valuable works. (For the artwork, they used auction prices and the number of times specific works appeared in text books. For literary works, they counted the words devoted to them in scholarly monographs.)

Their conclusion: Creative genius clusters into two categories: conceptual artists, who tend to do their best work in their 20s and 30s, and experimental artists, who often need a few more decades to reach full potential. Conceptual artists work from imagination, an area where the young have an advantage because they tend to be more open to radical new ideas.

People who are creative in older age aren't anomalies. There are Mark Twain, Paul Cézanne, Frank Lloyd Wright, Robert Frost, Claude Monet, James Michener, Morgan Freeman, Laura Ingalls Wilder, Grandma Moses and Virginia Woolf to name just a few of the creative people who did their greatest work in their 40s, 50s and 60s. These creative people rely on wisdom, which increases with age.

Twisted Belief No. 6: More Exercise Is Better. When it comes to improving health and longevity, most experts say exercise is key. But there is a growing number of studies that show that more exercise may not always be better. There is a point of diminishing returns. In a recent study, researchers tracked 1,098 joggers and 3,950 non-joggers from 2001 to 2013. Overall, the runners in this study lived longer than the non-runners: 6.2 years longer for the men, and 5.6 years longer for the women. However, the new study discovered that those who ran more than four hours a week at a fast pace—of 7 miles per hour or more—lost much, if not all, of their longevity benefits. The group that saw the biggest improvements were those who jogged from one to 2.4 hours weekly at 5 to 7 mph and took at least two days off from vigorous exercise per week.

Other studies have come to similar conclusions. In another study, scientists found that the death rate for runners is 30% to 45% below that for non-runners. But the mortality benefits were similar for all runners, even those who ran five to 10 minutes a day at speeds of 6 mph or less. Their conclusion was that fairly modest doses of running provided benefits as great as a lot of running. Their recommendation was to stick to a moderate cardiovascular workout of no more than 30 miles a week or 50 to 60 minutes of vigorous exercise a day, and take at least one day off each week.

THE WISE OLD MAN STORY[32]

A wealthy man requested an old scholar to wean his son away from his bad habits. The scholar took the youth for a stroll through a garden. Stopping suddenly, he asked the boy to pull out a tiny plant growing there.

The youth held the plant between his thumb and forefinger and pulled it out. The old man then asked him to pull out a slightly bigger plant. The youth pulled hard and the plant came out, roots and all. *"Now pull out that one,"* said the old man pointing to a bush. The boy had to use all his strength to pull it out.

"Now take this one out," said the old man, indicating a guava tree. The youth grasped the trunk and tried to pull it out. But it would not budge. *"It's impossible,"* said the boy, panting with the effort. *"So it is with bad habits,"* said the sage. *"When they are young it is easy to pull them out but when they take hold they cannot be uprooted."*

The session with the wise man changed the boy's life. Moral: Don't wait for Bad Habits to grow in you, drop them while you have control over it else they will get control you.

CHAPTER THREE

WHY DO WE NEED THE WISDOM OF OUR WISE ELDERS NOW MORE THAN EVER?

Those who think they have no time for bodily exercise
will sooner or later have to find time for illness.

— Edward Stanley

For the first time in 130 years, a young adult in 2014 was more likely to live with a parent than a significant other. This is the result of a Pew Research Center analysis of census data, which shows 32.1% of 18-to-34-year-olds lived in a parent's home in 2014, compared to the 31.6% who lived with a spouse or romantic partner. Historically, 5 percent or less of marriage age adults live with their parents. Men are more likely (35 percent) than women (29) to be living with their parents. How does this apply to Wise Elders? Well, we also know that more grandparents are becoming primary parents for their grandchildren.[33]

The numbers of grandparents raising their grandchildren has increased dramatically in the past few years to more than 2.7 million. Actually more than 13 million children are being raised or supported by at least one grandparent each year.[34] Here are some stories from contributors about their roles as grandparents who had a significant role in raising their grandchildren.

BEING A GRANDPA AND A GOD PARENT

Wise elder contributor, **Bob Brown**, tells a story of parenting his grandchild: *"Having been a high school music teacher for 31 years, I had many opportunities to mentor young people, but the one mentoring that took place over the* *second half of my life was thrust upon me without warning, and I approached it with some trepidation. However, it turned out to be the most gratifying experience of my life.*

"My 19-year-old middle daughter came to my wife and me with the news that every father dreads. She was pregnant. Furthermore, the young man who had participated in the pregnancy had hopped on his motorcycle and raced into the proverbial sunset, so there was no hope of a marriage resulting. I suggested to her, after I regained consciousness (I'm exaggerating) that it might be a good idea to arrange an adoption. No way, she was going to keep the baby, and my wife seconded her determination.

"When the baby boy was born, she decided to have him baptized, and conned me (not really, I'm a better man than that) into being his sponsor and godfather. How about that. Grandfather and godfather at the same time. As I held him and looked at his decidedly handsome face, I speculated about what his life would be like. I also realized that becoming a godfather involves a pretty serious commitment. So I made a vow to myself that I would do everything in my power to see that he would grow up to be a healthy and happy man with good values. At that very moment we bonded.

"For the first 3 years my wife and I served as his parent's, until our daughter got her life figured out. Then she married and took little Joe into her care. We still played a large part in his life, until he was 5, and then she moved to California. Our oldest son lived in Hollywood, so we had 2 good reasons to visit. We witnessed little Joe graduate from kindergarten.

"The next 6 intervening years involved many visits, and then unfortunately my wife died. I became a widower. It was hard. To seek some consolation, I invited 10-year-old Joe to take a midsummer trip with me. We started with a day-long visit at Universal studios, and then up Highway #1 on the California coast to the city of Vancouver British Columbia, with many interesting stops along the way, as well as many interesting conversations. For the first time we really got to know each other.

"The trip was so successful that we agreed to take another trip the next summer. It became a regular summer event for the next 7 years. One year, we went to Springfield, Illinois and visited Abraham Lincoln's home. The next year we started at Santa Fe and followed the Santa Fe Trail all the way to Kansas, visiting museums and historical landmarks along the way. Each summer became not only a trip, but also a lesson in US history.

"The climax to our travels came right after Joe graduated from high school. We traveled to Washington, DC, and spent 8 days there, which included Gettysburg, Mount Vernon, and a major league baseball game in Baltimore.

"Then Joe decided that he would enlist in the Air Force. I attended his graduation from basic training. I visited him at each of his stations in the US. Then he was stationed at Bagram Air Force Base in Afghanistan. Then in Seoul, Korea, where he met a lovely young lady from the Philippines, and married her. Then he was stationed at the US Ramstein Air Force Base near Kaiserslautern, Germany. At that point I was fortunate to visit him for a month and become acquainted with his wife and newborn son.

"This time it was Joe who gave me geography lessons. He took me to Paris, Cologne, Heidelberg and several other beautiful towns in Germany which names l can't remember, I also got to make a weekend trip to visit my oldest son's ex-wife and 2 of my grownup grandsons who I hadn't seen since they were infants.

"What a magnificent trip that was. I did not see Joe again until I went to Montgomery, Alabama. When Joe came back from Germany, after 10 years in the Air Force, he decided to enter officer's training. I went to his promotion ceremony to second lieutenant, and was privileged to pin his bars on him. That was 2 years ago. He has since been promoted to first lieutenant. So how is that for fulfilling a vow to be a godfather? I like to think that was the most important thing I have ever done in my life."

REDEFINING THE ROLE OF A GRANDPARENT.

Wise elder contributor, **Dean Tollefson**, tells a wonderful story about how he intervened in the life of a young girl: *"At an inter-generational gathering, I was sitting next to the children and listening to them chatter about how great their grandparents were…in considerable detail. (I tried to sit near the kids because they were more interesting.) All of a sudden, one of the middle school aged girls (ages 11-14) after being unusually silent blurted out that she didn't have any grandparents. She explained that they were either dead or lived so far away that she never sees them!*

"I came right back to her and assured her that we would be her grandparents. She looked at me like I had lost my mind! I suggested on the way home that night, and the next and all week if necessary that she talk about who would make good grandparents for her.

"The next week she came to us and asked my wife and me to be her grandparents.…and we took over being her grandparents… We took her out and

eat, or she dined with us at our home --- even for special occasions, or we took her to sports events of her choice. She still stays with us over weekends or other times when her parents are away, or we just talk and talk, or are silent together. It has all worked for all concerned!

"Grandparenting, like all forms of relationships, is first and fore-most an idea; …we conceive it, and practice it, and refine it, … again and again and we are better men (and women) because we do it. It takes thought and experience, trial and error, and tenacity and courage."

BEING THERE IN A CRISIS

Wise elder contributor, **Dean Tollefson**, shared another story involving his step-granddaughter. He wrote the following: *"My step-grand-daughter was bright & good, but troubled kid. She had been through too many family upsets. We talked lots; more correctly, she talked and we listened. One time in a fit of disgust she talked of just running away. I expressed my thought that it probably wasn't the best way to settle difficulties, but suggested that if she decided to run, she should run to our home for we would welcome you, and she would be safe.*

"Weeks later she was committed to a Juvenile Correction 'home' and then with another resident she ran away in the night. At 2:30 a.m. my telephone rang and an anxious little voice said, 'Grand-pa, do you remember...' I interrupted right there and said, 'Yes, where are you and I'll come and get you... ';and the next day started right there. They had waded Monument Creek not wanting to walk the bridge for fear of being picked up by the police so they were wet and muddy to their knees. So I found some night shirts and robes and my wife washed all their clothes, but deliberately did not dry them! This prevented them from running away again until we could make a plan and their clothes were dry. This all that took a while.

"My grand-daughter said that she thought she didn't belong on this planet, but was left here when her people visited here. So I suggested we send a message to them, I raised my arms in a big Y, fingers opened, asked them to do the same. We all crossed our arms at the wrists so we had a big antenna and sent the message: 'Oh good people we have one of your best here—whom we love and cherish but she wants to come home to you. We will miss her so much but we want her to be happy so she can get on with her life and use the fine mind she has.' Etc., etc., etc...

"Her friend thought we were all crazy... But she got the message of our love and care!! We asked each of them to identify one person who they trusted and who would call their parents and tell them that they are safe. It took them

a very long time to identify even one person. How very sad it was to be with them as they really struggled with all this.

"This episode all worked out, but her life hasn't as yet, and we have not abandoned her, and she knows that... Last winter we went to visit her in prison. She'll be out next spring into a vocation which she likes and we think can succeed at. Life is long and so often requires endless patience... with lots of love and care. What else really matters?"

WORDS FOR FUTURE GENERATIONS.

Wise elder contributor, **Michael Lightweaver**, wrote a 95-page book (*The World According to Michael*) primarily for his grandchildren and great-grandchildren, which he admits that he may never know. He wrote the following, *"This book is really being written for my great, great, great grandchildren who will be living into the 22nd century and whom I may never know. I remember as a child hearing scattered stories of my great grandfather, Anderson Hewitt: of how he fought in the Civil War, how he was educated for his time in a world of peasant farmers in Kentucky. How he used to go out in the fields and 'make speeches to the Black folks.' From the little I could piece together, he was apparently an abolitionist, which said to me that he marched to the tune of a different drummer than most of his peers and family in southern Kentucky.*

"Perhaps it was for that reason that he was always my secret hero. I also remember as a child an old trunk in the basement of our home that had some yellowed family ledgers and sepia photos of stern looking ancestors from the 1800's. As I looked into their eyes, even as a youth, I wondered about their stories. What had they experienced? What hardships had they endured? What did they think? What was their view of the world? At the time, I remembered that the greatest gift that I could imagine would be to sit down with them, hear their stories and see the world through their eyes and experience.

"So this is why I am writing this book; as a gift to you, my descendants; a gift that I would have loved to receive from my own ancestors. It is my attempt to give you a window into my world, back in 2014 and let you see what I thought and what made me tick. And to others who may read this, perhaps you will find something of value – or perhaps not." Later in the book you will be able to read more of what Michael shared in his book.

MENTORING YOUR SON

Wise Elder contributor, **Franz Schlink**, is from Bensheim, near Heidelberg, in Germany. Here is what Franz wrote about his relationship with his son: *"In our society in Germany older people are more likely to be seen as a burden. I notice little of a culture here that appreciates the elderly as experienced and wise people from whom we could learn much if we listened to them. I myself had many long conversations with my grandparents who lived in the same house as we did in my childhood and adolescence. They both had survived the First and the Second World War and independently ran a bakery. The life experiences of my grandparents affected me strongly and were certainly also responsible for my career choice.*

"Today, I am personally so busy that the feeling of being a 'wise elder' hardly comes up. Maybe that will change when I retire in three years. On the occasion of your book, I asked my children if they experience or experienced me in the role of a 'wise elder'. In everyday life, my children do not see me in this role. However, there was one situation that two of my children classified me under the motto 'wise elder'.

"For eleven years, once a year I participated in father-child camps for fathers with children between the ages of 5 and 14 for four days. The last camps I visited only with my son Martin. There, we ate together, talked, sung and planned in the group. Every year, we also implemented a small craft project. For example, we built a bird house in one year or made a boomerang in another year and then let it fly. We hiked, did a lot of sports together and learned a lot about the landscape, nature and architecture in different places. In the evenings, the fathers exchanged views and the children mostly organized the evening on their own and had a great pleasure to stay up late.

"My son Martin remembers that he learned a lot from the fathers and especially together with me, something that was not possible so intensively in the rest of everyday life. He is now 18 years old and very strong. At the moment, we have a lot of work with our two houses and the gardens. Since my back often hurts, especially during physical work, I am glad that Martin supports me on the weekends."

MENTORING YOUNG MEN

Wise Elder contributor, **Aric Rohrer** writes about his experience in mentoring two young men. *"For about 10 years now, I've been having weekly phone calls with two different young men. We focus mostly on what they're feeling* *about what's going on in their lives and what those feelings are asking of them. For example, fear, if they're not catastrophizing, is asking for a plan.*

"Most of what I'm doing is asking questions and listening, though I do chime in if I see there are some helpful distinctions they're not making. Overall, they seem to be able to solve their own problems simply through having an opportunity to talk about them.

"Talking with them has been very gratifying for me. It feels good to have an ongoing connection with them. I enjoy hearing their stories and watching them grow as people over time. And I feel proud of my part in that. Or at least I do when I allow the subtlety of being a catalyst through listening to shine through."

GERMAN WISE ELDERS TEACH HISTORY LESSONS

German wise elder contributor, **Franz Schlink**, reported that in German schools they are doing the following: *"In several schools in our region, contemporary witnesses are at times invited to history lessons or political education events. The idea is that the historical memory is of great importance for the political education and that the experiences of contemporary witnesses should not be lost. When certain topics are concerned, the local press reports about those events. This makes the experiences of contemporary witnesses accessible to a wider audience. Since history is just a record of what happened, having elders in the classroom to tell the young people what they experienced is extremely powerful. The Holocaust Project is another example where they have videoed survivors of the concentration camps to create a record of what actually happened to them to pass on to future generations so they do not forget. The Echoes and Reflections Project offers free educational materials to schools about the Holocaust. Their website is http://echoesandreflections. org/teach/?utm_source=google&utm_medium=cpc&utm_term=teaching%20 the%20holocaust&utm_campaign=Holocaust."*

MY DIALOGUES WITH SOPHIA

My two children decided not to have children, for various reasons, but I developed a close relationship with my step-granddaughter, Sophia. When she was very young, 4-8 years old, she loved to sit on my lap and have me read the Sunday *"funny papers"* to her (just the way my grandpa did for me when I was her age). When she was about 14 years old she came from Colorado to visit my wife and I while we were living in Swannanoa, North Carolina. She and I didn't see each other very often at that time, about once or twice a year, but when we came for a visit she always indicated she wanted to have some alone time with me so we could *"talk about things."* She was an expert *"debater"'* and was on her school's debate team, but our conversations were not *"debate-oriented,"* but instead consisted more like *"dialogues."*

"One evening she and I were sitting in our hot tub, 'talking about things.' She had very conservative ideas and often stated them openly and with great pride. She started our conversation that evening with the statement, 'I believe that abortion is murder.' Then, she looked at me for a reaction. When I didn't react to what she said, she asked me, 'Well, what do you think about abortion?

"Instead of trying to refute her belief, I told her about some of the experiences I had before there was a national law legalizing abortion. I told her that as the Director of the Counseling Center at the University of Wisconsin at Green Bay, I had a number of pregnant women students who came to me trying to decide whether or not to have an abortion. I told her that at that time it was illegal to have an abortion and that women at that time had very few good choices, if they decided to have an abortion. They could try to abort their fetus with a coat hanger that was very dangerous to their life. They could go to some illegal back room location where they could get an abortion from shady people who had poor or no credentials. Or they could travel to Canada where abortion was legal. None of these were great options, but for women who decided to have an abortion, they had to choose one of these poor options.

"After sharing this information with Sophia, I told her that because of my experiences when there was no law to protect a woman's right to an abortion, I was in favor of the law that protected a woman's right to choose. She was surprised by my admission, but she changed the subject and we talked about less charged subjects.

"The next time we met, about a year later, she announced that she had changed her mind on the subject of abortion. Later on we had other talks about relationships, what love is and the stresses she was facing in her relationship with a young man. She was open to share with me and I greatly appreciated seeing her and have her give me a hug with the exclamation, 'I love you, Grandpa Barry.'

"She loves to go fishing with me (I helped her catch her first fish). We also shared some important 'firsts' in her life. My wife and I took her to her first live concert at Red Rocks Amphitheatre in Denver. We saw her and our favorite performer, Neil Young. I also took her to her first major league baseball game at Coors' Field in Denver. She is now away at college so we talk regularly on Skype. She has become a strong advocate for women's rights and holds very progressive views about global climate change and protection for the 'Dreamers'.

"She and I watched with some dismay, the night of the 2016 Presidential election. She was hoping to witness the election of the first woman President. We cried and consoled each other after the results were in. We have had many discussions since then about the current political landscape."

She is clearly a different person from the young woman who told me she believed that *"Abortion is murder."* I can claim some credit for influencing her change of beliefs, but I know she made her own decision about these things by talking to others besides me. We still are very close and she seeks me out when she wants my opinion on some subject. She also seeks out my wife for advice on things that involve *"women's issues."*

WHAT DOES THE AUTHENTIC LIFE LOOK LIKE TO A WISE ELDER?

Here are the top 10 ways my life has improved at age 81:

1) I more am content just with being me. I do not fear being alone. Actually I long for it. Maybe some people know who they are at 30, but I sure didn't. Looking back, I doubt I even knew what I didn't know. Sure we all have attachments, opinions and perspectives but are they ours, or just products of our education, influences and upbringing? After 81 years of living, I've begun to embrace and discard enough to know what is really me and what isn't me. I have much clearer boundaries as a result. And while I'll never stop growing and learning, the me that I've found at 81 is at peace.

2) My writing is satisfying and purposeful. I started writing in my late thirties with far more doubt than talent. After writing for over 40 years and with 64 books published, I have suffering through the highs and lows my writing career. My first book took me 6 years to complete, after I had a contract. I had an *"editor from hell."* I would send her a copy of the manuscript and what I would get back from her was, *"Cut it, it's too long!"* It took six complete rewrites to finally satisfy her. Now I think I finally can claim the right to call myself a writer. While I still have room to grow and develop and continue to expand, right here is a really good place to be.

3) I'm healthier now than I was then. I ate a very unhealthy diet, drank plenty of sodas, and took very little tine to exercise. Thanks to a much-improved diet, regular exercise and an active mind, my vitality, stamina and optimism doesn't even compare to where I was at age 30.

4) My relationship and friendship with my wife is 100 times better than it was at age 30. I have been married, divorced and widowed by age 45. I remarried at age 47 and have enjoyed a transformational relationship like none I could have imagined. I had no idea that a relationship could be so completely satisfying. Janae and I have lived together and worked together as co-therapists with couples, taught classes together and wrote books together. We have abiding love for each other and a vision of service to others that we live out of every day.

5) My finances are much times better. When I was 30 through my 50s I had mortgages and lots of debt. Today, I am completely debt free and have a nice car and a nice home in a great neighborhood. While I am not wealthy, I have enough money to live comfortably. Many of our kids live near us (one just around the corner) and we seem to have a good relationship with them.

6) I love where I live and don't crave living somewhere else. I love living in Colorado Springs. That wasn't always the case. When we retired, we looked to move to some other part of the country. For a while, we lived half of the year in Florida and the other half here in Colorado. Finally, we moved to Asheville, North Carolina for 11 years, which was a lovely place to live. However, something deep within us pulled us to move back to Colorado Springs in 2014. I stated it as, *"You can take the man out of the mountains, but you can't take the mountains out of the man."* I look out at the view of Pikes Peak from my bedroom window every morning and thank my lucky stars to be living in such a beautiful place.

7) I don't crave things that I don't have. Although I never went overboard on buying things at age 30, like everyone else, I did want a bigger house, a nicer car, and all sorts of stuff that others had. Now 51 years later I realize that all that stuff did not produce any happiness and that integrity, peace of mind and loving connections with friends and loved ones are what really matters.

8) I'm much better able to be in and enjoy the moment. At 30, I was somewhat of a maniac about doing and seeing as much as humanly possible. I couldn't get enough of life. Yet, since I was so busy running to the next *"thing,"* I often felt stressed and overworked. It was as though I felt I had to do it all and if I didn't, I would never ever get another chance. At 81, I finally realize the gift of staying in the moment and just doing nothing at times. It is priceless.

9) I am far less controlled by the wants, needs and the expectations of others, and now I live more with the guidance of my own soul. I was a classic people-pleaser at age 30. Trying to please and sometime change my friends, my family, and yes, my spouse. One of the most important lessons I learned over the years is that you can't change anyone else or get anyone else to love you (let alone like you) if they don't want to. At 81, it is clear to me that I can only change myself and as for love, that starts in on the inside of me as well.

10) I am at peace about my understanding of Life, God and where I fit in the Universe. I didn't get exposed to an excessive amount of religious dogma as a child, but at age 30 I didn't really know what I believed. Now after years of contemplation, reading hundreds of books, spending many hours of study, and with the help of many smart people, I have pieced together my own understanding of a benevolent Universe and where I fit in it All.

Far too often, I hear people my age talk about the downfalls of aging. And of course, it would be pointless to deny there are some. But let's face it, there are just as many disadvantages to youth as well. So instead of focusing on all the negatives that are possible, I decided to focus on the rewards of growing older. I figured if I didn't value age as a gift with under-appreciated benefits, who would. When someone I meet says, *"I just turned 80,"* I often exclaim, *"Good for, you must be doing something right."*

THE WISE MAN OF THE HIMALAYAN MOUNTAINS[35]

Here is another story that comes from the Himalayan mountains: *"High in the Himalayan mountains lived a wise old man. Periodically, he ventured down into the local village to entertain the villagers with his special knowledge and talents. One of his skills was to "psychically" tell the villagers the contents in their pockets, boxes, or minds.*

"A few young boys from the village decided to play a joke on the wise old man and discredit his special abilities. One boy came up with the idea to capture a bird and hide it in his hands. He knew of course, the wise old man would know the object in his hands was a bird.

"The boy devised a plan. Knowing the wise old man would correctly state the object in his hands was a bird, the boy would ask the old man if the bird was dead or alive. If the wise man said the bird was alive, the boy would crush the bird in his hands, so that when he opened his hands the bird would be dead; if the wise man said the bird was dead, the boy would open his hands and let

the bird fly free. So not matter what the old man said, the boy would prove the old man a fraud.

"The following week, the wise old man came down from the mountains into the village. The boy quickly caught a bird and cupping it out of sight in his hands, walked up to the wise old man and asked, 'Old man, old man, what is it that I have in my hands?'

"The wise old man said, 'You have a bird.' and he was right. The boy then asked, 'Old man, old man tell me, is the bird alive or is it dead?' The wise old man looked at the boy and said, 'The bird is as you choose it.' And so it is with your life." Author unknown.

CHAPTER FOUR

WHAT DO WISE ELDERS WANT IN THEIR LIVES?

*I have reached an age when, if someone tells
me to wear socks, I don't have to.*

—Albert Einstein

WHAT IS THE PROCESS OF BECOMING A WISE ELDER?

The more challenging our world becomes, the more we need our wise elders to share the lessons they have learned, to lend us their problem-solving skills, and to enhance our lives by imparting their unique gifts. How can they prepare for this important task? Wise elders themselves need to embrace this role for themselves, their families, and their communities. The attitudes, disciplines, and life skills that elderhood demands are completely different from those would normally develop in the aging process. Wise elders want to totally transform their lives. However, what they often lack is a map to help them do this. There is a map that the great mythologist, Joseph Campbell, discovered by studying myths and fairy tales. The most complete myth he studied is *The Odyssey* by Homer.

WHAT IS THE JOURNEY OF TRANSFORMATION?

Campbell studied all the mythology and fairy tales of the Western world and some of the Eastern world as well in order to develop his map for the journey of transformation. Notice that the circular journey goes counter-clockwise because this journey does run counter to the normal journey through life that most people take. Most people have many trips around this circle in their life, but they can often identify the overall journey of transformation that they have lived.

Campbell, found that the myths and fairy tales he studied were not just children's stories or entertaining tales. They were carefully designed stories to teach people how to transform their lives. Below is a graphic map of the journey and under that is an explanation of the meaning of each step on this journey.

Figure 4-1. The Journey of Transformation

I created the Journey of Transformation by reading Joseph Campbell's book, *The Hero with a Thousand Faces*.[36] In this book, he shares his discovery of this journey imbedded in the myths and fairy tales of both Western and Eastern cultures. These were teaching stories that offered the listener a map to follow to transform his/her consciousness. Campbell brilliantly describes this journey as shown above. I have described the steps on this journey below in a modern context.

Interestingly, Andrew Harvey found a very similar map of the journey of transformation in the poetry of Rumi and in his book, *The Way of Passion*,[37] Harvey quotes Rumi's poem about transformation:

I burn away; laugh, my ashes are alive
I die a thousand times;
My ashes dance back—
A thousand new faces

Harvey explains the journey of transformation in Rumi's terms, *"When you consent to dance and burn away, you become the creation-destructor and creation creator all in one and your ashes dance back with a thousand new faces."* In Rumi's map of the journey of transformation the three stages are purification, expansion and union. Below is a description of each of the stages in Campbell's journey.

The Call to Awaken. This call usually comes as the result of an external event or some inner awareness that asks you to examine your life and the direction it is heading. This call can appear as an opportunity to do something new or as an obstacle that prevents you from living the way you have been. It can come at any time in your life and offer you a fork in the road where you can choose a new direction or pattern for your life. It can be precipitated by an illness or accident that interrupts your usual routine and gives you to reflect on your life. The call also can come from losing a job or from finding a new job that requires a move. It also can come from reading a book, seeing movie or play, from the loss of a loved one or the breaking up of a relationship.

Refusing to Answer the Call to Awaken. You may decide not to answer the call to awaken, At least not at first. Perhaps fear dominates your thinking and you decide this is not the right time to make changes. It is easy to find reasons to avoid the call to awaken. Perhaps you are in line for a promotion, or you decide to build a house or buy a car or boat. Whatever the reason, you may feel unable to breakout of your roles and responsibilities. Don't worry. If you refuse the call, it will come again and again, ringing louder and louder each time.

Some people spend a lifetime being stuck at this step of their life journey. They receive the call, refuse to answer it and go back to business as usual. As the calls keep coming, however, they keep getting a little louder each time. You may find that your life is getting more and more intense until you realize what is happening and you realize you are forced to change. Perhaps a family member gets sick; you get passed over for a deserved promotion or get fired from your job. If you don't pay attention to the inner call, something from the outside may force you to finally answer the call to awaken. You have no choice.

Answering a False Call. You may think you are answering the call, but instead you answer a false call by agreeing to do something that asks you to ignore your own needs and feelings, such as Rescuing others. You may believe you are doing what you are supposed to do, but you are really setting yourself up to be a Victim again. Perhaps old loyalty debts pull at you, asking you give up your own needs. You may become the chair of a committee at church, run for public office, or take a job you didn't want or even marry someone who you know will not support your spiritual growth. Only later do you finally realize that you have answered a false call.

Answering the Call to Awaken. This usually involves some kind of big risk, such as trying something entirely new, discovering your own inertia or identifying your own family patterns. Answering the call can be very difficult if you have refused it many times and you may feel backed into a corner when you finally answer the call. In any case, this decision usually involves a conscious choice to open yourself to a new pathway to growth and awareness. This decision is irreversible, although you may not realize it until much later that once you have taken this step, you cannot go back to being unconscious anymore.

Gathering Allies. At first, the new challenges related to answering the call to awaken can seem overwhelming. It is often necessary to gather allies to support you to take the next steps on your journey of discovery. The word *ally* comes from the Greek word meaning *"silly or fool,"* so you may meet allies who at first seem silly or foolish. Allies may also find you, rather than having to find them. Books may fall off the shelf into your hands in a bookstore, someone may give you a book to read or a tape to listen to, or you may have a chance meeting with an interesting stranger. You may also consciously seek allies by joining a class, a support group or getting into therapy. These allies help you realize that you are on the right track and can encourage you to become even more awake.

Crossing the Threshold of Consciousness. When we have gathered enough allies, we must risk crossing the threshold of consciousness into the unknown. This has been described in some myths as a crucifixion or dismemberment. This usually requires a leap of faith, to do battle with your inner demons or fears that tell you are doing the wrong thing. There are usually a number of different thresholds to cross before you can take the leap of faith into the unknown. The first is the *silliness threshold* that involves the fear of looking foolish to others. Another is the *sanity threshold*, or fearing you might go crazy if you leap into the void or that you will fall into a *"black hole"* and never return.

The *knowledge threshold* involves a fear of discovering something new that might invalidate the way of see yourself or the world. The *trust threshold* reflects your vulnerability and a fear of being hurt. You may also experience a *love threshold*, where you fear that you will lose the love of friends and family if you cross the threshold. Finally, you may find a *survival threshold* looming in front of you, fearing death or abandonment.

The Road of Trials. After the decision to cross the threshold into the unknown is made, you are immediately faced with the road of trials. These tests of your courage and commitment force you to rely on your newly acquired internal resources to handle the tests you encounter. There is no time to look back, to consult your notes, to think it over or talk to a trusted friend. The decisions must be made quickly and decisively.

The Dark Night of the Soul. Sometime during the road of trials, you may have to endure the dark night of the soul when the bottom literally drops out of your world. This might involve the death of a loved one, the end of a career, a betrayal in a close relationship, a serious illness or an accident that tests you beyond anything you have ever experienced. If you enter this stage fully you usually emerge from this experience feeling much stronger and more integrated.

Gathering New Allies. The kind of life-altering events around a dark night of the soul often help you attract new allies. The friends from before your shift in consciousness will probably seem shallow and unable to understand your despair. This step gives you an opportunity to go deeper into yourself to seek the meaning of your Dark Night of the Soul experiences. Some people return to therapy, travel, find new soul-partners or develop new interests and activities.

The Sacred Marriage. This very special step in your journey begins when you begin reclaiming your projections. It helps you develop a sense of inner unity between your masculine and feminine parts that helps you integrate your power and your love. It is described as the willingness to go on *"internal power"* and to consciously direct your life, instead of worrying about the opinions and reactions of others. It is also described as the *"psychological birth,"* or the birth of the individuated individual. In many sacred traditions, this step was ritualized and celebrated as a major step toward deeper consciousness.

The Apotheosis. This step involves casting off the False Self that you developed earlier in life in order to please others so that your Higher Self and lower Self can merge into your True Self. At this point, you have dealt sufficiently with your residue of developmental trauma and can feel compassion for yourself and your parents. This is a time of inner healing, a time to move out of old Victim or Rescuer roles and build healthy relationships with friends and loved ones. It is truly moving into the dimension of life where your heart opens fully and you feel the flow of deep feelings of love and compassion.

The Return to Consciousness. The transformational journey often seems complete at this stage, but actually this is only the halfway point. This is some traditions is described as a resurrection. Your task in the next stage of your journey is to be able to take all that you have learned during your inner journey and integrate it into your everyday life. In other words, to *get on with it.* This is not an easy task, for the everyday world still contains all the traps and family patterns that can lull you back to sleep again or pull you off center.

There are also unexpected costs to you for gaining access to your depths. Your friends and loved ones may not understand your experience or you may be tested and criticized by your peers about your new beliefs and visions for yourself. They may work very hard to get you to return to the old Drama Triangle dynamics. You also may find that the outer world that was once very comfortable to you now is experienced as very common, ordinary, dull and banal. You may even wish to retreat into the comfort and safety of your rich inner world. To put it simply, it becomes incredibly more difficult to live in the everyday outer world after having lived fully in your inner depths.

You must bring the knowledge from your inner depths back to the everyday world and learn how to integrate your inner and outer worlds. Crossing back over the threshold of consciousness into the outer world can activate some of the same fears that you had when you *crossed the threshold* the first time and took your leap of faith into the unknown. You may fear that people will think you are weird or silly for wanting to pray, spend an hour or more a day in meditation, write in a journal or do other strange daily spiritual practices. You may also fear that the split between your inner and outer worlds will drive you crazy or if you go into the outer world, you will lose contact with your inner world again.

Becoming The Master of Both Your Worlds. The last step on the circular journey is to become the master of both your inner and outer worlds. This means developing a *"passport"* that allows you travel back and forth over the threshold between them. At this stage of the journey you can enter your rich inner world, harvest your riches and bring them with you back into your everyday world. It means being able to navigate the interdependent world between oneness and separateness, free of major splits in your consciousness and the projections that go with these splits and free of your developmental trauma and the traps of the Drama Triangle.

This circular journey can be seen as one large life journey or as many smaller journeys that occur in your lifetime. As Rumi suggests, you may have to die a thousand times in order to reach the end of this glorious life-long journey of transformation.

WHAT ARE THE FOUR STAGES OF SPIRITUAL TRANSFORMATION?

Another map of transformation was developed by Scott Peck in his book, *A Different Drum* (1987).

There is a pattern of progression through identifiable stages of human spiritual development. I myself have passed through all of them in my own spiritual journey. Scott Peck described them this way:

1. Stage One: The Chaotic and Antisocial Stage. In this stage people pretend that they are spiritual or religious covering up their lack of principles. Although they may pretend to be loving (and often think of themselves that way), their relationships are filled with manipulation and self-serving. Being unprincipled there is nothing that governs their behavior except their own ego. Since their ego can change from moment to moment, there is a lack of integrity to their actions. Some can become quite disciplined in their service to themselves and their ambition and rise to positions of considerable prestige and power, even to become presidents.

2. Stage Two: The Formal, Institutional Stage. In this stage people obey the law, but they do not understand the spirit of the law. Consequently, they are legalistic, parochial and dogmatic. They are threatened by anyone who thinks differently from them and believe they are *"right"*. They then regard it as their responsibility to correct the people who are *"wrong."* They are *"true believers."* Their thinking is dominated by right-wrong, good and evil, etc. They have simplistic solutions to every problem and to try to escape the mystery of uncertainty. All those outside of Stage Two are perceived as Stage One people, because they do not understand those who might be in Stage Three or Four.

3. Stage Three: The Skeptical Stage of the Individual and the Questioner. These people include the atheists, agnostics and those who are scientifically minded and demand measureable, well-researched and logical explanations. Although frequently they may begin as *"non-believers,"* they are generally more spiritually developed many people who are content to remain in Stage Two. Although a skeptic, they are not antisocial and are often deeply involved in social causes. Despite being individualistic in their thinking, they are on a higher spiritual level than those in Stage Two. This questioning stage is a pre-requisite to entering Stage Four.

4. Stage Four: The Mystical, Communal Person. Out of love and compassion for others, this person uses his/her ability to transcend their own psychological background, their culture and limitations with all others, reaching toward a notion of a planetary culture. They seek answers to life's great mysteries. Mystics acknowledge the enormity of the unknown, but rather than being frightened by it, they seek to penetrate deeper into it so that they might better understand these mysteries.

They often use meditation, self-reflection and prayer to seek answers to these deep questions. This person regards conventional religion as a movement away from collective consciousness and inner truth to an acceptance of what I would call *"The Matrix"* or the simulated reality that they were taught in their family, church and schools. They can still be involved in religious practices in a church setting. They enter a religious community in search of answers about the mystery of life while others in the same congregation may be there to escape those same mysteries. This person sees the whole world as one community.

Wise elders are likely in Stage Three or Stage Four of their spiritual development. If they have doing their inner work, they are uniquely prepared to lead others from an internal perspective.

ANOTHER MAP OF TRANSFORMATION

Finally, Angeles Arrien,[38] created another map of transformation, *The Eight Gates of Wisdom*. She, like Campbell, says that all world tales and perennial wisdoms point to eight gates through which people must pass in order to fully develop into wise elders. Each gate has its own gift, task, and challenge. They include:

1. Facing new experiences and the unknown. This involves what Joseph Campbell says is crossing the Threshold of Consciousness into your inner unknown world.

2. Discovering one's true face or authentic identity. This is similar to Campbell's idea of gathering allies. At some point you hear an inner voice that tells you that you are not living out of your True Self and are not being an authentic person.

3. Exploring relationships from the crucible of love, intimacy and forgiveness. Here you explore the relationships you always have wanted, but were too scared to look for. This usually involves taking the risk to take the steps to establish the relationships that deep down you know you deserve.

4. Approaching service, creativity and generativity from a place of legacy. Wise elders often begin to look at their legacy. Most wise elders want to leave more than they took. They want to help to contribute to improving the conditions for others and reducing their suffering. This is part of what Eric Erikson called the seventh stage of development, Generativity vs. Stagnation. This stage takes place during middle adulthood (ages 40 to 65 years). Generativity refers to *"making your mark"* on the world through creating or nurturing things that will outlast an individual.

People experience a need to create or nurture things that will outlast them, often having mentees or creating positive changes that will benefit other people. We give back to society through raising our children, being productive at work, and becoming involved in community activities and organizations. Through generativity we develop a sense of being a part of the bigger picture. Success leads to feelings of usefulness and accomplishment, while failure results in shallow involvement in the world. By failing to find a way to contribute, we become stagnant and feel unproductive. These individuals may feel disconnected or uninvolved with their community and with society as a whole.

5. Developing character and deepening wisdom. The previous stage of development leads to the last stage in Erikson's progression: Ego Integrity vs. Despair. It is during this time that we contemplate our accomplishments and can develop integrity if we see ourselves as leading a successful life. Erikson described ego integrity as *"the acceptance of one's one and only life cycle as* *something that had to be"* (1950, p. 268) and later as *"a sense of coherence and wholeness"* (1982, p. 65).

He believed if we see our lives as unproductive, feel guilty about our past, or feel that we did not accomplish our life goals, we become dissatisfied with life and develop despair, often leading to depression and hopelessness. Success in this stage will lead to the virtue of *wisdom*. Wisdom enables a person to look back on their life with a sense of closure and completeness, and also accept death without fear.

Wise people are not necessarily characterized by a continuous state of ego integrity, but they experience both ego integrity and despair. Thus, late life for the wise elder is characterized by both integrity and despair as alternating states that need to be balanced.

6. Opening to the presence of grace. A simple definition of grace is "the experience of awe, gratitude and unconditional love when you are in harmony with yourself, with others and with the power that creates the cosmos. It is the harmonious integration of your body, mind and spirit with the way of nature. Grace is the spiritual freedom that arises when you realize that life is a gift. From this awareness you seek to live in harmony with the power that creates the cosmos. From this friendship arises a profound feeling of happiness as well as spiritual, emotional and mental freedom. When a wise elder can sustain a feeling of grace he has arrived.

7. Moving into surrender, acceptance, and equanimity. These terms may mean different things to others, but here is what they mean to me. It took me five years to be able to practice surrender on a regular basis and I mark it as the most important quality of a wise elder. Surrender is the key. There are two forms of surrender: a feminine and a masculine form. The feminine form means, *"The willingness to receive without resistance."* This involves acceptance and equanimity. The masculine form means, *"The willingness to take charge of your life without guilt or shame."* Wise elders need to be able to use both of these as the situation requires.

8. Practicing non-attachment and letting go.[39] Non-attachment has been said is the secret to happiness. It really means that the following is true:
- Expectations no longer rule your life.
- Emotions will inevitably go up, but you are in charge of them. You have perspective. Emotions don't have to catch you and torment you every time.

- You can relate to the world as it is rather than the way you would like it to be, which never brings lasting happiness.
- You have a clarity of mind so you're able to find the truth of things.
- You're not bothered by much of the mundane, but that doesn't mean you tolerate harmful behavior.
- The problems of this world evoke compassion in you rather than anger.
- You don't have to chase after happiness. You can just enjoy it when it's present.
- You're able to allow life to unfold without needing to control everything.
- You don't stop loving. You can love even more.
- Your heart only grows bigger and bigger and bigger particularly when you see all the unnecessary suffering in this world.
- You feel naturally compelled to help others, but you're not attached to the outcome.
- You experience a sense of spaciousness and freedom and you can feel bring a genuine contentment to whatever you are doing.

I may not have done justice to Angeles Arrien's *Eight Gates of Wisdom* people must pass through in order to become wise elders. If you are interested in learning more about her approach to transformation, I suggest you look into her course *"Becoming a Wise Elder with Angeles Arrien."* You can find this course at: https://www.spiritualityandpractice.com/ecourses/course/view/146/becoming-a-wise-elder

WHAT DO WISE ELDERS WANT IN THEIR LIVES?

I have compiled a consensus list of seventeen things that wise elders want in their lives. I will describe each of these and add what the contributors to this book have written about each of them. This list is not meant to be a complete list, so feel free to add your own if you don't see them there.

1. No more wars. We are tired of fighting and competing with everyone. Wise elders have found ways to resolve their conflicts peacefully. So many wars have been caused by splitting and projections. George Santana supposedly said, if we don't learn from our history we are destined to repeat it. Here is what **Michael Lightweaver** a wise elder contributor to this book has to say about wars and competition: *"Here is the dilemma. Is it possible to be informed by our personal or collective history without becoming its prisoner? Can our past experience inform our present and influence our future without* *putting our present and future in 'lock down' or solitary confinement? And furthermore is it possible to change?*

"Does our present view of an individual or group account for the possibility that they can or have changed, grown or evolved? And what about ourselves; have we changed or evolved over the past decade? If so, do we want our friends and families to take this into account or are we satisfied that they continue to hold us hostage to their perception of who we were ten or twenty years ago.

"At a social and international level, we see the same mechanism at work. Historical hatreds between ethnic groups, tribes, nations and religions are carried over from generation to generation like a genetic disease that is passed on from parents to children with no relief. The world is full of examples of this, the two of which come to mind most readily are the ongoing conflicts in Northern Ireland and Israel and Palestine. The parties in each case demonize the other side and perpetuate this poison from generation to generation and act it out in wars."

2. Come home to love to be with family, friends, and community. Here is what wise elder contributor, **Lloyd Wright**, wrote about this topic: *"I think the journey of finding consciousness is the way to Self. If I cannot find it, I will never be able to serve others and will not be prepared for death. I know this because in the last 10 years I have lived in my home town. I moved back here for a job, but reconciled the move because it would re-connect my wife and I to our families.*

"Within four years of that move, I lost 4 cousins (dear friends as well). I lost my only brother and my only sister. I am the last surviving member of my nuclear family and I am moved by that place. There are more of my people at the cemetery then walking around my old home town.

"My sister died in an accident, all the cousins died from disease and my brother died from a long, lingering lung disease and it was a horrible way to die. He was 78, ten years my senior and he never found Self. He never was able to see life as anything other than a huge party filled with laughter and travel with friends. He went to church. I know he believed in God, but not sure how he defined God.

"My brother was a good friend and first to jump in to help everyone. From the outside, you would see a guy who was doing God's work every time he got out of bed in the morning. He was a private pilot both fixed wing and helicopter. I saw him transport kids to the Shrine Hospital when they were in need. When his friend was injured and became paralyzed from the waist down, he had him on the plane to the best hospital in the country for rehab.

"I spent every other day with him in his room while he was dying. Many times, and I am not exaggerating here, I had to wait downstairs because there were too many people in his room visiting him. This went on for months. Clearly he was revered by his friends."

3. We want to help others. This is what almost all wise elders say they want. Wise elders need to develop a *"service to others"* life orientation rather than a *"service to self"* life orientation.

Wise elder contributor, **Michael Harder**, added the following: *"If we accept that we are all one, there is only one so helping what appears to be another is helping yourself. I caution you to avoid the tendency to help others to be viewed as special and a "good" person. This is not the correct motivation for helping others."*

4. We want to share our lives with others. We want to tell our stories and offer our wisdom, humor and experiences for the sheer joy of sharing this great adventure of life. I get to do this every Monday night with my Men's Group. It is the highlight of my week. I am a story-teller and I am proud of it. I also enjoy my sense of humor. Wise elder contributor, **Michael Harder**, added the following ideas: *"As wise elders we want to share our experience to help remove the blocks to love from our collective conscious. From the False Self-perspective, we have to guard against the tendency to share our experiences in sort of a one up man ship manner – 'Spiritual Specialness.'"*

Wise elder contributor, **Mike Holtby**, added his thoughts about this specific want of wise elders. *"We want to tell our stories and offer our wisdom, humor and experiences for the sheer joy of sharing this great adventure of life.*

"This life is a great adventure, and I have had a blog: http:// GrandAdventures.org for many years. It is based on Helen Keller's saying, "Life is a grand adventure or nothing at all." My blog details, with many photographs, my seven decades of adventures. As a psychotherapist I often asked my clients, "What do you want most out of life?" I had a client with AIDS early in the epidemic when few survived. His answer was, "I want lots of adventures, so when I'm sick I'll have lots of good memories to fall back on." I thought that was a great philosophy, and I've tried to live it ever since. I hope it also serves to inspire others as well.

"So I've set about collecting adventures by traveling to 42 different countries, and trying to document the disappearing cultures of indigenous people, as well as endangered wildlife. As a photographer I have teamed up with the Jimmy Nelson Foundation in Amsterdam with the same mission. Both the

Foundation and I are inspired by the work of Edward Curtis, a photographer at the beginning of the 20th Century who documented American Indian tribes with the knowledge their cultures and languages were disappearing. The Foundation is sending me to Tanzania in February, 2019.

"I want to pass on to the next generation, at least to those in my own family, a heritage rich in the images I have taken of cultures and wildlife that may not exist when they are my age. It is my legacy. So I am not only printing those images in the form of books, and individual photographs; but also video slide shows they can keep in a digital form. Many of these can be seen on my website: http://DenverPhotography.com

5. We want forgiveness. We know we have made mistakes and may have hurt others. We deeply regret these things we caused and now ask for forgiveness. We also have to forgive ourselves. Wise elder contributor, **Michael Harder**, again helps us as wise elders to understand the underlying purpose of forgiveness. He writes *"From the perspective of a wise elder, forgiveness means you forgive yourself for realizing nothing really happened and the perceived other is helping you with a lesson to remove a block to love. The realization that nothing happened is at the eternal or spiritual level. Forgiveness can help us see the truth in the statement that we are one.*

"From the perspective of the False Self, forgiveness can be just another ego tool to strengthen your sense of separation. If any forgiveness has any element of choosing a "good" or a "bad" person, place or thing, it is ego or False Self-based forgiveness."

6. We want to matter to others. We want to know we are needed and included, not just looked after. Many aging people feel more and more alone. A wise elder seeks to be included and not forgotten. He builds a network of friends where he can truly be himself. Because of geographical location, this is often as virtual circle of friends that he communicates with regularly by phone, text, Skype or just emails. This is an important value to wise elders.

7. We want to stay involved. We love life and now have time to truly enjoy the things that enrich our lives. Many wise elders volunteer their time to charitable organizations. There are a wide variety of opportunities to serve and stay involved at the same time. For example, we serve the homeless at the Soup Kitchens or drive for Meals-on-Wheels or in a myriad of ways provide service to others.

8. We want passion. We want a life filled with love and meaningful work. We know our gifts are born from passions still inside ourselves and we want to express them. Wise elders who have done their personal work often to restore a sense of passion to their lives. They are passionate and excited about everything they do. For most of the wise elders, they have reached a stage in life where they only do the things that bring more passion into their life.

9. We want to have fun. Fun for elder may be slightly different from what younger men see as fun. What is fun for elders is completing whatever *"bucket list"* they have created. This may mean going to a live concert of the Rolling Stones or Tony Bennett or Neil Diamond. It may involve traveling to some place you have always wanted to see, but never took the time to do it. It may involve reading that good book you never got to or going out to eat at a fancy restaurant or just playing with your grandkids.

10. We want to be seen as unique individuals. We are not all alike and resist labels. One of the most insulting things you can say to a wise elder is to address him by his first name without first getting their permission. It is a kind of personalized discount. As has been mentioned, the elderly is treated differently by many of the people they encounter. Stereotyping is rampant toward people with white hair or a wrinkled face. Elders are very sensitive to people who display their stereotypes.

11. We want to keep learning new things. Wise elder contributor, **George Butte**, wrote the following: *"As a college teacher for almost 50 years, I know it's easy to settle into familiar ideas about literature and film (which I teach), and about the world my students come from. And there are similarities: I protested the Vietnam War years ago, and some of them protest our wars in Afghanistan and Iraq. I know everyone says young people have different brains because of social media and electronic exposure. Perhaps. But some qualities of youth are the same: especially an impatience with social injustice and evils like inequity and oppression/violence linked to gender, race, or sexual orientation.*

"I remember well how impatient I was at 20: Why does it take so long to change things? Why did the Vietnam war drag on? (Think of Afghanistan!!) Why are the effects of slavery so long-lasting in contemporary America (think of the riots of the late 1960's)? Now I know more about the past—how the British made many of the same mistakes in Afghanistan in the 1850's, and the French in Indo-China in the 1890's. I still feel the sadness of suffering that keeps going on and on. After years of seeing change—that to some eyes is a lot, to others not nearly enough—what do I need to learn that is new? Do I need to remember the urgency of the young, to keep moving to a better place? Or do I need to remember patience—because disappointed urgency can sour

into cynicism? How do I keep my eye on the prize, and wait for the moral arc of the universe to manifest itself? Am I learning something new, or relearning something old?"

12. We want to find meaning in life. Wise Elder contributor, **Michael Lightweaver**, writes that lives are determined by our questions. He writes, *"For me the big questions have always been 'Why Are We Here?' 'What is this all about?' 'Are we here just to experience the joys and pain of childhood; the challenges of puberty and our teen years, school – endless school – followed by the fun and fiction of relationships, family, kids, mortgage, jobs, debt, old age and death? Is life just a bouncing between ecstasy and agony?'*

"It took me about 50 years to figure this one out, or at least to come to some conclusions that made sense to me and gave meaning to the whole comedy/ tragedy drama of human existence.

"It began with the early 1980's when I created the Human Potential Institute: a clinical hypnosis practice in Nashville, Tennessee (USA). In the course of using hypnosis to find the source of a client's concern in some event or a situation in their childhood, I would occasionally do regressions. Needless to say, it came as a big surprise when individuals would sometimes regress back to a supposed past life – especially when they did not even believe in reincarnation.

"At the time I had no special belief about the subject, as it was not a part of my Christian upbringing. But as it began to happen on a regular basis I launched into a lot of reading to get a better understanding of what it could all mean. From personal experience with clients as well as historical research into early Christian teachings, exploring other cultural and religious beliefs, and common sense born from observing nature, I came to see that we don't have to get it all done in one lifetime. Each of our lives is but a very brief chapter in a very long book. If this is true, then what is the plot? Gradually I came to see that it is really all about "soul growth."

"If this is true, then ultimately all of our experiences in life are just the curriculum. Some of it is pleasant and a great deal of it is unpleasant, but it is all instructive to those who have ears to hear and eyes to see. It has been my experience that our curriculum falls roughly into four categories: finance, romance, our bodies and our egos."

Wise Elder contributor, **George Butte**, wrote the following related to finding meaning in his life: *"This goal has remained constant in my life since I became a conscious adult in college, I guess. Then meaning was mostly in the future—hoping to do useful things, meet good people, find and give love, make a difference. To look back at 71 (my age now) is of course different: Now I ask* *how many of those hopes were realized? It is an important satisfaction is to see that there was some movement forward on these matters—actions, relationship, projects—many of them very imperfect, and only imperfectly realized: but still, they are something that I accomplished. Family, children, students, classes held, people loved, however imperfectly, ideas communicated. But what about the future? There is still time to make things even better. I don't know how to abandon my teleology.*

"A big goal for me has been to manage the loss of the traditional narratives of Meaning. For me the closure and comfort of traditional gospels is missing something - I don't believe in the empty tomb, Judgment Day, and holy orders, in anything like the received sense of Grace. We make community and meaning every day, and sustaining that work isn't always easy. Sometimes it's hard to believe, but I always believe in my beliefs."

13. We want physical connections and experiences. Hugs, making love, exercise, sports and being in nature are as important as ever. I think these things become even more important to wise elders. They strive to be vital in their old age and are reluctant to give up physical activities such as sports. Because of my scoliosis, I was forced to give up playing tennis. I loved the competition of tennis and the social aspects of meeting with my tennis buddies after a match.

It was extremely hard for me to do it, but I was faced with a choice: Either give up tennis or suffer from chronic lower back pain. I tried Pickleball thinking that would be less harmful to my back, but the bending over to reach a wiffleball that barely bounces, was actually harder on my back than tennis was. I still love fly fishing, and I can still pull on my waders and stand in the middle of a trout stream and catch fish. I like to hike, but now I have to limit the distance. My relationship with my wife of 34 years, Janae, has been a source of great connection on all levels: physical, emotional, intellectual, and spiritual.

14. We want to stay as independent as possible. This is a big desire of wise elders and most other elders. More and more wise elders are choosing to live independently and yet they have to build networks of friends so they are not alone. A recent survey showed that 61 percent of persons over the age of 65 prefer to live independently. I intend to live independently for as long as I can. I am never going to retire. I have at least 10 more books to write. Three are already on the drawing board. My parents and their parents all died at home and I plan to do the same.

15. We want to prepare for death in a conscious manner. Wise elder contributor, **Lloyd Wright**, had this to say about preparing for death: *"I want to prepare for death in a conscious manner. I have fought all the wars. There may be some yet to fight, but I want to consciously cobble together all my experiences for the time I have left and use them to come to terms with why I came here and why I will one day go.*

"I don't do a very good job of managing my ego and it could be the single most important element of my existence on this earth. I think it has been difficult for me because I don't remember my dreams much. When I do though, they are big and powerful.

"An amazing friend, left with me before she died, a valuable point that I believe is the answer to my desire. She said: 'I want you to remember, the only reason the Self dreams is to put the ego back on track, because we are only in this World to correct the ego's course and to make our contribution. The ego does not have the road map to our contribution...the Self does.'

"I think the journey of finding consciousness is the way to Self. If I cannot find it, I will never be able to serve others and will not be prepared for death. I know this because in the last 10 years I have lived in my home town. I moved back here for a job but reconciled the move because it would re-connect my wife and I to our families.

"Within four years of that move, I lost 4 cousins (dear friends as well). I lost my only brother and my only sister. I am the last surviving member of my nuclear family and I am moved by that place. There are more of my people at the cemetery then walking around my old home town.

"My sister died in an accident, all the cousins died from disease and my brother died from a long, lingering lung disease and it was a horrible way to die. He was 78, ten years my senior and he never found Self. He never was able to see life as anything other than a huge party filled with laughter and travel with friends. He went to church. I know he believed in God, but not sure how he defined God.

"My brother was a good friend and first to jump in to help everyone. From the outside, you would see a guy who was doing God's work every time he got out of bed in the morning. He was a private pilot both fixed wing and helicopter. I saw him transport kids to the Shrine Hospital when they were in need. When his friend was injured and became paralyzed from the waist down, he had him on the plane to the best hospital in the country for rehab.

"I spent every other day with him in his room. Many times, and I am not exaggerating here, I had to wait downstairs because there were too many peo-

ple in his room visiting him. This went on for months. Clearly he was revered by his friends."

16. We want to awaken our spiritual comprehension of life. What changes significantly for wise elders is an interest in the inner journey. Numerous scholars have observed that middle and later life involve an experience of increasingly transcendent aspects of inner life. Some have tied the development of wisdom to an increasingly transcendent attitude toward oneself, toward relationships with others, and toward worldly aims. As age increases, many people perceive themselves as having increasingly transcendent attitudes. They take more delight in their inner world, are less fearful of death, and feel a greater connection to the entire universe.

A study of active spiritual seekers among a representative sample of people born during the baby boom period found that 62 percent of active seekers were middle-aged or older, and most felt that *"People have God within them, so churches aren't really necessary."*[40]

These findings affirm the ancient wisdom among groups as diverse as the Navajo and the Jewish cabalists that a person must be age fifty to begin serious spiritual study. Many spiritual traditions assign special significance to age or life stage in terms of increased receptivity to spiritual development.

Evidence that spiritual growth is common in later life includes gradual increases with age in self-acceptance and perceptions of one's life as having integrity; service to others, especially community service and providing long-term care to family and friends; and interest in the young. With their exposure to the recent heightened cultural interest in spirituality, upcoming cohorts of wise elders may be even more interested in spiritual journeys as a focal point of later life.

Increased perceptions of life meaning and integrity, service to others, and generativity all require an attitude of transcendence and a measure of selflessness. They suggest that becoming a wise elder can represent a return home to the silence from which one came, and that on the way home, a nonpersonal state of consciousness may be gradually uncovered by conditions common in later life: a quiet mind, a simplified daily life, and a let-be attitude toward the world. The deepening spirituality of later life is often subtle and non-deliberate; it may occur naturally and spontaneously as a result of the physical, mental, and social processes of aging. It has been described as the conditions under which many people experience aging as a "natural monastery."

Contributing wise elder, **Michael Harder**, writes the following on this topic: "*Wise elders want to experience more and bring more oneness to the physical plane. Basically, we want to bring more love into the world.*

"*However, there may be tendency to be distracted away from removing the blocks to love. For example, multiple advanced degrees, sporting activities, political activities, or social activities that add to our thought constructs distract us into believing this will make you more valuable, knowledgeable or above others.*"

17. We want our culture to wake up from the incessant drumbeat of fear, competition and war. Wise elders want to contribute to helping people wake up and they often choose to do that by spending more time contemplating the world around them. They no longer have to march to the drumbeat of fear, competition or war. As a result, they can see the *"big picture."* They also are better able to zero in on the root causes of problems rather than get caught up in the symptoms of these problems. They know how to use their time wisely.

Wise elder contributor, **Aric Rohrer**, wrote the following about this topic: "*As part of my own unplugging from the drumbeat, I unplugged from the news. In fact, I haven't watch television for many years. Information about what's going on in the world is available out there when I'm ready for it and want to reach out to get it.*

"*There's no need to be bombarded with sensationalism. I reached out to a Political Theory professor that I know. We've been having ongoing conversation about how much skill and effort it takes to sift through the vast sea of information that's out there -- to sort the true from the false and the relevant-to-my-values from the irrelevant. We've been looking at how to empower everyone to do so. In social media I neither read nor pass on any gossip or fear-mongering.*"

WHAT IS THE SECRET OF HAPPINESS FOR WISE ELDERS?

Here is what wise elder contributor, **Michael Lightweaver**, has to say about this topic: "*The secret of happiness has always been the holy grail of human pursuit. Perhaps that secret is different for each person. In my younger years, I believed it was the attainment of goals – very often material ones – that would lead to happiness. But as I dutifully attained each of these goals, I realized that they brought only a moment of satisfaction, but no lasting happiness. Finally, I came to realize that my only true source of happiness was Gratitude and Generosity.*

"Regardless of our circumstances in life, we always have the choice of looking at those who have more or those who have less. Regardless of your station in life there will always be those who have more than you do; more money, more possessions, more fame, more love and better health. And there will always be those who have less. I found that my happiness largely depends on what I focus my attention on; whether I am in a state of gratitude for what I have or in perpetual angst for what I lack. It is that simple.

"I have heard it said that studies have shown that pessimists are more realistic, but optimists live longer and happier lives. At this stage in my life I can say that I am indeed happy. Yes, I still have worldly cares and challenges but I have found over the years, truth in the saying, 'in every seeming adversity is the seed of an equal or greater benefit.'

"And in spite of any momentary unpleasantness or sense of loss, I have always found a gift; something to be grateful for. And not only this, but the simple habit of Gratitude – for even the simplest of things – creates a personal frequency of joy that builds upon itself and is self-perpetuating. Deep appreciation and gratitude have become the cornerstone of my joy.

"A natural product of that Gratitude is Generosity. Living in a state of natural gratitude & deep appreciation for all that is, spontaneously opens my heart. As fear, anger, disappointment and hurt melt in the sunshine of Gratitude, my heart smiles and opens to a state of grace and giving.

"There is a deep desire and joy that comes from giving to others from the bounty of one's own life; whether it is money, love, possessions or simply good vibes, and the more one gives in the spirit of grace, the greater the joy and happiness. And since life is a two-way street and 'what goes around, comes around' that bounty returns in many forms and usually in greater measure. This is the second cornerstone of my joy."

CHAPTER FIVE

WHAT ADVICE DO WISE ELDERS HAVE FOR YOUNG MEN?

By the time you're eighty years old you've learned everything. You only have to remember it.

—George Burns

When I decided to write this book, I was unaware of another similar book on the market. It is titled, *Aging Wisely: Wisdom if Our Elders.*[41] What makes this book unique is that it was written by 97 year old Irving Silverman. It too contains the words of contributors that Irving recruited for his book. When asked why he wrote the book here is what he said, *"mostly, because I love older people because their lives are so full of exciting stories of living well and accomplishing so much."* Congratulations Irving, at your age you are truly remarkable and this book is filled with the wisdom of men and women like you. The book is available at Amazon at: https://www.amazon.com/Aging-Wisely-Wisdom-Our-Elders/dp/128414173X

I, like Irving, reached out to many friends and colleagues who I regard as wise elders. I was able to get 18 of these men to share with me a number of their mentoring stories and their experiences related to the 17 things that wise elders want in their lives that were listed in the previous chapter. This chapter contains the advice they wished to offer young men. They covered many topics in their advice including work, relationships and general advice that they wished they had gotten when they were young. In passing on their advice it is clear they hope it will help young people avoid some of the traps and pitfalls they encountered. Wise elders have a deep desire to share what they have learned from their experiences so that younger men do not make the same mistakes that they made.

As you read their advice listed below consider, if you are a wise elder, what advice you would want to pass on to your children or other young people you know. Do not hesitate to share what you know in the form of witnessing your story. If you give advice in that manner it will not seem like you are talking down to the readers, but rather just sharing what you have learned that you think might be helpful to young people. Use the online forum described in the last chapter to share your stories.

WHAT DO OTHER WISE ELDERS HAVE TO SAY?

Wise elder contributor, **Mark Joyous**, echoed these sentiments when he wrote, *"I feel like words of wisdom might be lost on many younger people today who realize that words are merely symbols. We can preach and teach, but reading about making a campfire is not the same as making one. The best I could offer would be stories and examples of Life from a heartfelt perspective that connect with deeper feelings.*

"I guess I would try to pass on the wisdom I gained from my elders and whatever I can add to it from my own experiences. The rapid pace of change in modern life has erased a lot of similarities and truths that once were shared by many generations. The secrets of the seasons and wisdom gained from nature came more easily and readily when each generation worked the soil and farm the land.

"But now the most honest teachers can only say that most of the jobs the children will be working in the future haven't even been invented yet. So how does one prepare for the unknown in a world that is constantly changing? The best the most honest teachers can say is that most of the jobs children will be working in the future have not even been invented. So how does one prepare for the unknown in a world that is constantly changing?

"The first thing is to discover that there are basic patterns and similarities even though the actual experiences are different. It's easy to get distracted by the fast pace of instant information and the desire for instant gratification as we grow into a global society. Surely it's hard to sip from fountains of knowledge when the firehose of information found in the media today can blast you apart. So the timelessness of real wisdom is found in messages like Desiderata or sacred texts and whatever speaks directly to your heart in ways that send chills or shivers up your spine. I'd say trust your instinct and intuition more often. If you trust that automatically in life and death situations, why don't you trust more in your more banal every day circumstances?

"I'd say don't be confused and learn the difference between wisdom and knowledge. For example, knowledge is knowing that a tomato is a fruit. But wisdom is knowing not to put it in a fruit salad.

"I'd say that slowing down to the pace of life will help you enjoy more and savor the fullness and richness of living, rather than simply running to or from our errands and accomplishments. I'd say time is precious quantity and one should be mindful of how we spend our time in things that bring us joy and help bring joy and harmony to others.

"I'd say look for ways to enjoy being of service as GHANDI said; there's more to life than increasing its speed. And I would finally say the best words of wisdom came to me from a woman rocking a baby who said as I was about to become a parent to simply learn to be positive, stay calm, build bridges, and grow strong."

Wise elder contributor, **Aric Rohrer**, put it very simply when he wrote: *"I wish someone had taken the time to be with me and show me that it was ok to be me, that how my parents raised me wasn't ok (even though it looked perfectly ordinary from the outside), and that there's such a thing as developmental trauma. I've been seeing therapists for decades. I only recently discovered any of this and it wasn't from them. I hurt for a long time and I didn't have to."*

Wise elder contributor, **Michael Harder** has similar, brief but pointed, advice: *"As you build your identity in this physical plane, locate all the blocks that prevent you from extending unconditional love in each and every moment here. It is much easier to build a true self then to undo a false self later in life."*

Wise elder contributor, **Larry Lawn**, sent me this list to share:

1. *"The passing of time alone will not make you a wise elder."*
2. *"The outer world is a reflection of how you see yourself, and the law of cause and effect can be used as a feedback loop for a life of self-discovery and spiritual growth."*
3. *"Don't waste time trying to change people, places, or things with outer actions only."*
4. *"Start now to increase your inner self-awareness. First look inside and notice patterns of recurring thoughts and feelings and see how they relate to your outer world."*
5. *"Take responsibility for how you are creating your version of a recurring 'problem' by noticing the specific meaning you have been automatically giving the outer situation. If there are other people involved, try to understand the meaning they are each projecting onto the same outer circumstances."*

---

6. *"Taking responsibility for your inner beliefs and feelings will give you the freedom to consciously choose your actions and to get different results."*

7. *"With awareness, responsibility, choice, and the willingness to learn from the consequences of your actions, you will live more peacefully and grow wiser over time."*

Wise elder contributor, **George Butte**, was very modest in sharing his thoughts: *"I don't have much Wisdom. Maybe that's wisdom. To my son and daughter, I say: keep the faith, but question. Understand your own wounds, and the wounds of others, and then commit to action; don't be paralyzed. Protect yourself, but always be open to the new and the Other. Truly accepting the Other is very difficult, and those difficulties could destroy our ever-more-closely-connected world, where differences of language, culture, tribe, belief (homosexuality is evil, etc.), gender, history, are more unavoidable than ever in the past.*

"Here is a favorite thought from the narrator of George Eliot's Middlemarch (1872): "If we had a keen vision and feeling of all ordinary [tragic] human life, it would be like hearing the grass grow and the squirrel's heartbeat, and we should die of that roar which lies on the other side of silence" (Ch. 20). I believe we can hear the grass grow, and not die of the roar that lies on the other side of silence; we learn to hear, to bear up, to move out into the world, and to make it better in all kinds of ways. I try to say this to my sons."

Wise elder contributor, **Lloyd Wright**, is very brief but specific about his advice: *"Slow way down. Listen more than make proclamations. Never make a decision on Mondays and take care of your wife and family. It is the most important thing you promised to do in your life. Your career means nothing without it."*

Wise elder contributor, **Richard Shulman**, shares several stories about mistakes he felt he made and offers them as suggestion of what not to do if you want to be successful and happy: *"I learned some lessons along the way that I would like to pass on so you don't have to learn them."*

*"**My Main Lesson:** The combination of arrogance and ignorance is deadly! I've been a working musician and composer since 1971. The combination of my ignorance and arrogance has made my career stall many times and required me to reinvent myself over and over for lack of traction in the professional music community. In one of the following examples it could be said that I made choices where I stuck to my principles but I now realize that I held my principles*

too rigidly, and unknowingly closed off opportunities. I was also holding other people to my own standards... It's enough to hold myself to my own standards!

"**Sub-Lesson #1:** *Don't talk about money early in the game if you are aspiring to get a job, deal or create a relationship. In the late '80s I had recorded a really great jazz album with my NYC band and was in the process of looking for a major label to work with me. I got a call from the legendary A&R guy at Atlantic Records, Aziz Goksel. He asked me if the album was still available. I said yes and that I had already spent $11,000 and was ready for a label to help. I immediately felt the energy between us droop and we ended the conversation. He called me back in a half hour and told me that their marketing people didn't think it would sell. End of that deal... Ten years later I released the album on my own label without the support I could have had, had I not sabotaged myself by complaining about money.*

"**Sub-Lesson # 2:** *Decide if you want to be right or win. When I moved to NYC a friend hired me to do some playing for an advertising music company he was working for. I had some reservations about participating in advertising, but the sessions paid pretty well and I was playing with some of the best musicians in the world. One time I had to wait around before getting to play and someone had told me that you're supposed to get paid for waiting to play. I asked my friend for the correct money. I was paid and that was the last time I was hired by that company. Yes, I was right, but I was also an unnecessary thorn in their side. So in a way, I kept myself "clean" of the advertising business, but I also lost all the support that was available through that network.*

"**Sub-Lesson #3:** *Learn to be more flexible in finding business arrangements that work for everyone. The Universe is seeking to help us in myriad ways, and I no longer am quite so picky about how those ways should work or how they should look. The story about the guy stuck on his roof in the middle of a flood illustrates my own learning process, and fortunately it's not too late for me to learn these lessons...*

"*The story goes something like this: A man has great faith in God. His neighborhood is flooded in a natural disaster. His first floor is filled with water so he goes up to the second floor and opens a window. A neighbor floats by in a boat and offers him a ride to safety. He replies, no thanks, God will save me. The flood gets higher and the man climbs out the window and onto the roof. Two more boats come by offering help, and he replies, no thanks, God will save me. The flood waters get higher and the man is forced to the very top of the roof. A helicopter flies by and the pilot offers him a rope ladder to climb up into the cockpit.*

"He says, no thanks, God will save me. Soon after this the flood rises above the house and the man drowns. His soul meets God and he says 'Why didn't you save me? I had such great faith!' God answers, 'I sent you three boats and a helicopter; wasn't that enough?'"

Wise elder contribution, **Rafa Flores**, has this to say to young men: *"What would I say to a younger person...??? I would ask them a question. How will I know what a younger person is needing if don't ask them, or if I am not there to offer an opinion on the task at hand, or add to the discussion? To be a wise Elder, (and everything that a wise elder stands for... insert super hero status) requires us to be PROACTIVE and to be present in their lives and activities. Society, as it is currently, needs a paradigm shift. Youth/society need to know it is acceptable to seek guidance from elders, and in fact, it should be a cultural norm for youth to seek this advice. We have to start by asking young people, 'What do you need?'"*

Wise Elder contributor, **Troy Lee**, has the following advice to young people about their relationships: *"One of the common themes I hear from young men is the frustration with dating and finding love that results in a long term relationship. I often hear men talk about the how all women are 'crazy' or are too critical and unrealistic, or are just looking for men with money.*

"This belief that woman are unrealistic and just want to be treated like a princess, or how all the good ones are already taken, is just not just something young men say, but is a belief I've seen many men hold on to, well into their later years. If you keep ending up in disastrous relationships or just can't find a woman who is not crazy or too demanding and unrealistic, or even just ANY woman (because you may be so lonely and desperate that crazy and high maintenance are characteristics that don't sound so bad in comparison) there might be a common denominator in all your unsatisfactory relationships. Yep, you guessed it. It's YOU!

"It is so easy to point your finger at the other person and reduce them to terms like crazy and high maintenance, absolving yourself from any responsibility. You're right those female archetypes are real, and those types of women do exist, and I absolutely can tell you those are not the majority of women. Yet somehow you keep ending up with the crazy ones? Hmmmm...

"My wife and I have an axiom we like to follow, in that healthy personalities do not attract unhealthy personalities, and unhealthy personalities do not attract healthy ones; at least not in the long term. If you find that you have never been in a healthy relationship, you may want to start looking in the mirror for the cause of the problem.

"I have been down the road of way too many failed romantic relationships, most of which I played a leading role in helping to destroy. When I was finally tired of my life being a disaster (which manifested itself in just about every other area of existence, not just relationships) I had to take a long hard look at myself and come to the realization that I was unhealthy.

"In fact, I was a giant immature man-child, and found myself in relationships where my partner accepted my immaturity, because they were just as unhealthy as I was. Or they were healthier than me, or were on the way to getting healthy, which means they dumped me as soon as they figured me out, which usually took all of five minutes. Oh what a victim I was!

"My first marriage failed (certainly not MY fault) or all my other relationships that fizzled out or went up in a giant flaming ball of dysfunction, all because those women were just so... nuts? Turns out it was me all along. I finally figured out that if I wanted to be in a healthy loving relationship, I had to do some work on myself.

"As it turns out, after finally discovering this secret and moving forward with being a healthy grown up, low and behold my now wife shows up. It wasn't fate and I don't know if I believe in soul mates, but I can tell you that we found in each other a perfect match. There are many reasons behind our compatibility, but the main component to our successful relationship is our commitment to grow in our health for ourselves and one another. I have learned so much from her.

"My wife and I are friends with several beautiful, successful, competent women. We also have many similar friends who are married or in relationships, and are soon to be single because the relationship is failing. A commonality among these friends is when we are with them when my wife and I interact, or just when they hear stories my wife tells them about me, seeing their eyes fill with tears and hearing the common refrain of "I hope someday I find my Troy (that's me)," or them telling my wife "you married a cross between Jesus and a unicorn. Dudes like him don't exist. You lucked out Sam (that's my wife.)

"I am not embellishing these statements, nor does it happen infrequently. So, what is it about me that makes me such a catch and successful in my marriage and makes my wife the envy of her friends? How did I wind up with such a smart beautiful mature woman who loves football, cage fighting, deeply intellectual conversation, and frequent crazy sex? (Again, I am not embellishing.) It's not that I'm wealthy or tall or ridiculously good looking or have a much sought after six pack. The secret is simple, but is incredibly difficult, even painful, to accomplish. Here it is... you have to work on yourself.

"We're talking about self-discovery, introspection, looking in a very realistic way at your own shortcomings and faults. Even seeking out (gasp!) counseling. It means: learning how to communicate, becoming emotionally intelligent, discovering how to be a generous and competent lover, learning to be well groomed in your appearance, being a man worthy of respect because it's hard to love someone you do not respect, working to resolve any past parental issues and traumas (you have those by the way. How do I know? Because you're human.) Not projecting your bullshit on to your partner, and learning how to be a grown up. Please understand that all these elements of growth need not be fully present as you search for a partner, but you should be moving towards them. Finally, it's important to know that the work is never done. Growing and learning is a lifelong endeavor, and it's hard.

"It's the most amazing thing in the world to have someone moving forward with you. If you find yourself in a relationship where you are the only one willing to put in this kind of self-improvement, it is a relationship that will stagnate and fail. If it is the opposite, and you are standing still and your partner is moving forward, the relationship is doomed. Part of becoming a healthy grown up is becoming wise and learning patience.

"When you get healthy, you will not find yourself in unequal relationships. You will not tolerate it. It may feel lonely for a while, because loneliness can be a temporary side effect of growth and epiphany. It makes it harder to relate to those people in your life who continue to stand still, and as you grow it can make them feel uncomfortable. It's sad, but people do not like being reminded they need to mature and grow, and seeing you grow will emphasize that point.

"You may even feel unhappy for a while, but happiness is not the goal. What's the whole point behind all that introspection and hard work if not happiness? Contentedness, wisdom, clarity, self-awareness, and joy are the goal. Happiness is a pleasant by product. When you are working to obtain these goals you will be amazed at the sheer number of likeminded people, and potential partners, which will be drawn to you. Like minds seek each other out.

"Here is a hard truth. Men can be immature emotionally stunted narcissistic slobs. Then they complain how women won't give them the time of day, except for the 'crazy' ones. And working on yourself will not make you a beta male /soy-boy/ incel /snowflake/, or whatever other moronic names men want to heap on you. Be a real man, resolve your fears, and find someone who is like minded and loves you because you have worked hard and are worthy. It starts with you."

Wise elder contributor, **David Wheeler**, has a long list of wise suggestions for young people, based on his experiences:

1. *"Always think big. And when you think you're thinking big, think again, you can think much bigger than that. Always look for ways to break through any limits anyone (including yourself) might set you.*

2. *"If you have something that lights your fire, feed that flame, and don't ever let anyone extinguish it. That fire is your life. That passion is your reason for existence. Without that flame burning brightly, you will die.*

3. *"In pursuing your passion, you will encounter many obstacles. The only people without problems are dead. Realize that as long as you are alive, you will have obstacles, you will have problems to solve. Solve them. If you don't know how to solve them, ask for help, look for many ways those problems can be solved, those obstacles surmounted. Those problems and obstacles are there as opportunities to help you grow.*

4. *"Yes, punching through those problems, those obstacles may be difficult. You may find yourself knocked down again and again and again. You may fail more times than you can count. Pick yourself up each time and go again. Each time. You're beat only if you quit. Every failure is nothing more than a learning opportunity. Use each experience to lift yourself closer to your goals.*

5. *"Almost any fear or other negative emotion you have is most often only your body's way of telling you an adventure is about to begin. When you push past your fear and accept that adventure, you get to watch your entire life open up.*

6. *"Be a problem hunter. Listen for anyone complaining about anything. You can build a business that will finance any dream you have from the intersection of three things: 1) problems you can solve well; 2) problems you enjoy solving; and 3) problems that many other people have, because those people will be your best customers. If you hear anyone complaining about anything, chances are that many other people have the same complaint. The more people you can serve by solving their problems, the more you will be paid.*

7. *"Some parts of any business you may not enjoy, or may not even be good at. Hire people to do those tasks. But hire only the best, and pay them well for their contributions. If you don't think you can afford to pay them what they deserve, get creative. Money is not the only thing many people want in exchange for their services. Take time to discover what your employ-*

ees want, and pay them in those ways. Keep in mind that those ways can be myriad!

8. "Live life from your heart. Always look for heart connections with anyone you encounter or interact with. Those connections are there, if you look for them, no matter how painful any relationship you have may be.

9. "Find a partner who will both encourage you and challenge you, and for whom you can do the same. Don't ever settle for a second-rate partner. And once you have that partner, do whatever it takes to keep her in your life.

10. "Surround yourself with like-minded people who also have big goals and dreams. Select 6 – 10 of them to be your master-mind group, your closest companions and supporters. Stay in close touch with them and support them at least as generously as they support you.

11. "Always look for the good, the useful, the constructive in everything. And when you find it, build on it."

Wise elder contributor, **Michael Lightweaver**, focuses on what he calls "the curriculum of life:" finance, romance, our bodies and our egos. Here is his advice under each of these categories:

a. How to Handle Money. "Let's start with money as an example. They say that money can't buy you happiness. This is probably true, but it is equally true that the lack of money can certainly bring you a great deal of pain, stress or sadness. Anyone who has experienced this understands. From the time you leave home as a child or youth until the time that you lose direct control of your finances as a result of an accident, illness or old age – you will be dealing with money and learning all that it has to teach you. You will have the opportunity to learn about spending, budgeting, generosity, greed, honesty, integrity, how to manage with too little and how to manage wisely with too much.

"Your money and how you handle it will give you an opportunity to learn a great deal about yourself, your values, your goals, your discernment, your self-image. And how you use it will give others a clear snapshot of who you are; your strengths, your weaknesses, your beliefs, what you really value in life. Money can become a great mirror for you to take a close look at yourself, seeing what you like about yourself and what you may want to change.

b. Be Careful with Your Relationships. "Our human relationships begin with our parents or early care givers. I ascribe to the idea that we do in fact choose our parents before we pop in for any given incarnation. They become our initial teachers – not just in terms of information – but also in terms of experience.

Our early experience with parents can give us a good hint as to the level of difficulty of the curriculum we have chosen for this incarnation.

"The more issues you have with your parents, the richer the curriculum and opportunities you have for soul growth. For a moment, step away from the blame game related to what they did or didn't do, and pretend – just pretend – that all of this occurred as a part of the curriculum that you chose. I'm not asking you to believe it. Just pretend because this will give you a new set of glasses through which you can view the situation and open you to new learnings. As long as we are locked into the blame game and our victim mentality, we limit our vision for seeing the bigger picture.

c. Your Body. *"Like money, your body is going to be with you all of your life. You will have to deal with it as a teenager, whether it is facial blemishes, unruly hair or the dramatic changes of puberty. Your body will be constantly talking to you and seeking your attention in a thousand different ways. As you get older and wage the battle against weight, sagging, wrinkling and the gradual breakdown of various functions, your body may demand more and more of your attention. And then there are those who experience illness or accidents in which the body suddenly requires 100% of your attention. But guess what? It is all just curriculum. A great deal of it related to the body, is unpleasant but oh so instructive.*

d. Your Ego. *"A big part of our human training has to do with individuation; coming to see ourselves as individuals distinctly different than others. In this piece of curriculum, the Ego becomes our guru. It likes nothing better than to feel special and it can do it in a thousand different ways. Sports, academics, trophies, degrees, the biggest house, the most expensive car, the most popular, the most friends, the most bling, the most spiritually enlightened. All of them are egos way of making you feel special, better, or at least different than others. From the moment we wake up in the morning until the last moment before falling asleep, we are experiencing the curriculum of one or more of these four gurus – and most of it unconsciously.*

Wise elder contributor **Michael Lightweaver** was the only contributor who gave advice to young people about sex, so I included it below: *"Sex is a big topic. First and foremost, it is a natural appetite, which is one of the components that come with the human vehicle you are traveling in this time around. Like the need for food, water & air, it is neither good nor bad. It simply serves a biological function to perpetuate the species. However, unlike all other species, we have attached a ton of baggage to sex. We have attached it to love, owner-*

ship, domination, religion and a host of other issues. Unlike breathing, however, which flows naturally and neutrally, we have made certain expressions of our sexuality good and bad, often with dire consequences.

"OK, I agree. Sex isn't exactly like breathing. Because it involves reproduction, it can have long term consequences that any parent, and particularly single parents with full parental responsibility can attest to. So yes, it is a biological function, but it can also have consequences that an individual may or may not want. For this reason, it does involve some exceptional responsibility for those with reproductive capacity.

"Sex can also be one of our most profound pieces of your curriculum. When attached to the concept of love, it becomes much more than a biological function. In this case it becomes an emotional expression of the love which two people share or, in some cases, the love that one person holds for another. In addition to this, nature has created it with the same intensity as hunger, thirst or the need to breathe – with the added ingredient of intense pleasure.

"So without real love or the desire to procreate, it can be enjoyed for the pure pleasure of endorphin overload. And then there is the concept of ownership so prevalent in traditional patriarchal societies. Women 'belong' to men and sex becomes an expression of that ownership, and often domination. In practice the man is free to have sex with whomever he will but, in some societies, such freedom can mean death for the woman.

"Ownership in such societies also extends to the offspring. Family and linage are the household goods of such societies. How can you know that the children 'belong' to you if your wife isn't 'faithful?' And so sexual expression becomes an integral element in maintaining the patriarchal hierarchy.

"So here we have four different meanings for sex: procreation, an expression of love, an expression of ownership and/or domination, and pure pleasure. Is it any wonder that this has become such a rich piece of curriculum for the human experience? Any one of these alone could offer a lifetime of learning, but when you begin to mix them up and weave them together, it often results in a knotted tangle rather than a beautiful tapestry.

"It is important to note here that, in spite of the prevalence of patriarchal societies that have prevailed into modern times, there are exceptions. Whereas an unmarried woman might be stoned to death in certain cultures for any expression of romantic love, in the traditional pre-missionary culture of certain islands of Polynesia, such as Tahiti, a woman was not deemed fit for marriage until she had given birth to her first child as a result of her nocturnal frolics with the village lads. Why? Because the issue was fertility, not virginity. Until

she proved that she was fertile she was not considered 'wife material.' And the children? They belonged to the village. Perhaps this is the origin of the saying 'It takes a village to raise a child.'

"The only advice I can offer is to be clear of your intent before allowing your hormones to dominate your experience. Are you seeking only pleasure? If so, be honest with yourself and others. Do not lead them to believe that it is an expression of authentic love. If you are primarily seeking love, do not fool yourself in to believing that every sexual experience will be just that. There are those who give sex to get love and there are those who give love to get sex. Be clear before you start as to whether you want to bring children into the world with the lifetime of responsibilities this entails, and then handle things accordingly. Above all, go into any situation which you encounter with your eyes wide open. And whatever the results or consequences, remember that ultimately it's all just curriculum."

Wise elder contributor, **Michael Lightweaver**, has this to say about "falling in love." Here are his ideas about how to handle this kind of situation: "Beware of falling in love. Ah yes! Another 'biggie.' This is something that you will likely have to deal with at least once, and perhaps many times in life. It's natures' design (trick?) to keep the species going and much of it is based on myth: Fall in love, get married and live happily ever after. Oh, if it were only true! But simple observation seems to indicate otherwise.

"Why is this so? It is because the very foundation of the myth is a lie. We never fall in love with another person. We actually fall in love with the fantasy of what we want that person to be for us. The truth is, what we call 'love' is in fact infatuation; an intense passionate attraction to another person that blinds us to everything about that person except their highest and best, whether real or imagined. However, as time passes and with some experience together, the veil of infatuation which clouds the eyes begins to fade and you begin to see a real person and not a fantasy. 'This is commonly referred to as "the honeymoon is over.'

"But infatuation plays an important role in the human condition so I'm not condemning it. I'm only shinning a little light on it so that we can really see what it is and what it isn't. First of all, it plays an important biological role in holding two peoples' attention long enough for them to perhaps – learn to love each other and/or potentially propagate the species. Authentic love is a learning process and something that can only be learned once the fantasy has faded and reality has set in. It is only when you see the real person, with all of their imperfections, that you can begin to love them.

"Until that time you are simply infatuated with the fantasy you have of them. This is the basis of the term 'love is blind.' It's also the basis of the common phenomena of 'The honeymoon is over.' It means the two people have woken up to the reality of who each is and what they do and don't have together. Infatuation is emotional based and temporary while authentic love includes an emotional element but involves much, much more, and is grounded in commitment. It's going to be around even when the going gets rough, as it inevitably will.

"Unfortunately, because we have been lied to as to the nature of love when the infatuation fades, we believe that we have 'fallen out of love' and too often go in search of a new 'high' that the infatuation brings. Infatuation is oh so delicious! It is also very deceiving if one isn't clear.

"Don't get me wrong. I'm not opposed to 'falling in love' or infatuation. It is one of the grandest feelings in the world and I 'love' it!!! But at my age, I see it for what it is and isn't, and don't take myself too seriously.

"One of the things I have noticed in myself is that when I 'fall in love' I get totally stupid, so one of the commitments I have made to myself is not to make any big decisions while I am 'under the influence.' I've made some pretty stupid 'mistakes' in the past while under the influence of cupid's spell. Or we could say that I've attracted some very challenging 'curriculum.'

"When the infatuation fades, as it ultimately will, you have the opportunity to really learn to love the person you are with including all of their imperfections. No, they will not fulfill all of your hopes, desires or fantasies. They aren't on the planet to make your dreams come true. And yes, they fart in bed sometimes.

"It's when you come to this reality that you have the opportunity to learn to love in spite of it all. What is learning to love? Learning to love is like learning anything else. It has its curriculum and it is work and sometimes it's hard."

Wise Elder Contributor, **Gary Scott**, who is a successful international entrepreneur, has the following advice for young men:

#1: **"Start something that follows your dreams.** *There are many ways to create a joyful lifestyle. Each path may bring happiness. Some may pay their way and some may create significant income and wealth. The key is let pleasure and joy be the motivators of your activity, as much as is possible. Even if you have to work at something you do not enjoy to pay your bills and make your current way, also start something at least part time that you enjoy. Don't worry if it's a lifelong dream. We can never know how much we love doing something until we try, so start and learn.*

#2: "Start small. Starting small is nature's way. *This is how all of nature expands… always starting small and growing at a steady pace. Consider this. During a recent recession, a German billionaire quietly put on his coat, told his wife "I have to go to the office for a while," and drove to a railway embankment near his home, where he lay on the frozen tracks and waited patiently for a train to crush him to death. This man was ranked as one of the 100 richest men in the world, with a personal fortune that reached over $10 billion. But even though he was worth billions, the global recession left him feeling out of control.*

"He did not need the money. He lived so modestly that he cycled to work on a 15-year-old bike for most of the year, and in bad weather he drove a four-year-old VW Golf. He had no bodyguards or servants, lived in the same unimposing chalet-style house for 60 years and stopped off at his local pub on his way home each night to share a drink with the regulars.

"The blame for his demise was placed perhaps most importantly on loss of control. His companies were his life and when he was going to lose control of them he obviously felt he would lose control of his life. Fortunately to be happy, we do not have to be financially rich. We do not have to wait to be happy either. All we have to do is start to gain freedom, purpose and a sense of control. We can start taking that power, right now, by having one small win. A small win sets forces in motion that favor another small win. That's it, take a small step forward today. Find controllable opportunities that produce visible results. Examine…what is your passion, your purpose and figure out how to do good or earn with it in the process. Here is the process.

"Passionate ideas or dreams allow you to learn what you really like and what you can really do. The passion creates enthusiasm. Enthusiasm leads to education. Education leads to action. Action leads to profit or loss and experience. Experience leads to new ideas. The process grows, more refined each time. So don't worry if what you love is the right thing or the ultimate idea for your life. Just pick something that's attracting you now and start!

#3: "Have staying power. *If you have a decent idea, enjoy what you are doing and can manage to stick with it long enough, you'll attain success. This is why it's good to focus on doing what you love. If you are not having fun or gaining some great fulfillment or satisfaction, then it's hard to have staying power. Determination and follow-through are a part of staying power, but this is not the key. We'll always need 'sheer determination and follow-through' to do some of things you do not enjoy so much, but when you do something you love, these disciplines come more easily.*

"Also live within your means! No matter how big or small your activity, there will be ups and downs and a learning curve. There is always learning to be gained and the need to adapt.

"You cannot focus on this process and enjoy doing the things you love if you are hounded by payments and cannot afford the essential requirements of life. Living within your means is simple. Just don't spend what you do not have! Always save something. Make your savings a bill that you must pay! Avoid debt for consumption. There are times when debt to invest makes sense, but never borrow to spend! Invest your extra money in a business or diversify into an investment portfolio rather than fashion and consumer goods!

"Dr. Thomas Stanley in his book the 'Millionaire Mind' lists the twenty most important factors that 733 millionaires (whom he interviewed) which made them rich. None of the factors have anything to do with having a high IQ, a good education or a sharp stock broker. Some of them may surprise you but learning these factors and how to attain them are perhaps more important. Most of the millionaires did not live in the most upscale neighborhoods. These wealthy people don't dine out much, are likely to drive four-year-old Buicks, and own very few (if any) Armani suits. Life is a series of cycles. Some will be up. Some will be down. What you love and want to do today may not make you happy in the future.

"You can never truly know what life will bring, but if each day you follow these three rules - Follows your dreams - Start small and have staying power, your odds of living a fulfilled, productive, happy and contented life are dramatically improved."

WORDS OF WISDOM

I found an article that contains 15 different kinds of advice. These seemed to me to be words of wisdom.[42] These are suggestions for young people to help them avoid some of the pitfalls that wise elders have encountered. Some of them are humorous. Here they are:

1. Life isn't tied with a bow, but it's still a gift.
2. Worrying doesn't take away tomorrow's troubles, it takes away today's peace of mind.
3. Get outside and travel.
4. Miracles are around every corner.
5. Your job won't take care of you when you are sick. Your friends and family will. Stay in touch.

6. You don't have to win every argument. Agree to disagree.

7. Make peace with your past so it won't screw up your present.

8. However good or bad a situation is, it will change.

9. Don't compare your life to others'. You have no idea what their journey is all about.

10. Life is too short for long pity parties. Get busy living, or get busy dying.

11. When it comes to going after what you love in life, don't take 'no' for an answer.

12. Over prepare, then go with the flow.

13. Be yourself. Everybody else is taken.

14. Life isn't fair, but it's still good.

15. Don't take yourself so seriously. No one else does.

CHAPTER SIX

HOW CAN WISE ELDERS MAINTAIN GOOD HEALTH AND LONGEVITY?

Do not try to live forever, you will not succeed.

—George Bernard Shaw

Longevity is a goal for wise elders, but they have to live life in ways that promote their longevity. Here are some tips:[43]

ALL AGES:

+ **Stay active.** Cut your chances of being mowed down prematurely by major degenerative diseases like heart disease and cancer by exercising regularly. Get your heart rate up for 150 minutes each week through moderately intense aerobic activities, such as brisk walking, or for 75 weekly minutes through more intense activities, such as jogging. Strength training at least twice a week is also important, according to the Centers for Disease Control and Prevention.

+ **Stay lean.** Packing on extra pounds not only jeopardizes health, but can set the stage for arthritis and mobility problems later in life.

+ **Eat wisely.** Fruit, vegetables, whole grains, low- and nonfat dairy, legumes, lean meats, and fish are staples of a healthy diet.

+ **Limit red meat** to no more than 18 (cooked weight) ounces per week, suggests the American Institute for Cancer Research. Harvard School of Public Health researchers recently linked daily consumption of red meat—particularly processed varieties—with increased risk of premature death, especially from cancer and heart disease.

+ **Keep alcohol to a minimum.** No more than two daily drinks for men and one for women.

+ **Floss daily** to prevent the buildup of gum-disease-causing bacteria, which are increasingly being implicated in heart disease.

+ **Prioritize sleep.** Getting too few winks may lower your immunity and invite everything from obesity to accidents. Aim for a minimum of six nightly hours.

+ **Kick the habit.** It bears broken-record repeating: Even at older ages, quitting smoking may still add years to your life and health to your years. Up your odds of success with this research-tested trick: When the urge to light up strikes, imagine, say, having to breathe through a tracheotomy tube as opposed to the feel-good sensation of taking a drag. Evoking smoking's serious potential consequences can help quell cravings.

+ **Flex your mental muscle** by writing, reading, or playing games, such as crossword puzzles. Despite there being no proven way to cut the chances of Alzheimer's, some research suggests that keeping the brain active from childhood on may somewhat armor against the disease.

+ **Apply and reapply sunscreen** and sport a brimmed hat and UV-blocking shades whenever you're exposed to the sun's harmful rays. Overexposure can lead to skin cancer and cataracts.

+ **Get only the healthcare you need.** Excessive testing—even preventive screenings—and overreliance on medications, such as antibiotics, can actually be harmful. Before taking any medication or agreeing to any procedure, discuss with your doctor the pros and cons before deciding what's best for you. If you're uncertain, don't hesitate to get a second opinion.

+ **Watch out for anti-aging treatments.** Nothing can turn back the clock and some therapies can be dangerous. Your money and health are on the line.

+ **Get a ballpark idea of how long you can expect to live** with centenarian researcher Thomas Perls' *Life Expectancy Calculator* (http://www.livingto100.com/). The roughly 10-minute, 40-question test helps reveal the affect your health-related behaviors could have on your longevity, and suggests ways to adjust your lifestyle to add years.

AGES 20S AND 30S:

+ **Remind yourself:** These aren't the *"freebie"* decades. Your lifestyle at this stage of your life can affect how well (or poorly) you age.

+ **Develop "positive coping skills,"** or healthy ways to manage life's stressors. Deadline looming? Rather than shoveling chips into your mouth, go on a run or bike ride. Meditate. Now's the time to lay down a lifelong foundation for healthy living.

+ **Cultivate a positive outlook on aging.** No one wants to grow old, but evidence suggests a link between harboring a negative view and heart attack and stroke susceptibility.

+ **Safeguard your hearing.** Noises over 85 decibels, roughly the volume of a hair dryer, can inflict permanent damage.

+ **Maintain a healthy weight.** Tools like the United States Department of Agriculture's *SuperTracker* (http://www.choosemyplate.gov/supertracker-tools/supertracker.html) can help you plan, log, and analyze your eating and exercise patterns.

40S AND 50S:

+ **Beware of creeping weight gain.** Obesity is increasingly affecting adults in middle age and beyond. As you enter midlife, you need fewer calories, your metabolism ebbs, and it's harder to drop pounds. Limit processed foods that combine sugar and fat; research suggests this combo is highly addictive.

+ **Keep up with weekly strength-training sessions.** Lean muscle mass starts disappearing at a rapid clip around midlife.

+ **Don't skimp on calcium and vitamin D**—both promote bone health. The Institute of Medicine (IOM), outlines recommended daily intake by age and gender. Men and women ages 51 to 70 are generally advised to get 1,000 milligrams and 1,200 mg of calcium, respectively, and 600 international units (IU) of vitamin D each day.

AGES 60S AND OVER:

+ **Once you turn 65, make sure to get an annual eye exam.** Age-related vision problems can arise slowly, often unnoticed.

+ **Take care to avoid falls—the No.** 1 cause of injury-related death for the 65-plus set. Potential preventives include balance-building activities such as tai chi, and making practical changes around the house, like installing *"grab bars"* near the shower.

+ **Maintain your fitness to prolong good health and ability to live independently.** If 150 minutes of physical activity per week seems daunting, try dividing it into three 10-minute blocks, five days per week.

+ **Know the warning signs of top killers, such as stroke.** Call 911 immediately if you notice symptoms. For stroke, they include numbness in your face and limbs, sudden difficulty seeing or speaking, dizziness, and/or a sudden severe headache.

WHY IS THE LIFE EXPECTANCY IN THE U. S. GOING DOWN?

Life expectancy in the United States has dropped again this year following last year's decline, which marked the first multiyear downturn in more than two decades. On average, Americans can now expect to live 78.6 years, a statistically significant drop of 0.1 year, according to a report on 2016 data published recently by the National Center for Health Statistics. Women can now expect to live a full five years longer than men: 81.1 years vs. 76.1 years. The last time the agency recorded a multiyear drop was in 1962 and 1963.

The two main causes are an alarming increase in deaths from substance abuse and despair. There has been a 21% increase in overdose deaths from the year before and cited a 137% increase in opioid-related deaths between 2000 and 2014. The opioid drug use crisis seems to be one of the main causes with over 62,000 deaths.

By contrast, in Canada, the average life expectancy was 80 years for males and 84 years for females in 2018. Life expectancies across the globe are projected to rise by an average of 4.4 years over the next two decades, but a recent study predicts the United States will continue to linger far behind other high-income nations, reaching an average lifespan of just 79.8 years by 2040. Comparatively, frontrunner Spain is forecast to boast an average lifespan of 85.8 years by that time, while Japan sits at a close second with an expected lifespan of 85.7 years. The U.SA. currently ranks 31st among all nations.

WHAT IS THE DIFFERENCE BETWEEN GROWING OLD AND LIVING LONGER?

Until the 20th century life expectancy was around 40-50 years. Longevity is the largely unexpected consequence of improvements in general living conditions during the 20th century. Longer life was the byproduct of better living conditions for the young. The challenge today is to build a world that is just as responsive to the living conditions of very old people as it is to the very young.

The aging mind is slower and more prone to error when processing information. It is less adept at considering old information in novel ways. Memory suffers. In particular, working memory—the ability to keep multiple pieces of information in mind while acting on them— declines with age. The ability to inhibit extraneous information when attempting to focus attention becomes impaired. In spite of these facts, the subjective experience of normal aging adults is largely positive. Most older people remain active and involved in families and communities. The majority of people over 90 still live independently.

One study focused on validating a life-span theory of motivation they called socioemotional selectivity theory (SST). One finding was that older people are more satisfied with their social relationships than are younger people, especially regarding relationships with their children and younger relatives. They also found that despite losses in many areas, emotional well-being is as good, if not better, in older people as in their younger counterparts.

Findings from this initial study suggested that in older people, memory of emotional information was superior to memory of other types of information. Older people were also better at remembering positive emotions than younger people. Younger adults performed better than older adults on the negative emotion trials, but older adults outperformed younger adults on the positive emotion trials. This points to the increased development of the pre-frontal cortex where our positive emotions are stored.

Psychological researchers have recently focused on the role of the pre-frontal cortex in improving emotional responses to life circumstances. This part of the brain seems to be the major part that improves in the studies cited above.

NUTRITIONAL SUPPORT FOR AGING GRACEFULLY[44]

Ty Bollinger offers some of the vest advice on how to age gracefully with the proper nutritional support that I have run across. I have summarized below what he wrote about this subject.

Cellular Regeneration: How Things Are Supposed to Work. In a healthy biological environment, your body's vast cellular network of nearly 100 trillion cells is almost always dying. Cells that have reached the end of their life cycle are constantly being purged and eliminated in order to make way for new cells that pick up the baton where they left off. If a cell is no longer able to do its job, it will either repair itself or commit *"suicide"* via a process known as apoptosis. This is a streamlined process that keeps everything in the body balanced and running smoothly.

Since cells are the building blocks behind every organ and system in the body, it's important that all of them meet the highest quality standards. Defective cells can put the entire system at risk, and thus have to be eliminated. It functions a lot like the quality control unit at a manufacturing plant, where only the best components make it off the assembly line and into the final product, while everything else ends up in the scrap heap.

Cellular Regeneration and The integrity of human DNA. Healthy cells act as an airtight bunker to keep these blueprints of life locked away and fully protected in their nuclei, where they can't be tampered with or corrupted. Expired cells, on the other hand, are like an old house with a leaky roof, where the genetic code is exposed to all sorts of damaging elements.

This is why it's vitally important for cells that no longer work, or that have reached the end of their lives, to either regenerate themselves or die. When they do this, the cellular system is kept in good working order. Your body is able to absorb nutrients from food, convert them into energy, use them to keep organs and tissue healthy and strong, and reproduce and proliferate as needed. This is the very bedrock of human life.

Cellular Senescence: When Cells Turn to the Dark Side and Refuse to Die. When we're young, it's easy for our bodies to do this. They swap out used-up cells and replace them with new ones. But as we grow older, life catches up with us: poor diet, lack of exercise, and a stressful lifestyle all contribute to the demise of this important, life-sustaining process. If cellular maintenance continues to degrade, it can eventually bring about chronic disease.

One manifestation of this is cellular senescence, a state in which bad cells no longer complete their normal life cycle and instead stick around in a type of *"zombie"* state. Senescent cells are those cells that have somehow been damaged by stress – either internally or from some outside source – but that don't either repair themselves or self-destruct. Though they're no longer capable of doing anything beneficial, senescent cells remain present within the cellular terrain. As children and young adults our cells easily repair and replenish, but this process slows down as we age

To clarify, healthy cells that become worn out or damaged are programmed to either repair themselves or commit suicide: this is how life persists. But senescent cells are different in that they do neither of these things. They actually impede the life cycle by getting in the way of it. Like a clogged drain, senescent cells gunk up cellular pathways and obstruct the flow of activity that's responsible for regulating energy levels, sleeping patterns, organ functionality, and many other things.

One study explains cellular senescence as an *"irreversible arrest of cell proliferation (growth) that occurs when cells experience potentially oncogenic stress"* [Note: Oncogenic refers to the potential of cells to become cancerous and form tumors.] Senescent cells are permanently damaged, in other words, meaning they have no capacity to ever serve a useful purpose again. And yet they never go away.

This is an obviously problem, especially when considering the fact that these senescent cells can accumulate in the body over time. The health effects of this process are significant and may include symptoms you're familiar with. Things like:

- Accelerated signs of aging
- Poor metabolism
- Fat accumulation
- Joint stiffness and pain
- Blood sugar imbalances
- Age-related memory loss

Just about the only good thing about senescent cells is that, in some cases, they appear to be somewhat tumor-suppressive. They don't replicate like cancer cells do. The fact that senescent cells even form in the first place is seen by some as being a good thing because at least they're not cancer cells that reproduce and cause even more problems.

It's kind of the lesser of two evils, but unfortunately it still doesn't tell the full story. The more that senescent cells collect, it turns out, the more they generate pro-inflammatory cytokines. Studies suggest these cytokines directly contribute to increased abnormal cell growth. For this reason, senescent cells are really no better than cancer cells if they eventually provoke the formation of cancer cells. Added to that, inflammation isn't exactly a good thing when it comes to keeping cancer at bay, either.

One of the studies that looked at aging and cancer in relation to cellular senescence concluded that, because of their propensity to drive degenerative pathologies, senescent cells are definitively cancer-forming. As they accumulate, senescent cells create a tissue environment *that is permissive for the development, or at least the progression, of cancer,*" the study concluded.

In other words, any perceived benefits to senescent cells are greatly overshadowed by their immense detriments. Inflammation aside, senescent cells are known to disrupt the structures of healthy tissue throughout the body, provoking all sorts of degenerative effects.

These include damage to the brain, as well as other typically age-associated pathologies such as:

- Memory loss and dementia
- Immune suppression
- Muscle loss
- Muscle loss that's replaced by fat

What You Can Do to Minimize Cellular Senescence While Optimizing Cellular Health? From an official standpoint, there's not much that you can do to get rid of senescent cells. Once they're there, they're not going anywhere – or so goes the claim. However, the truth is that there are many ways to help combat cellular senescence that work to give your body an upper hand in maintaining an optimal state of cellular regeneration. Perhaps the most obvious way is through your diet (which many mainstream health experts ignore).

A Healthy Diet to Combat Cellular Senescence. Nutrition, it turns out, can be a powerful weapon against these cells. It not only helps the body get rid of them, but also prevents them from forming in the first place. The scientific literature is replete with evidence to show that nutritional deficiency is directly linked to cellular senescence. It is often the determining factor behind common health conditions like type-2 diabetes, obesity, chronic inflammation, hypertension, and various other markers of metabolic syndrome.

Low glycemic diets rich in micronutrients – things like vitamins, trace minerals, phytochemicals, and antioxidants – have been shown to induce the opposite effect. Functional foods free of processed ingredients, refined sugars, and other damaging chemicals are protective against these types of conditions. The complexity of micronutrients they contain is essential for keeping the body well-tuned. These micronutrients aid in the production of digestive enzymes and hormones that further help to guard cells against senescence. Beyond this, micronutrients help to:

- Convert carbohydrates, fats, and proteins into usable energy
- Support a strong and robust metabolism
- Minimize oxidative and free radical damage that leads to inflammation
- Protect against brain degeneration
- Support bone remineralization
- Synthesize DNA
- Repair damaged tissue
- Support muscle movement and flexibility

ATP: Fuel for Your Mitochondria. One of the key elements that cells require in order to function properly is adenosine triphosphate, or ATP. Also known as the *"universal cellular energy molecule,"* ATP is the fuel that cellular mitochondria need in order for cells to breathe, generate energy, and do their respective jobs.

This is another area where micronutrients come into play. They function as metabolic cofactors in food to ensure that healthy cells are given all of the building blocks they need to produce ATP. Without these micronutrients, cellular mitochondria would starve – leading to the exact opposite of the above listed benefits. Current research suggests that humans require more than 50 different micronutrients from three unique categories for health optimization.

1) Vitamins are essential for maintaining cellular health, helping to protect the body against oxidative stress. In the process, they aid in slowing the aging process and protecting against cancer as well. There are 13 vitamins in particular that are considered to be absolutely essential for human health, including both water-soluble and fat-soluble types.

The 13 Vitamins Considered Essential for Human Health. This includes water-soluble vitamins like the entire B vitamin complex: B1 (thiamine), B2 (riboflavin), B3 (niacin), B5(pantothenic acid), B6 (pyridoxine), B7 (biotin), B9 (folate), B12 (cobalamin), as well as vitamin C.

Because these water-soluble vitamins tend to be easily lost via sweat and urine, it's important to consume plenty of them on a daily basis. Here are some of the bodily functions they each support (and take note that many of these nutrients overlap and work together with one another in synergy):

- B1 (thiamine) – hair, skin, brain, heart, nervous system
- B2 (riboflavin) – metabolism, immune system, nervous system
- B3 (niacin) – digestion, hair, skin, brain, heart, circulation
- B5 (pantothenic acid) – energy, adrenal glands, nervous system, heart, hormones, brain
- B6 (pyridoxine) – protein digestion, mood, appetite, immune system, blood
- B7 (biotin) – glucose synthesis, metabolism, skin
- B9 (folate) – reproduction, heart, nervous system, mood, digestion, eyes
- B12 (cobalamin) – metabolism, nervous system, blood
- C -immune system, nutrient absorption, cardiovascular system

Fat-soluble vitamins are equally as important, but because they're more easily stored in the body long-term, but we generally don't need as much of them (though I would suggest erring on the side of too much rather than too little). Fat-soluble vitamins include vitamins A, D, E, and K, and they are vital for the following systems:

- A (beta-carotene) – immune system, mucous membranes, immune system, bones, eyes, skin
- D – nutrient absorption, bones, immune system
- E – immune system, muscles, blood
- K – protein activation, blood, wound healing, bones

2) Minerals Hold a Top Spot in Cellular Health. Minerals help to support healthy bone development, metabolism, brain function, and longevity. There are at least 18 different minerals that the body needs in order to maintain optimal functionality, including *"macrominerals,"* or electrolytes. These include things like calcium, magnesium, potassium, and sodium, along with *"trace"* minerals like copper, iodine, iron, manganese, selenium, and zinc, each of which offers the following benefits:

- Calcium – bones, digestion, blood
- Magnesium – nervous system, muscles, digestion, heart, blood, energy, brain
- Potassium – blood, heart

- Sodium – muscles, nervous system, fluid balance, enzyme function
- Copper – inflammation, brain
- Iodine – growth and development, thyroid
- Iron – oxygen delivery, energy
- Manganese – bones, blood, metabolism, inflammation
- Selenium – prostate, inflammation, reproduction
- Zinc – immune system, brain, cardiovascular system, reproduction

3) Antioxidants as Well as Other Free Radical-Fighting Compounds. Antioxidants are commonly found in whole, nutrient-dense foods like vegetables, fruit, seeds, nuts, ancient grains, legumes, and pasture-raised animal products. Healthy living is contingent upon having enough antioxidants, including what's considered to be the most important antioxidant of all: the *"master"* antioxidant known as glutathione peroxidase.

Maximizing Glutathione, "the Master Antioxidant". Glutathione peroxidase represents the essence of cellular vibrancy. It lives inside every single cell in the body, and is absolutely critical for maintaining a healthy immune system. Glutathione further facilitates enzyme expression, detoxification, inflammation support, and programmed cell death as well – all things that directly counteract cellular senescence.7

Maximizing glutathione intake in order to optimize cellular health can be as simple as knowing the right things to eat. By consuming the following foods regularly, you can help your body to naturally produce more glutathione, and thus stave off cellular senescence and its life-destroying effects:

Cruciferous Vegetables and Leafy Greens. Foods like broccoli, Brussels sprouts, cabbage, and cauliflower are all rich in sulfurous amino acids that help to keep the body's glutathione stores in an optimal state. Other sulfur-rich veggies worth adding to the mix include arugula, collard greens, Bok Choy, kale, mustard greens, radishes, watercress, and turnips.

One of the most beneficial glutathione precursor nutrients known to man is the mineral selenium. And one of the world's richest sources of natural selenium is the Brazil nut. Just one ounce (6-8 nuts) of which contains about 544 micrograms of selenium. This is more than 100% of the recommended daily value. Other selenium-rich foods include grass-fed beef, wild-caught fish like yellow fin tuna, halibut, and sardines, pastured chicken and eggs, and spinach.

Folate-Rich Foods. Consuming the full spectrum of bioavailable B vitamins, or what are often referred to as methylation nutrients, is critical for the body to produce glutathione. These include vitamins B6, B9, B12, and biotin. Not to be confused with folic acid, its synthetic counterpart, folate is one of the primary components that the body uses to generate fresh, new cells. It also helps in transcribing DNA to these new cells from the old ones. Folate-rich foods include garbanzo beans, liver, pinto beans, lentils, spinach, asparagus, avocado, beets, black eyed peas, and broccoli.

Whey Protein. Considered by many to be a premiere food for increasing glutathione levels, whey protein contains a special amino acid known as cysteine that's directly involved in the body's production of the master antioxidant. Clean whey protein derived from grass-fed cows or goats is ideal, containing the full spectrum of other vital amino acids that are also necessary for cellular support.

Camu Camu Berry and Acerola Cherry. Vitamin C is one of the most beneficial antioxidants and it's also a precursor to glutathione. Vitamin C-rich foods are thus an important part of a healthy cellular optimization lifestyle. Camu camu berry and acerola cherry top the list as the densest natural sources of 100% bio-available vitamin C. Other vitamin C-rich foods include citrus fruits as well as red peppers, kale, Brussels sprouts, and broccoli.

Foods Rich in Vitamin E. While vitamin C is busy increasing glutathione levels in red blood cells and lymphocytes, vitamin E helps to protects them, along with vital enzymes, against oxidative stress. The perfect pairing, these two classes of vitamin wield a death blow to cellular degeneration. This is why it's important to eat foods rich in vitamin E. These include almonds and other raw nuts and seeds, leafy greens, sweet potatoes, and avocado.

When I speak of vitamin E, by the way, I'm talking about eight different varieties of fat-soluble antioxidants that fall into two distinct categories: *"tocopherols"* and *"tocotrienols."* These include alpha, beta, gamma, and delta varieties – four in each category – that each possess their own protective benefits in support of cellular optimization.

This collective of *"tocols,"* as they're called, are what constitute true *"vitamin E"* – the full spectrum of which has been shown to aid in protecting against heart disease, cancer, and a variety of other chronic ailments.

Beef Liver. It might seem gross to some people, but the liver of animals is where nutrients tend to congregate. Liver from grass-fed cows, in particular, is densely packed with glutathione-producing nutrients like selenium that offer copious benefits with regards to cellular optimization. This offers added protection against cellular senescence.

Milk Thistle. A flowering herb commonly used in traditional folk medicine, milk thistle (silymarin) has been shown to directly enhance glutathione levels in the body. Studies reveal that it helps to protect the liver and biliary tract against disease, and can even help to offset liver toxicity induced by alcohol consumption (which, for the record, is also known to substantially decrease glutathione levels).

THE EVOLUTION OF THE PREFRONTAL CORTEX

The prefrontal cortex has remarkably expanded in size throughout human evolution, culminating in modern Homo sapiens. This suggests a strong selection pressure in favor of its continued growth and development throughout our evolution. While the brain itself has only increased in size about threefold in the past five million years, the size of the PFC has increased six fold.

Medical studies have shown that the PFC is the last section of the brain to mature. In other words, while all other brain regions are fully developed early in life, its development is not complete until around age 25. Magnetic resonance imaging (MRI) research has revealed that the prefrontal cortex changes a great deal during adolescence, as the brain's myelin matures and connects all regions of the brain together.

This late growth and development is likely the reason that some otherwise intelligent and sensible teens engage in high-risk or excessive behaviors even though they understand the potential dangers. This probably is why men have a shorter life expectancy than women because young men take unnecessary risks that end up taking their lives. Once the PPC matures, as the research above suggests, it continues to develop throughout our lifetime.

THE PRE-FRONTAL CORTEX OF THE WISE ELDER[45]

When you are using your skills as a wise elder you are building neural connections to the pre-frontal cortex that help support the following important psychobiological functions that increase longevity:

1. **Body regulation.** Helps you regulate your body to handle any sudden or unexpected experiences. This allows you to remain calm in the middle of a crisis.
2. **Attuned communication.** When connected to the PFC you can connect with another person's mind as well as your own mind. You can attune to another person without words only by looking into their eyes.

3. **Emotional balance.** It helps us reregulate our emotions quickly when we get triggered by the memory of an unhealed trauma.

4. **Response flexibility.** It allows us to think before we act and then act only after we have more completely assessed the situation.

5. **Empathy.** It enables us to know what someone else is feeling and be able to connect with them at a feeling level.

6. **Insight.** The PFC helps us begin to make sense of our thoughts and feelings by connecting past and present behaviors to predict any potential future behavior at any given moment. It is essential for self-reflection and self-correction.

7. **Fear modulation.** Has the capacity to help us calm down when the *"fear factory"* in our limbic brain goes into over-production.

8. **Intuition.** It is where we process signals from various parts of our brain and enables us to intuitively decide the best course of action. It also helps awaken our imagination.

9. **Morality.** It is where we construct our sense of morality and can apply that to our beliefs about ourselves, other people and the world around us.

Access to an integrated pre-frontal cortex enables us to live a flexible, adaptive, coherent, energized and stable life with a fully realized Self. If the pre-frontal cortex is disintegrated or disconnected, it cannot transmit information to help override the more primitive impulses from the lower brain containing memories of unhealed developmental trauma. Interestingly, people who are diagnosed as Narcissists or Psychopaths often lack the ability to perform the above mentioned pre-frontal cortex functions.

Early emotional memories are stored in the amygdala part of the brain as pictures, symbols, or icons rather than narrative language. Severe traumas from wars, natural catastrophes, and collective traumas such as global catastrophes, for example, are also symbolically stored in the amygdala as a form of epigenetic or race memory.

During episodes of reenacting unhealed childhood traumas, visual images related to the original event are re-experienced, and they fire in the brain as flashbacks. These images also hold memory traces containing certain visual scenes that are stuck in the brain's processing.

Symbolic memories, unavailable to the conscious mind, emerge in dreams, artwork, body memories, feelings, and events that trigger an image of earlier traumas. A second kind of memory, called narrative memory, uses language—words and meanings based on words. Narrative memory, which begins being stored in the hippocampus around age 4 or 5 years, forms the memory found in the conscious mind.

In order to release a traumatic memory from the amygdala, it is necessary to convert the pictures or symbols that are filed in the amygdala into narrative language that is stored in the hippocampus. This transfer of information between these parts of the brain has become a key component of trauma reduction and trauma elimination therapies. Creating narrative memory is also a critical component of helping people make meaning of their traumatic experiences, as it allows an experience to be integrated into the person's life experience. Reframing a life experience is a powerful healing mechanism, one that follows the adage, *"when life hands you lemons, learn to make lemonade."*

Trauma also disrupts the circuitry in the corpus callosum, a structure found in mammalian brains that connects the left hemisphere's cognitive function with the right hemisphere's emotional, relational and symbolic functions. Short circuits in the corpus callosum can impair not only your ability to recognize your feelings, but also your ability to express them. This impairment creates *alexithymia*, or the lack of words to express feelings.

What does this have to do with the physical and mental health of wise elders? If you had childhood trauma and have not healed it, the neural connections between the amygdala and the pre-frontal cortex either did not develop or are severed. In the section below, I explain how this predicts the physical and mental health of wise elders.

THE ACE STUDY: THE LONG-TERM EFFECTS OF CHILDHOOD TRAUMA ON THE PHYSICAL & MENTAL HEALTH OF WISE ELDERS

The initial phase of the ACE (Adverse Childhood Experiences) Study was conducted at Kaiser Permanente from 1995 to 1997 by Dr. Vincent Feletti of Kaiser Permanente and Dr. Robert Anda of the Centers for Disease Control. This was the largest epidemiological study aver attempted with more than 17,000 participants from the San Diego Area. They were given a standardized physical examination and asked to take a confidential survey that contained 10 questions about childhood maltreatment and family dysfunction, as well as items detailing their current health status and behaviors. This information was then combined with the results of their physical examination to form the baseline data for the study. Since the original study there have been over 80 follow-up studies with similar results.[46]

In order to determine the possible long-term effects of ACEs on your physical and mental health fill out the questionnaire below and record your score. If you had four or more ACEs, you are at risk for long-terms effects to your physical and mental health.

ACE QUESTIONNAIRE:

Prior to your 18th birthday:

- Did a parent or other adult in the household often or very often... Swear at you, insult you, put you down, or humiliate you? or Act in a way that made you afraid that you might be physically hurt?
  No__ If Yes, enter 1 __

- Did a parent or other adult in the household often or very often... Push, grab, slap, or throw something at you? or Ever hit you so hard that you had marks or were injured?
  No___ If Yes, enter 1 __

- Did an adult or person at least 5 years older than you ever... Touch or fondle you or have you touch their body in a sexual way? or Attempt or actually have oral, anal, or vaginal intercourse with you?
  No___ If Yes, enter 1 __

- Did you often or very often feel that ... No one in your family loved you or thought you were important or special? or Your family didn't look out for each other, feel close to each other, or support each other?
  No___ If Yes, enter 1 __

- Did you often or very often feel that ... You didn't have enough to eat, had to wear dirty clothes, and had no one to protect you? or Your parents were too drunk or high to take care of you or take you to the doctor if you needed it?
  No___ If Yes, enter 1 __

- Were your parents ever separated or divorced?
  No___ If Yes, enter 1 __

- Was your mother or stepmother: Often or very often pushed, grabbed, slapped, or had something thrown at her? or Sometimes, often, or very often kicked, bitten, hit with a fist, or hit with something hard? or were ever repeatedly hit over at least a few minutes or threatened with a gun or knife?

No___ If Yes, enter 1 __

- Did you live with anyone who was a problem drinker or alcoholic, or who used street drugs?

  No___ If Yes, enter 1 __

- Was a household member depressed or mentally ill, or did a household member attempt suicide?

  No___ If Yes, enter 1 __

- Did a household member go to prison?

  No___ If Yes, enter 1 __

Now add up your *"Yes"* **answers: ___ This is your ACE Score.**

The higher number of ACE experiences you had prior to your 18th birthday, the higher your risk is of developing serious adult physical and mental health problems. According to the original findings, adults who had four or more *"yes's"* to the ACE questions were, in general, twice as likely to have a number of degenerative diseases such as heart disease, cancer, diabetes, stroke, when compared to people whose ACE score was zero. Adult women with five or more *"yes's"* were at least four times as likely to have depression as those with no ACE *"yeses."*

Adults who listed 6 or more ACEs had a reduced life expectancy of 20 years. Dr. Rob Anda, epidemiologist and co-developer of the original ACE study shared this about his work. *"Just the sheer scale of the suffering—it was really disturbing to me,"* Anda remembers. *"I actually ... I remember being in my study and I wept."*

A major follow-up study was conducted by the CDC in 2009 with 26,229 randomly selected adults living in five different states. They found that almost 60 percent of the respondents had at least one ACE and about 9 percent had five or more ACEs.[47]

Here is a summary of the health outcomes related to the results of the ACE studies:

Table 6-1. Adverse Childhood Experiences Are Associated With Numerous Measures of Poor Mental and Physical Health

I. Social Functioning
 a. High perceived stress
 b. Relationship problems
 c. Married to an alcoholic
 d. Difficulty with job

II. Mental Health
 a. Anxiety
 b. Depression
 c. Poor anger control d. Panic reactions
 e. Sleep disturbances
 f. Memory disturbances
 g. Hallucinations

III. Sexual Health
 a. Age of first intercourse
 b. Unintended pregnancy
 c. Teen pregnancy
 d. Teen paternity
 e. Fetal death
 f. Sexual dissatisfaction

IV. Risk Factors for Common Diseases
 a. Obesity
 b. Promiscuity
 c. Alcoholism
 d. Smoking
 e. Illicit drugs
 f. IV drugs
 g. High perceived risk of HIV
 h. Multiple somatic symptoms

V. Degenerative Diseases
 a. Ischemic heart disease
 b. Chronic lung disease
 c. Liver disease

d. Cancer

e. Diabetes

f. Skeletal fractures

THE ROLE OF DEVELOPMENTAL TRAUMA IN CAUSING DEGENERATIVE CONDITIONS

The research of an American physician, W. Douglas Brodie, confirmed my research that unrecognized effects of developmental trauma from childhood is a major cause of physical and mental diseases later in life. He found that some inescapable shock or unhealed emotional trauma showed up in this patient's life within 2 years of being diagnosed with cancer. In addition, in working with cancer patients for over 30 years, he discovered a set of personality traits that were consistently present in all cancer-susceptible individuals. Many of these personality characteristics correlate with my research on chronic stress caused by unhealed developmental shock, trauma, stress, and unresolved emotional conflicts. FN Brodie, W. (1997). *Cancer and Common Sense, Combining Science and Nature to Control Cancer.* Reno, NV: Winning.

WHAT IS THE CANCER PERSONALITY?

Brodie describes the following characteristics as part of his *"cancer personality"* profile.[48]

1) Being highly conscientious, dutiful, overly responsible, and hardworking. (These characteristics describe parentized children who were forced to take care of their parents' needs and deny their own needs. We also found in our research that people with this personality trait experienced developmental shock, trauma, or stress during the codependent or bonding stage of development in the first year of life.)

2) A strong tendency to carry the burden of others and worrying excessively about others. (These are also characteristics of parentized children and people with codependency-related developmental shocks, traumas, or stresses.)

3) People-pleasers who try to make others happy. (This is also characteristic of those with unhealed developmental shocks, traumas, or stresses during the codependent stage.)

4) A tremendous need for approval and acceptance. (This is a classic symptom of the long-term effects of unhealed developmental shock during the codependent stage.)

5) A history of a lack of emotional closeness with one or both parents. (This is another sign of the long-term effects of unhealed developmental shock, trauma, or stress from the codependent or counterdependent stages.)

6) A tendency to harbor long-suppressed toxic emotions and difficulty expressing them. (This is also a classic symptom of people coping with the effects of unhealed developmental shock, trauma, and stress.)

7) Adverse reactions to developmental shock, trauma, or stress, typically to an especially stressful event beyond the individual's ability predict or control that happens about 2 years before the onset of cancer. The *"last straw"* reaction to this event comes after years of suppressed reactions to developmental stress. (This precisely describes people coping with the long-term effects of unhealed developmental shock, trauma, or stress.)

8) An inability to resolve deep-seated emotional problems anchored in childhood, the presence of which the individual is often totally unaware (This correlates with our research on the long-term impact of unrecognized and unhealed developmental shock, trauma, and stress.)

Brodie understood that chronic developmental stress suppresses the immune system just as much as episodes of shock or trauma. He saw patient after patient with the same patterns of developmental trauma and stress and underlying personality traits that he associated with cancer.

These are the same symptoms of adults who had a disorganized attachment with their mother and/or father during their first year of life. He also found that if a person could resolve the inescapable shock or heal the emotional trauma, the cancer would disappear.

My research has shown that these symptoms do not go away unless you can *"connect the dots"* and understand the connections between what happened to you as an infant and what symptoms you are displaying as an adult. This helps you transfer the images stored in the amygdala to the hippocampus and finally to the pre-frontal cortex. One of Brody's most significant finding was his six stages of cancer growth in your body. Below is a description of this developmental process.

WHAT ARE DR. BRODIE'S SIX DEVELOPMENTAL STAGES OF CANCER GROWTH IN THE BODY?

Brodie carefully describes six stages of how cancer grows in our bodies. His work clearly shows how events involving unrecognized or unhealed developmental shock, trauma, and stress within the previous two years are strongly related to the onset of cancer.

Stage One: An Inescapable Shock or Emotional Trauma. According to Brodie the conditions that produce cancer start with some kind of inescapable shock or emotional trauma. Again, he said this *"last straw"* event happens within 2 years of the onset of the cancer. This event affects deep sleep and the melatonin production in the body.

Melatonin is necessary for inhibiting cancer cell growth and is the primary hormone responsible for regulating the immune system. During this stage, a place in the emotional reflex center of the brain slowly breaks down, creating a dark spot on the brain actually visible via an x-ray. Brodie also found that this emotional center of the brain is connected to a specific organ in the body, and when this center begins to break down while attempting to process the unhealed trauma or shock, so does the organ or body part associated to it.

Stage Two: Stress Suppresses the Immune System. Elevated cortisol levels then begin to suppress your immune functioning. The immune system also receives subconscious messages from the affected emotional center of the brain to slow down and to even stop working altogether. The experience of the trauma or shock often feels like an emotional death to the brain and so it sends messages to the immune system causing it to give up the fight.

This causes somatids to appear, which are sub-cellular microbes akin to DNA molecules known to predict degenerative health conditions by up to 18 months, to react in the blood cells. Normally these somatids are limited to three stages in their life cycle, but when the immune system is impaired or suppressed they change into 16 stages that begin to create viral, bacterial, and yeast-like forms in your body.

Stage Three: Stress Causes Cell Glucose Levels to Rise. Over time, the elevated stress hormones deplete your adrenaline levels, causing your glucose (sugar) levels to rise in normal cells. Adrenaline serves to remove and convert glucose from the cells into energy for the body. When your adrenal hormones are depleted, glucose levels increase sharply within the cells, leaving less room for oxygen to be taken in from passing blood. This is why so many cancer patients become weak and lethargic at this stage.

Stage Four: Fungi Enter Cells to Feed on the Glucose. Here the pathogenic microbes (the somatids) establish themselves in the weakened part of the body and begin to feed on the high glucose levels in the cells. The fermentation of the glucose causes highly toxic waste products to be released into the body that further rob the cells of oxygen and energy. This lack of oxygen and cell energy causes normal cells to mutate during cell division, creating rogue cancer cells. The body's tissue and cells become highly acidic due to the waste products caused by the actions of somatids. Over-acidification of the body is due to fermentation of the excess stress hormones in the body. We now know that cancer cells cannot grow in an alkaline body.

Over-acidification can also be caused by poor diet, a lack of exercise, a high stress lifestyle, or the effects of unrecognized and unhealed developmental traumas. Viruses, bacteria, yeasts, mold, candida, and cancer cells thrive in a highly acidic environment. It is now known that cancer and candida albicans, a fungus that grows on your mucous membranes, are co-dependent. If one is present, the other is also.

Stage Five: Fungi and Cancer Form a Symbiotic Relationship. The somatids help the yeast-like fungus to form a symbiotic relationship with newly created cancer or tumor cells. This fungus feed on the high levels of glucose in the cells to produce new somatids. The yeast-like fungi also feed on the glucose in the cancer cells giving them energy to grow and reproduce. This eventually causes the cancer cells to form a mass or a tumor. The fungi prevent the cancer cells from reverting back to normal healthy cells as they produce more of an acidic condition in the body, which provides an environment that stimulates their growth.

Stage Six: Stress Stimulates Tumor Cell Growth or Metastases. The elevated stress hormones, norepinephrine, and epinephrine levels in the body stimulate cancer cells to produce chemicals. He believes that stress hormones make it easier for cancer cells to travel to other parts of the body through a process called metastasis.

Dr. Brodie died in 2005, but his colleagues still carry on his work at their clinic in Reno, Nevada. Information on Dr. Brodie's Reno Integrative Medical Center can be found at <https://www.renointegrativemedicalcenter.co>. He was ostracized by most of his colleagues in the medical profession, who saw his findings as a threat to their *"cancer industry."* While Dr. Brodie was able to communicate with the cancer patient's conscious and unconscious minds, he realized that it was his relationship with his patient that carried the most healing potential (Walker, M., 2002).

WHAT IS THE ROLE OF ADRENALINE IN CAUSING DEGENERATIVE DISEASES?

In Brodie's Six Stages of Cancer Growth note that a key is the increased depletion of the adrenal hormone. Research has shown that our adrenaline is the most addictive substance to the human body. Even more addictive than heroin or cocaine. It is a contributing factor in most of our degenerative diseases. Because of this fact, it is imperative for wise elders to keep their stress levels low and to have healed their developmental traumas that can cause a sudden uptick of their adrenal hormones when they get triggered by a memory of an unhealed developmental trauma. I will discuss this in more detail in Chapter Nine.

WHAT ARE SOME ALTERNATIVE CURES FOR CANCER?

As I mentioned in my dedication of this book to Bill Henderson, he was a pioneer in identifying over 400 alternative cures for cancer that work. You can sign up for his Newsletter at bill@beating-cancer-gently.com. This newsletter provided up-to-date information on the latest alternative cancer cures.

His book, *Cancer Free: Your Guide to Gentle, Non-Toxic Healing* is available at Amazon. In his book he has a recommended protocol for those who have been diagnosed with cancer. It can also be used as a preventative tool for those who do not have cancer and do not want to get it. The Bill Henderson Protocol is an inexpensive yet potent cancer treatment. This protocol can be used by any cancer patient with any type of cancer. *However, if the cancer is fast-spreading, has already spread significantly, or is a particularly dangerous type of cancer, he recommends a stronger protocol, such as the Cellect-Budwig, Cesium Chloride or High RF Frequency Protocol.*

CHAPTER SEVEN

WHAT ARE THE PERSONAL/ PSYCHOLOGICAL BARRIERS TO OVERCOME IN ORDER TO BECOME A WISE ELDER?

*He who is of a calm and happy nature will hardly feel
the pressure of age, but to him who is of an opposite
disposition, youth and age are equally a burden.*

—Plato

The difference between someone who is just growing old and someone who is becoming wiser is related to the amount of personal/psychological work they have done on themselves. If they are self-reflective and self-corrective, they have a good chance of becoming a wise elder. There are predictable barriers that have to be overcome in order to develop wisdom. You will see, as you read this list, it is not necessarily easy to become a wise elder. (There are many challenges or barriers to overcome in order to become an effective wise elder.) I have made a list of the challenges that men have to face in order to become a wise elder. They are listed below, with a short explanation about each of them:

1. Don't repeat the past. Look at how the past is influencing the present and determining the future. This is probably the most important challenge to overcome. There are two truths that come into play here:

- Everything you ever experienced in this lifetime is stored in your body somewhere. Situations and people can trigger memories of these experiences.

- The second truth is that if there was anything left unfinished, unresolved or unhealed, it will show up to be finished. This is the natural learning style of humans. They repeat anything left unfinished until they get it finished. In Chapter Nine I present some tools to help you finish what was left unfinished earlier in your life.

2. Don't go to sleep. Be aware of what is happening to you and learn something new every day. This can be a huge challenge if you do not consciously take control of this process. Going to sleep in this context means not paying attention to all the signals you get every day to help you grow and develop. It is easy to get distracted by the complexity of modern life and not pay attention to the lessons and experiences that come your way.

3. Get in touch w/ your true self w/o judgment. Almost all of us developed a False Self mostly to please others and to get along with others. This is not who we really are. A wise elder must do the work to recover his true self if he wants to be effective as a wise elder. He must do this without any guilt or shame. You didn't do anything wrong (guilt) and there is nothing wrong with you (shame). Everybody adopted a False Self and if you are not aware of the elements of your False Self, you may be prone to believe that is all there is of you.

4. Remember, being self-sufficient is not necessarily growth. We are all social beings and we learn best when we are in relationship with others. It is also important to learn how to ask directly for what you want or need from others. Many people fear they will be rejected if they ask directly, so they manipulate others to give them what they want without having to ask. This is a terribly inefficient way to get your need met. Later in this chapter, I discuss the Drama Triangle and how that can become a dysfunctional way to try to get your needs met. You will need to accept help from others and be willing to ask directly for what you want, in order to be an effective wise elder.

5. Eliminate all self-hatred. This is a huge obstacle for many people. We all grew up in a world that tried to socialize us by pointing out all the things they didn't like about us. This includes parents, teachers, bosses and clergy. It is no wonder when asked to produce a list of good and bad qualities, our list of bad qualities always out-numbers the good list.

6. Open yourself to love however it appears in your life. What is love? Well, there is a lot of confusion about what love means. Most of what we considered love given by our parents or others was not really love at all. It was conditional and therefore was at best a form of manipulation to get you to behave the way they thought you should behave. Love has to be given without conditions or it is not love. The only love worthy of its name is unconditional love. I believe we desperately need unconditional love in order to evolve. Without it we stay stuck in responding like Pavlov's dog in a conditioned way. A wise elder needs to be able to give and receive unconditional love.

7. Strive to understand the meaning and purpose of living, dying and death. This mean being gable to ask the *"big"* questions like, *"Who am I?"* *"Why am I here?"* and *"What is my purpose in being here?"* What is happiness?" *"What does death really mean?"* Wise elders regularly ask these questions. Wise elder contributor, **Michael Lightweaver**, sent me his thoughts on *"The Secret of Happiness."* I include here some of what he wrote: *"The secret to happiness has always been the holy grail of human pursuit. Perhaps that secret is different for each person. In my younger years I believed it was the attainment of goals – very often material ones – that would lead to happiness. But as I dutifully attained each of these goals I realized that they brought only a moment of satisfaction but no lasting happiness. Finally, I came to realize that my true source of happiness was Gratitude and Generosity."*

Michael also sent me his thoughts about death and I am including some of his words here: *"I am going to die. Everyone that you know at this moment; all of your friends, all of your family, all of your colleagues and co-workers, everyone you read about in the newspaper – world leaders, celebrities, heroes – all of them will be dead within a hundred years."* With that in mind, let's take another look at your issues.

Such a statement, while abrupt and shocking, brings us back to basics and helps us to put things in perspective. This sojourn on the Earth and all of our experience – whether pleasant or problematic – is quite temporary, just a brief moment in time. When we are tempted to get caught up in our daily dramas, it is helpful to pause and remember this, not as a cause for despair but to offer a perspective that allows us to laugh at ourselves and our inclination to suffer the deadly disease of *"seriosity."* Bottom line, when you get really bogged down with your problems, put them in perspective and lighten up.

8. Resist all illusions and addictions that help you stay in denial. For some people *"de-nial"* is a river in Egypt. Most people strive to live their lives in their *"comfort zone."* This takes a lot of energy and often a hypervigilance to prevent anything from coming into our lives and unexpectedly *"upsetting* *the apple cart.*" Unfortunately, this can lead to stifling control behaviors that become addictive. My definition of an addiction is *"a ritualistic, compulsive comfort-seeking behavior."* Using this definition, how many addictions do you have? How much of your time and energy goes to trying to stay in your comfort zone? Wise elders are able to take risks that often take them outside of their comfort zone. This is actually a defining quality of a wise elder. He is not trapped by his addiction to remain confined in his comfort zone.

9. Face any fears and depressions related to these illusions or addictions. Fear is often the biggest motivator and depression can set in if you *"brood"* about your present and future. This is often called anxiety about the unknown, or the fear that we will not be safe in some way or things will happen to us that take us out of our comfort zone. You might ask yourself the following question: *"What is my biggest fear?"* Drill down to see if you can find your bottom-line most fear.

10. Prepare to let go of your attachments to material security. This is extremely difficult for many older people. Either they or their parent lived through the Great Depression in this country. The memory of having to do without so many things has made many of these people become hoarders or people who get very attached to *"things."* Fortunately, I have learned this lesson, even though I grew up with parents and grandparents who lived through the Great Depression. One experienced helped me get over my attachments, was when Janae and I moved to Europe. We expected to live there for at least five years so we sold almost everything we owned. Because we could not afford to ship very many belongings overseas, we reduced our *"stuff"* down to 17 boxes, of which 12 of them were our books. A great experience in letting go of our attachments.

11. Surrender the need to be perfect. It took me five years to learn how to *"surrender"* the need to be perfect. I discovered that there are two forms of surrender: a feminine form and a masculine form. The feminine form involves not needing to be perfect by being right all the time. It requires you to be willing to receive what information you are getting from others, without resistance. Most of us when we hear or see something that we don't agree with, we don't even let it in and immediately start thinking of ways to refute it. The feminine form of surrender asks us to receive or let in what we are receiving and then thinking about what we want to do with this information. Currently, there are many people we see on television, who need to be right so when anything that challenges the *"rightness"* of their belief, they resist it and actually try to convince themselves even more that they are right and the other person is wrong. This generally goes nowhere.

The masculine form of surrender means to *"take charge of your life without guilt or shame."* Again, if you have an attachment to being right or perfect, you will not take charge of your life and look for someone to blame for what is not working in your life the way you would like it to. Wise elder need to be able to use both the masculine and feminine forms of surrender in all situations in their life.

12. Maintain a healthy sense of humor and a Positive Mental Attitude. This starts by not taking yourself too seriously and being able to laugh at yourself at times when you do something silly or stupid. Having a healthy sense of humor involves just that. Having a Positive Mental Attitude (PMA) is highly correlated with longevity. Also people who have a negative mental attitude are not fun to be around. I remember my aunt was one of those people. When you asked her how she was, she would reply, *"Not so good."* Then she would tell you all the woes she had in her life.

Nobody wanted to be around her and most of the time we didn't dare ask how she was, because we didn't want to hear her complaining. I had learned breathwork techniques that I used with both my parents and others relatives. After experiencing some relief from her burdens, my mother suggested I do breathwork with my aunt. I did, and it worked miracles. She had MS and was confined to wheelchair most of the time. The session involves someone lying down and doing connected breathing. It took several of us to get her off her wheelchair and onto the bed. After one session, she literally leapt off the bed and never went back to her wheel chair again. In addition, her mental attitude changed radically. She became a happy person and was fun to be around. She died about ten years later and was a totally peaceful person during that time.

13. Be humble, perceptive and plan well. Humorously, I used to say, *"I used to be conceited, but now I am perfect."* I often said it as a joke, but the truth behind it was that I did carry some one-up beliefs that grew out of being treated as *"special"* while growing up in my extended family. I have had to change this attitude in order to do what I do. Wise elders need to be humble and be perceptive in order to be effective.

14. Give up your warrior motives and actions. Become an inner warrior. This one was hard for me. I have always been a warrior to defend the rights of those who I perceived were being *"un-faired against."* This strong desire to help the less fortunate sometimes led me to *"chase windmills"* like Don Quixote. As I began to use this motivation on myself, I became more of an inner warrior and worked really hard to understand himself better and surrender by being more in charge of my life without guilty or shame and receiving more without resistance. Wise elders choose their battles carefully and are committed to working on themselves so they can work more effectively in service to others.

15. Be patient with yourself and others. Boy, this one continues to be a challenge for me. I am extremely patient with others but still have a hard time being patient with myself. My Dad was this way. He used to say, *"When they were handing out patience, I got tired of standing in the line."* I have high standards for myself and I am impatient with myself if it fails to meet my high expectations of myself. I consciously work on being more patient with myself every day and I can see progress. Perhaps I eventually will find some middle ground on this one.

16. Understand and be open to receive the many gifts of aging. It is a hard sell for many elderly people to see the gifts of aging. They mostly experience the limitations that aging has brought to their lives and the aches and pains they have to endure. Janae's Dad used to say, *"Where are the 'golden years' they promised me?"*

I count blessings every day. I live in beautiful house with a beautiful view of Pikes Peak out all my windows. I have no worries about money. I have a transformative relationship with a wonderful woman. I have great kids who I talk with often and I have a great relationship with my granddaughter. Finally, I am able to do want pleases me the most: Writing, teaching and helping others change and enrich their lives. I have a lot to be grateful for.

17. Find peace and forgiveness w/ your family and community. Peace is an internal state where you don't let whatever problems you have pull you off center. Forgiveness is another issue. The way I define what it means to *"for-give,"* is to *"give back"* all that you mistakenly took on as yours that actually belonged to someone else. You were born innocent and in the process of growing up you were told things about yourself that simply were not true. They were values, beliefs, thoughts, ideas and feelings that belonged to someone else, usually a family member, a teacher, or a minister.

To forgive them then means consciously giving back to them all that belonged to them in the first place. It is impossible to become emotionally separate from someone by making them *"bad."* The only other way to get separate from them is to give back all these things that you took on thinking they belonged to you. They never did belong to you and it is important for a wise elder to give back all the negativity that they were given by others. This is the only way to reclaim who you really are. I present strategies for meeting this challenge in Chapter Nine.

18. Experience the sacred nature of all life. This is one of the most important parts of my life. I remember being at a conference where Ted Turner was a speaker. At the break, I overhead a young women talking to Ted to convince him to give money to preserve a sacred site somewhere. He turned to her and said, *"Young lady, this whole Earth is a sacred place. That means there are no special sacred places, it is all sacred."* I feel connected to the beauty and sacredness of all life. The sacredness overwhelms me at times.

It is important for wise elders to know their place in the universe and are able to experience everything they do as being connected to the sacred nature of all life. I recall an insurance salesman coming to our house and he found out that I grew up Lutheran. He was a member of a local Lutheran church and I could see he was interested in recruiting us to attend his church. He asked us, "Do you go to church?

We replied immediately, *"Oh, yes, we go to church every day."* He looked puzzled by our answer, so we added, *"We believe that church does not just happen on Sunday morning, it is everywhere and everything we do is like "going to church."* He then quickly changed the subject because this concept was a bit outside of his belief system.

WHAT IS THE GREATEST PERSONAL/PSYCHOLOGICAL CHALLENGE FOR WISE ELDERS?

The successful resolution of the conflicting drives between the desire for oneness and the desire for separateness occurs by age 3 is the biggest challenge in their development as a wise elder. It is called *"individuation"* or *"the psychological birth."* This occurs when your normal, healthy, narcissistic needs are acknowledged and met by caring, self-assured, aware, and psychologically whole parents and adult caregivers. You, like most people likely did not get this kind of effective support to complete your individuation process as infants. So you are left to complete it as an adult.

To complete your psychological birth as an adult, it is necessary to resolve your internal struggle between two seemingly opposite forces: the natural drive toward oneness and closeness and the equally powerful drive to be an emotionally separate, self-determining individual.

If you have not completed your psychological birth, the need for the intimacy of oneness can also bring up intense fears of being engulfed or consumed. This experience can feel like a psychological annihilation and dismemberment of your Self. The counterforce of separation can produce intense fears of existential alienation, aloneness, and abandonment by others, even God.

Navigating these intense emotional experiences as an adult requires spiritual courage. Carl Jung identified such experiences as an integral part of individuation. Jung saw it as both a psychological and a spiritual process that generally is not completed by most people until mid-life. I believe wise elders have to be able to move beyond the conventional wisdom in order to discover gnosis, or the knowledge of the heart that renders human beings free. [49]

Jung also realized that humans cannot fulfill their potential if they become too attached to the trappings of the external world. He urged people to be *"in the world, but not "of the world"* in order to feel individuated. He cautioned people to look for their spiritual truths inside themselves and not in established religions.

In either case, understanding what happened in your childhood, identifying and healing your developmental shocks, traumas, and stresses and developing new relationship skills will help you complete your psychological birth as an adult and prepare you to be an effective wise elder. You may ask, *"How will I know if I have completed it?"* You will know because you will have a keen sense of who you really are and are able to handle life's challenges and conflicts with a minimum of stress, while feeling good about yourself and good about others. You will be able to maintain your object constancy in the midst of most of your life challenges. You will be comfortable with being both close and intimate and being separate and alone when you want or need to. Triggers from past developmental shocks, traumas, or stresses that used to elicit an intense emotional response no longer have the same negative effects.

Another benchmark is your ability to ask for what you want and need from others in such a way that they are delighted to give it to you. Only those who have worked on themselves psychologically and spiritually can expect to successfully complete this essential developmental process as an adult. At this point in our individual evolution as a species, most people have not had sustained experiences of deep emotional attunement and biological synchrony to fully enable them to perceive reality as it is. They have projections on others and on situations that prevent them from seeing things as they really are.

WHAT IS THE DRAMA TRIANGLE?[50]

The biggest challenge to master is to be able to get off and stay off the Drama Triangle. One of the most common ways that people try to get their needs met is by using the Drama Triangle. The Drama Triangle consists of three rotating roles: Rescuer, Persecutor and Victim. The objective of the game is to get your needs met by manipulating others to meet your needs without having to ask them directly. The Persecutor is the *"bad guy"* role in the Drama Triangle. For this reason, you avoid it unless you have a need to vent your *"justified"* negative feelings such as anger or rage.

In these instances, you must identify some reason to feel justified or right so you can express these negative feelings. Once you have found a good reason for making someone bad, you can dump your repressed feelings. This is one of the Persecutor payoffs. Righteous indignation, the most common form of Persecutor behavior, is putting others down by using guilt and shame.

According to Berne, there are first-degree games that just involve making someone uncomfortable or wrong. Second-degree games involve threatening someone's safety. Third-degree games can actually be life threatening. While the Drama Triangle can be played at any of these three degrees, people typically begin at the first degree and then escalate to second or third degree. Below is a brief description of the three roles plus the psychological games that they can play using that role and a list of the payoffs they want by using a particular psychological game:

THE PERSECUTOR ROLE/GAMES:
"NIGYSOB" "It's All Your Fault" & *"See What You Made Me Do."*

The Rules of These Games:
1. Set unnecessarily restrictive rules & limits.
2. Blame others for whatever happens.
3. Criticize all actions of others.
4. Keep the Victim oppressed.
5. Express justified and righteous anger.

6. Use guilt and shame to put the other person down.
7. Provoke conflict and drama.
8. Take a rigid, authoritative stance.
9. Act and sound like a critical Parent.
10. Come from an I'm okay/good, you're not okay/bad position.

The Payoffs for These Games. A Persecutor gets to be *"right"* and therefore is justified in releasing pent-up emotions. The Persecutor role allows a player to remain in control and dominate others. When someone rejects the heavy-handed behavior and expresses justified anger in return, this catapults them into the Victim and victim consciousness.

The Rescuer is the *"good guy"* role in the Drama Triangle. It provides people with a look-good opportunity to get their ego needs met. Rescuing allows people to look important and competent and to feel superior. Rescuer acts are often accompanied with woeful messages of self-sacrifice and martyrdom that also obligate the Victim in some way, if they buy into the guilt.

The Rescuer's attempts to help someone usually fail in some critical way, which then permits the Victim to get angry. This is also where people can quickly switch roles—from Persecute the Rescuer. The Rescuer then switches into the Victim role, saying indignantly, *"I was only trying to help you!"*

I discovered that most Rescuers are usually acting out their own unmet need to be rescued. They unconsciously project this need from unhealed childhood trauma, and then use it to justify rescuing of others. Here's a summary of the Rescuer role.

The Rescuer Role/Games:
"I Am Only Trying to Help You" & *"Look How Hard I've Tried."*

The Rules of These Games:

1. Feel obligated to rescue & often really doesn't want to.
2. Do things for others that they don't ask for and could do for themselves.
3. Feel guilty if they don't help others.
4. Act and sound like an *"authoritative"* Parent, keeping the Victim dependent and helpless with their Rescuing.
5. Support the Victim's perception of being weak and a failure.
6. Expect to fail in your own attempt to Rescue the Victim.
7. Often a pleasing, marshmallow person who avoids conflict and drama.
8. Come from an I'm okay/good, you're bad/not okay position.

The Payoff of These Games. You get to look okay, strong, capable and be one-up and the other person gets to look like they are weak and one-down. **Ultimate Payoff:** Become a Victim when your Rescuer's attempt to help you doesn't work.

The Victim role is key in the Drama Triangle, because the whole game revolves around getting to be the Victim. It is the one role where you can get your needs met without having to ask for anything from others. Those in the Victim position also can avoid taking responsibility for their behavior or feelings. They can blame whatever isn't working in their lives on someone or something else.

There are two types of Victims: the *"Pathetic Victim"* and the *"Angry Victim."* The Pathetic Victim plays one-down games, holds pity-parties, uses woeful, poor me facial expressions and body language, and uses one-down verbal language.

The Angry Victim pretends to be powerful, using guilt and shame to get others to feel sorry for them. The underlying motive of the Angry Victim is revenge. Both types want someone to blame for the feelings they have and for their troubles. Always operating in the background, of course, it is their desire to attract a Rescuer who can take care of them. Here's a summary of the Victim role.

The Victim Role/Games.
"Poor Me," & *"Ain't It Awful."*

The Rules of These Games:

1. Act victimized, oppressed, helpless, hopeless, powerless and ashamed in order to manipulate others.
2. Look for a Rescuer to help perpetuate your negative self-beliefs and to try to get your needs met without asking directly.
3. Use the Victim role to avoid making decisions, solving problems and taking responsibility for your actions.
4. Use conflict situations to play Victim.
5. Refuse to learn how to avoid or create conflict situations.
6. Have a slouched dejected body posture.
7. Operate from a *"I'm not okay/bad, you're okay/good"* position.

The Payoffs for These Games: You can get what you want and need without asking.

Martyrs are a special class of Victims. Sometimes described as *"emotional vampires,"* they act out toxic theatrical vignettes that escalate into hysteria and *"high drama."*

Martyrs use their Victim status to try to invoke extreme pity from others, and to prove that there is nothing that will improve their situation. Rather than blaming other people for your troubles, you can blame them on God or some other omnipotent force that no one could win against. Martyrs are the most eloquent and committed kinds of Victims. They are often seen as *"drama queens."*

The drama part of the Triangle comes from the fact that game-players rotate roles. They typically start out in the Rescuer role, but usually end up as the Victim. This rapid role switching is confusing to others. It disrupts their attempts to think logically and to express their authentic emotions. In dysfunctional families, this scene plays out as the *"Talk fast, Don't Listen"* game.

Drama Triangle players must become adept at switching roles in order to insure confusion in their social interactions. They use the *"Three Rules of Chaos"* to help them switch roles quickly and defend, deny and protect themselves.

1. Make a game out of everything,
2. deny everything, and
3. blame others for everything and put them on the defensive.

The faster that roles the change on the Triangle, the more the drama increases. As people's brains short out, they become more frustrated and angrier. At some point the emotional intensity peaks. Then the player can express rage, scream and lose control of his/her emotions, and maybe even get violent.

What Keeps the Game Going? Competition for the Victim role keeps the game going. Let me repeat this. It is competition for the Victim role that keeps the Drama Triangle game going. Each player secretly strategizes in order to get to the Victim role. The Victim role is the prize! Here you can get others to help you meet your needs without having to ask them directly, and you can blame others if their attempts to help you don't work out.

The Persecutor initially feels righteous in his/her anger at the Victim, but then may feel guilty after attacking someone who is so weak and helpless. The Victim can then push the Persecutor's *"guilty"* button and blame him/her for a lack of compassion or appreciation about the Victim's challenging situation.

What Is the Purpose of the Need/Obligate System? The purpose of the Need/ Obligate System clearly is manipulation and control. It is how the Drama Triangle works in the larger world around us. It is designed to make you take care of other people without them having to ask for it. This is also the defining quality of all co-dependent interactions.

The Need/Obligate system is also a way of controlling large groups of people at one time. Like families, large groups can use Persecutor, Rescuer and Victim dynamics in ways that turn people into *"examples"*—humiliating, shaming and dehumanizing them ways that make those witnessing this *"punishment"* more compliant and less assertive. This is also known as *"vicarious traumatization,"* a very effective form of mind control.

How Do Lobbyists Use the Need/Obligate System to Manipulate the Lawmakers? Washington lobbyists and politicians use the Need-Obligate system all the time. A lobbyist approaches a member of Congress, for example, and donates a sum of money to his campaign fund without the Congressman ever asking directly for it. Then the Congressman knows that he/she is obligated to vote a certain way on legislation that related to the lobbyist's interests.

Nothing is ever transacted directly or written down. The members of Congress know that if they do not vote the way this lobbyist wishes, that will be the end of any future campaign contributions from that source.

Once the Supreme Court's Citizen's United decision legitimized corporations as people, it made it easy for corporations to secretly give large sums of money to support candidates for reelection. Super-PACs are able to receive money without ever disclosing its sources, which makes the Need-Obligate System a real game. The Citizen's United decision permits secret Need/Obligate System transactions to occur legally in both the national and state legislatures.

I believe that the best way to protect yourself from the Need-Obligate System and other dysfunctional, codependent Drama Triangle structures is to know yourself very well. The better you understand yourself, the better your bullsh*t detector will work. It will help you to avoid manipulation and entanglements that could interfere with being an effective wise elder.

What is Betrayal and How Do You Heal It?
Another big challenge for the wise elder is to heal his/her major betrayals. If you don't find a way to resolve the feelings around a betrayal you experienced, you are destined to encounter another betrayal with similar elements.

James Hillman[51] in a ground-breaking article lists the typical ways that people try to handle the feelings around a perceived betrayal as follows:

Revenge. You may feel a very strong desire to get even with the person or persons who betrayed you. When someone says or does something hurtful to you, the immediate impulse may be to hurt them back in some way. Hillman says that this choice is the most common response and the one that creates the least amount of growth in consciousness. Seeking revenge and getting even means placing your focus on what other people did or didn't do or say and allows you to avoid looking at your role in helping to create your betrayals. It usually leads you to plotting ways to get even with the perceived betrayer.

Splitting. If you are betrayed in an intimate relationship, you may lose your internal object constancy or sense of self. You may resort to splitting. You either split against the betrayer or you split against yourself. Triggered by post-traumatic stimuli from the past, you may feel regressed and then make either yourself or the other person the *"bad guy."* This kind of split immediately activates automatic fight/flight/flee behavioral responses. Splitting responses to betrayal may indicate a need for trauma reduction therapies and/ or individual counseling that focuses on identifying and healing any hidden developmental traumas from your first three years of life

Denial. A third choice in a betrayal situation is to deny the value of the other person. This choice may also involve splitting, or making a person once perceived as *"all good"* into someone who is now *"all bad."* You may be surprised at how quickly this defense mechanism can be activated, often with little awareness.

Cynicism. This easy choice may be the disease of our contemporary times. It is easy for you to get cynical because of your inability to stop reenacting or predicting your betrayal traumas and the subsequent lack of understanding of the patterns inherent in them. Cynicism, unfortunately, also doesn't lead to much growth or awareness.

Paranoia. Paranoia, or not trusting your potential betrayers, is another common response to betrayal. If you were betrayed in a loving, trusting relationship it may require that you put others through a lot of tests before they are allowed to get close to you. Paranoia also leads to very little growth. It requires a lot of time to constantly monitor the other person's behavior to determine if he or she is passing your various trustworthiness tests. Rather than focusing on the source of the betrayal or the patterns being reenacted in the relationship, paranoia is a way for you to avoid self-responsibility.

Self-Betrayal. The final sterile choice, according to Hillman, involves the betrayal of yourself. The inner response to a betrayal might be, *"How could I have been so stupid!"* Such responses often include a self-judgment about the risks that were taken. Rather than seeing the risk-taking as a potential for learning, you classify it as a mistake that you can use for self-judgment and disempowerment.

Hillman goes on to say that none of these ways to cope with betrayals actually heal the underlying feelings related to the betrayal. He suggests that we have to forgive ourselves and the other person in order to heal the wounds associated with a betrayal. Again he states what I believe that we cannot heal our wounds by making ourselves and/or the other person *"bad."* In Chapter Nine, I describe some strategies for healing your major betrayals.

CHAPTER EIGHT

WHAT ARE THE SOCIAL AND CULTURAL BARRIERS TO OVERCOME TO BECOME A WISE ELDER?

Old people at weddings always poke me and say,
"You're next." So I started doing that at funerals.

—Unknown

Some of the biggest social/cultural barriers to overcome are based on misperceptions of aging by the media and the general public. This is the first barrier to overcome if we are going to honor our wise elders.

WHAT ARE THE PUBLIC'S MISPERCEPTIONS OF AGING?[52]

Three categories of (mis)perceptions of the American public became clear. The first concerns older adults' capabilities (more accurately, their perceived lack thereof), the second is about the role of older adults in the broader society, and the third concerns culpability.

Capabilities: Aging=Decline. The prevailing thinking by the majority of the American public sampled was the association between aging and decline. The most common words used to describe aging was of *"loss," "slowing down,"* and *"breaking down."* There is a strong belief that a loss of control and deterioration are inevitable as one grows older. Consistent with that belief is an emphasis on the increased need by the elderly for healthcare and the difficulty of them meeting their healthcare needs. The public also believes older adults can no longer learn anything new—they believe the elderly stagnate, and they are digitally incompetent. The public characterizes the aging process as one in which identity, knowledge, skills, success, and other aspects of life become increasingly in decline and unable to be changed.

139

The experts, on the other hand, emphasize that aging is not necessarily synonymous with disease or disability. With the right kind of contextual and social support, most older adults remain healthy and maintain high lives of independence and functioning. Implicated in the belief about older adults' lack of capabilities is that *"nothing can be done"* to change their decline. If decline is inevitable, they reason, why bother investing in preventive and support services that would help the elderly to maintain independence, health, and social involvement?

Elders' Role in Society: Older Adults Seen as "Other." The second grouping of misperceptions that shows up in most surveys is the role of older adults in the broader society. These surveys reveal that society in general sees the elderly *"other."* Older adults are being compartmentalized from the rest of society and the language of *"battling"* or *"working against"* aging dominates in people's attitudes. Rather than recognizing that aging is relevant to all of us, those interviewed perceive older adults as an external group that competes with the rest of society for limited resources.

However, the experts' view is that older adults are integral parts of society. In fact, they recognize that the elderly has an enormous economic and social impact on American society—an impact often not well accounted for in our social discourse, media, and public policy. Experts are clear that older adults represent an enormous source of consumer spending and economic productivity. They also emphasize that older adults are a large source of social productivity, even if it is not currently being recognized by society.

According to many surveys, Americans recognize that societal changes can create greater challenges for older adults. Extended families are dispersed, offering less support for the perceived needs of older adults; the country's economic landscape can make it more challenging for older people to get and keep jobs, despite the belief that some older adults need or want to work longer before retiring. There also is a fear that Social Security is doomed and will not be there for future generations of people as they age.

The belief that older adults are *"other"* contributes to a zero-sum game thinking wherein policy discussions about aging are characterized as by allocating more resources for *"them"* it means fewer resources for *"us."* Such thinking makes it difficult to see aging as a public health issue. Also, there is a belief that the past—when generations of families lived close to each other and there was a booming economy— was better than today. All this reinforces fatalism and the belief that *"nothing can be done."* This dissuades people from even thinking about implementing public policy and community-based solutions.

Culpability: Elders Are Accountable for Their Circumstances. The final set of misperceptions that shows up in surveys of public perceptions of the elderly has to do with culpability. The responses from the public about older individuals are consistent with a basic American cultural belief each person is accountable for his or her circumstances. The public believes the lack of well-being of older adults is exclusively the result of having made poor individual lifestyle choices and financial planning. By extension, it implies that those who did eat well and exercise throughout their lives are the healthy older adults and those suffering disabilities must not have adequately taken care of themselves. This is a Social-Darwinism belief, that those who took good care of themselves and are the fittest are destined to survive and thrive, while those who are poor and did not take good care of themselves deserve their fate.

Similarly, the public believes all people need to take control of their financial security throughout their lives and plan for retirement. Therefore, if, as an older person, you are economically strained, it must have been a result of poor planning. Finally, the public asserts a belief in *"mind over matter."* This means that elderly people's experience of aging is determined by their attitude, willpower, and choices. Their prevailing attitude is *"they made their bed now let them lay in it"*.

The implication of the public's focus on individual responsibility is that it minimizes the consideration of systemic social, economic, psychological, cultural influences on the well-being of the elderly and clouds the consideration of policies that could be an important driver of older adults' full participation in society. It denies our collective responsibility, it ignores any concept of a social contract, and it creates an obstacle even to the aging community's efforts to improve the quality of life of the elderly.

The experts, on the other hand, emphasized the need for public policy and social determinants to help create the environments necessary for older adults to secure and maintain a good quality of life. For example, issues about work opportunities, the health of the Social Security system, policies to address ageism, and the adequacy of our healthcare workforce to meet the demands of the elderly predominates. The experts also recognize the role social determinants such as geography, race, and social supports play in how people live their later years.

WHAT ARE SOME OTHER MISPERCEPTIONS OF AGING IN THIS COUNTRY?[53]

America is well known for its obsession with youth. Youth and beauty are glorified across all forms of our media and we are taught from a very young age that *"youthing"* not aging is what to go after. Ageism is a significant social problem. Researchers and academics need to place more emphasis on studying the needs of this larger cultural problem and try to figure out ways to minimize the impact of our social and cultural misperceptions and biases on our aging population. In America, those 65 years of age and older is the fastest growing segment of the population. The baby boomers have now joined the ranks of the elderly. It is going to be necessary to change the social/culture misperceptions and people's general attitudes about aging and the elderly.

People in this country are fixated on trying to look much younger that they are. Plastic surgery for both men and women is at an all-time high. Most forms of plastic surgery are elective and have more to do with vanity and physical appearance than anything else. Hollywood movies typically only cast young women in leading roles, and leading men are typically the strongest, fittest, and most virile men. Fashion magazines that are marketed to women only put young, beautiful, and thin women on their covers. Men's magazines pretty much do the same, but they use male models, actors, and famous athletes. What are the messages being sent here? What does this do to our attitudes toward aging? How does this shape our views toward the elderly, and our own concerns about getting old?

Even though the United States has an ever growing aged population there is still a clear bias against aging and a general fear of getting old. Even though the emphasis on youth and beauty has traditionally been directed more toward females than males, we are now seeing an increasing concern by males about aging and getting old. The elderly used to be a highly respected group and were admired for their experience and wisdom. This has changed and we need to address this as a social/cultural problem.

Changes in the political, social, and economic landscape has altered perceptions about aging and ultimately has decreased the status and position of the elderly in our society. With a growing sense of rugged individualism and an increasing concern with staying young, the elderly has had to face an escalating level of disregard, disrespect, and marginalization. These prevailing social and cultural issues have social and academic significance that merits far more attention and applied action than it is now receiving, particularly in academia.

The mass media in this country is at the center of this marginalization and devaluing of the elderly. The mass media is largely the central nervous system of American society and has a massive influence on people's values, beliefs, and perceptions. This has been demonstrated across all research in the social and behavioral sciences that show the overall beliefs of the general public about the elderly are largely negative and stereotypical.

Common feelings toward the elderly are that they are of low status and incompetent and this is a common theme running across the media representations of the elderly. Elderly people are often depicted as weak, unattractive, and senile. Other cultural stereotypes often seen in a media portray of the elderly as frail, feeble, financially distressed, and not contributing to society.

If American society moves further in the direction of secularism, materialism, and individualism, we can expect an increase of these negative attitudes and perceptions toward the elderly, and aging in general. If our primary social institutions, such as the mass media, continue to represent old age as something to be feared and avoided, then we can expect to see harmful stereotypes and a general prejudice toward our oldest members of society to increase.

WHAT DO THE ELDERLY THINK: GROW OLDER, FEEL YOUNGER?

A recent survey confirmed that the elderly believe you're never too old to feel young.[54] In fact, it showed that *the older people get, the younger they feel–relatively speaking.* Among 18 to 29 year-olds, about half say they feel their age, while about quarter say they feel older than their age and another quarter say they feel younger. By contrast, among adults 65 and older, fully 60% say they feel younger than their age, compared with 32% who say they feel exactly their age and just 3% who say they feel older than their age.

Moreover, the gap in years between actual age and their *"felt age"* actually widens as people grow older. Nearly half of all survey respondents ages 50 and older said they felt at least 10 years younger than their chronological age. Among respondents ages 65 to 74, a third said they felt 10 to 19 years younger than their age, and one-in-six said they felt at least 20 years younger than their actual age. Related to this upbeat way of counting their felt age, older adults also displayed a *"count-my-blessings"* attitude when asked to look back over the full arc of their lives.

Nearly half (45%) of adults" ages 75 and older say their life has turned out better than they expected, while just 5% say it has turned out worse (the remainder say things have turned out the way they expected or have no opinion). All other age groups also tilted positive, but considerably less so, when asked to look at their lives so far compared against their own expectations.

WHAT DO THE ELDERLY SAY IS THE DOWNSIDE OF GETTING OLD?

To be sure, there are burdens that come with growing old. When any of my older friends complain about some ache or pain, I always say to them very authoritatively, *"I know what is causing that problem."* They look at me and ask, *"Well, what?"* I then say to them, *"Old age."* They groan and then they laugh with me. Here are more results from the Pew Research Center survey:

About one-in-four adults ages 65 and older report that they experience memory loss. About one-in-five say they have a serious illness, are not sexually active, or often feel sad or depressed. About one-in-six report they are lonely or have trouble paying bills. One-in-seven cannot drive. One-in-ten say they feel they aren't needed or are a burden to others. These are real problems.

But when it comes to these and other potential problems related to old age, the share of younger and middle-aged adults who report expecting to encounter them is much higher than the share of older adults who report actually experiencing them. In other words, the fear is greater than the reality.

Moreover, these problems are not equally shared by all groups of older adults. Those with low incomes are more likely to face these challenges than those with high incomes. The only exception to this pattern has to do with sexual inactivity; the number of older adults reporting this as a problem is not correlated with income.

Not surprisingly, troubles associated with aging accelerate as adults advance into their 80s and beyond. For example, about four-in-ten respondents (41%) ages 85 and older say they are experiencing some memory loss, compared with 27% of those ages 75-84 and 20% of those ages 65-74. Similarly, 30% of those ages 85 and older say they often feel sad or depressed, compared with less than 20% of those who are 65-84. And 25% of adults ages 85 and older say they no longer drive, compared with 17% of those ages 75-84 and 10% of those who are 65-74.

But even in the face of these challenges, the vast majority of the elderly surveyed appear to have made peace with their circumstances. Only a miniscule share of adults ages 85 and older–1%–say their lives have turned out worse than they expected. It definitely helps that adults in their late 80s are as likely as those in their 60s and 70s to say that they are experiencing many of the good things associated with aging. Here they include time with family, less stress, more respect or more financial security.

WHAT DO THE ELDERLY SAY IS THE UPSIDE OF GROWING OLD?

When asked about a wide range of potential benefits of old age, seven-in-ten respondents ages 65 and older say they are enjoying more time with their family. About two-thirds cite more time for hobbies, more financial security and not having to work. About six-in-ten say they get more respect and feel less stress than when they were younger. Just over half cite more time to travel and to do volunteer work. Their responses do indicate that the phrase *"golden years"* is actually something more than just a syrupy greeting card phrase.

Of all the good things about getting old, the best by far, older adults say, is being able to spend more time with family members. In response to an open-ended question, 28% of those ages 65 and older say that what they value most about being older is the chance to spend more time with family, and an additional 25% say that above all, they value time with their grandchildren. A distant third on this list is having more financial security, cited by 14% of older adults as what they value most about getting older.

WE ARE ALL LIVING LONGER?

Older adults now account for record shares of the populations of the United States and most developed countries. In 2017, 15.6% of the U.S. population were age 65 and older–up from 4% in 1900. This century-long expansion in the share of the world's population that is 65 and older is the product of dramatic advances in medical science and public health as well as steep declines in fertility rates. In this country, the increase in our older population has leveled off since 1990, but it started rising again after the first wave of the nation's 78 million baby boomers turned 65 in 2011. By 2050, according to Census Bureau projections, about 80 million Americans will be over age 65, and about 5% will be ages 85 and older, up from 2% now. California has the largest number of elderly people, but Florida has the highest percentage of elderly in their population. These ratios will put the U.S. at mid-century roughly where Japan, Italy and Germany–the three *"oldest"* large countries in the world–are today.

WHAT ARE OLDER ADULTS PERCEPTIONS ABOUT AGING?

In a 1969 Gallup Poll, 74% of respondents said there was a generation gap, with the phrase defined in the survey question as *"a major difference in the point of view of younger people and older people today."* When the same question was asked a decade later, in 1979, by CBS and The New York Times, just 60% perceived a generation gap. But in perhaps the single most intriguing finding in a new Pew Research survey, is that the share that say there is a generation gap has spiked to 79%–despite the fact that there have been few overt generational conflicts in recent times of the sort that roiled the 1960s.[55]

It could be that the phrase now means something different, and less confrontational, than it did at the height of the counterculture's defiant challenges to the establishment 40 years ago. Whatever the current understanding of the term *"generation gap,"* roughly equal shares of young, middle-aged and older respondents in the new survey agree that such a gap exists. The most common explanation offered by respondents of all ages has to do with differences in morality, values and work ethic. Relatively few cite differences in political outlook or in uses of technology. Here are some of the key questions they asked the elderly and some of their responses.

When Does Old Age Begin? The age of 68 was the average of all answers from the 2,969 survey respondents. But as noted above, this average masks a wide, age-driven variance in responses. More than half of adults under 30 say the average person becomes old even before turning 60. Just 6% of adults who are 65 or older agree. Moreover, gender as well as age influences attitudes on this subject. Women, on average, say a person becomes old at age 70. Men, on average, put the number at 66. In addition, on all 10 of the non-chronological potential markers of old age tested in this survey, men are more inclined than women to say the marker is a proxy for old age.

Are You Old? Certainly not! Public opinion in the aggregate may decree that the average person becomes old at age 68, but you won't get too far trying to convince people that age that the threshold applies to them. Among respondents ages 65-74, just 21% say they feel old. Even among those who are 75 and older, just 35% say they feel old.

What Age Would You Like to Live to? The average response from our survey respondents is 89. One-in-five would like to live into their 90s, and 8% say they'd like to surpass the century mark. The public's verdict on the most desirable life span appears to have ratcheted down a bit in recent years. A 2002 AARP survey found that the average desired life span was 92.

What Do Older People Do Every Day? Among all adults ages 65 and older, nine-in-ten talk with family or friends every day. About eight-in-ten read a book, newspaper or magazine, and the same share takes a prescription drug daily. Three-quarters watch more than an hour of television; about the same share prays daily. Nearly two-thirds drive a car. Less than half spend time on a hobby. About four-in-ten take a nap; about the same share goes shopping. Roughly one-in-four use the internet, get vigorous exercise or have trouble sleeping. Just 4% get into an argument with someone. As adults move deeper into their 70s and 80s, daily activity levels diminish on most fronts–especially when it comes to exercising and driving. On the other hand, daily prayer and daily medication both increase with age.

Are Older Adults Happy? They're about as happy as everyone else. And perhaps more importantly, the same factors that predict happiness among younger adults–good health, good friends and financial security–by and large predict happiness among older adults. However, there are a few age-related differences in life's happiness sweepstakes. Most notably, once all other key demographic variables are held constant, being married is a predictor of happiness among younger adults but not among older adults (perhaps because a significant share of the latter group is made up of widows or widowers, many of whom presumably have *"banked"* some of the key marriage-related correlates of happiness, such as financial security and a strong family life). Among all older adults, happiness varies very little by age, gender or race.

Retirement and Old Age. Retirement is a place without clear borders. Fully 83% of adults ages 65 and older describe themselves as retired, but the word means different things to different people. Just three-quarters of adults (76%) 65 and older fit the classic stereotype of the retiree who has completely left the working world behind.

An additional 8% say they are retired but are working part time, while 2% say they are retired but working full time and 3% say they are retired but looking for work. The remaining 11% of the 65-and-older population describe themselves as still in the labor force, though not all of them have jobs. Whatever the fuzziness around these definitions, one trend is crystal clear from government data3: After falling steadily for decades, the labor force participate rate of older adults began to trend back upward about 10 years ago. In the Pew Research survey, the average retiree is 75 years old and retired at age 62.

Living Arrangements. More than nine-in-ten respondents ages 65 and older live in their own home or apartment, and the vast majority are either very satisfied (67%) or somewhat satisfied (21%) with their living arrangements. However, many living patterns change as adults advance into older age. For example, just 30% of adults ages 65-74 say they live alone, compared with 66% of adults ages 85 and above. Also, just 2% of adults ages 65-74 and 4% of adults ages 75-84 say they live in an assisted living facility, compared with 15% of those ages 85 and above.

Old-School Social Networking. The great majority of adults ages 65 and older (81%) say they have people around them, other than family, on whom they can rely on for social activities and companionship. About three-quarters say they have someone they can talk to when they have a personal problem; six-in-ten say they have someone they can turn to for help with errands, appointments and other daily activities. On the flip side of the coin, three-in-ten older adults say they *"often"* help out other older adults who are in need of assistance, and an additional 35% say they sometimes do this. Most of these social connections remain intact as older adults continue to age, but among those 85 and above, the share that say they often or sometimes provide assistance to others drops to 44%.

The Twitter Revolution Hasn't Landed Here. If there's one realm of modern life where old and young behave very differently, it's in the adoption of newfangled information technologies. Just four-in-ten adults ages 65-74 use the internet on a daily basis, and that share drops to just one-in-six among adults 75 and above. By contrast, three-quarters of adults ages 18-30 go online daily. The generation gap is even wider when it comes to cell phones and text messages. Among adults 65 and older, just 5% get most or all of their calls on a cell phone, and just 11% sometimes use their cell phone to send or receive a text message. For adults under age 30, the comparable figures are 72% and 87%, respectively.

Religion and Old Age. Religion is a far bigger part of the lives of older adults than younger adults. Two-thirds of adults ages 65 and older say religion is very important to them, compared with just over half of those ages 30 to 49 and just 44% of those ages 18 to 29. Moreover, among adults ages 65 and above, a third (34%) say religion has grown more important to them over the course of their lives, while just 4% say it has become less important and the majority (60%) say it has stayed the same. Among those who are over 65 and report having an illness or feeling sad, the share who say that religion has become more important to them rises to 43%.

Staying in Touch with the Kids. Nearly nine-in-ten adults (87%) ages 65 and older have children. Of this group, just over half are in contact with a son or daughter every day, and an additional 40% are in contact with at least one child–either in person, by phone or by email–at least once a week. Mothers and daughters are in the most frequent contact; fathers and daughters the least. Sons fall in the middle, and they keep in touch with older mothers and fathers at equal rates. Overall, three-quarters of adults who have a parent or parents ages 65 and older say they are very satisfied with their relationship with their parent(s), but that share falls to 62% if a parent needs help caring for his or her needs.

Was the Great Bard Mistaken? Shakespeare wrote that the last of the *"seven ages of man"* is a second childhood. Through the centuries, other poets and philosophers have observed that parents and children often reverse roles as parents grow older. Not so, says the Pew Research survey. Just 12% of parents ages 65 and older say they generally rely on their children more than their children rely on them. An additional 14% say their children rely more on them. The majority–58%–says neither relies on the other, and 13% say they rely on one another equally. Responses to this question from children of older parents are broadly similar.

Intergenerational Transfers within Families. Despite these reported patterns of non-reliance, older parents and their adult children do help each other out in a variety of ways. However, the perspectives on these transfers of money and time differ by generation. For example, about half (51%) of parents ages 65 and older say they have given their children money in the past year, while just 14% say their children have given them money. The intra-family accounting comes out quite differently from the perspective of adult children. Among survey respondents who have a parent or parents ages 65 or older, a quarter say they received money from a parent in the past year, while an almost equal share (21%) say they gave money to their parent(s). There are similar differences in perception, by generation, about who helps whom with errands and other daily activities. (To be clear, the survey did not interview specific pairs of parents and children; rather, it contacted random samples who fell into these and other demographic categories.) Not surprisingly, as parents advance deeper into old age, both they and the adult children who have such parents report that the balance of assistance tilts more toward children helping parents.

Conversations About End-of-Life Matters. More than three-quarters of adults ages 65 and older say they've talked with their children about their wills; nearly two-thirds say they've talked about what to do if they can no longer make their own medical decisions, and more than half say they've talked with their children about what to do if they can no longer live independently. Similar shares of adult children of older parents report having had these conversations. Parents and adult children agree that it is the parents who generally initiate these conversations, though 70% of older adults report that this is the case, compared with just 52% of children of older parents who say the same.

WHAT ARE SOME WAYS WE COULD HONOR OUR ELDERLY?[56]

We know that the elderly has a lifetime of experience to share. They comprise a generation that has survived The Great Depression, World War II, Vietnam and The Great Recession. These wise elders have a lot to teach us about enduring change and handling life's adversity. It's one thing to read about Pearl Harbor, but it's more engrossing to hear about it from someone with first-hand knowledge. Younger generations must learn the importance of making time to listen and spend quality time with them. Here are some ways we can appreciate and recognize them:

1. Ask for advice. Sadly, we know that even though elders are some of the wisest people in society we do not ask them for their advice. It's a shame to think that an elder, with a lifetime of experience, would be overlooked for his advice. Elders have a lot to contribute to society through their life experiences, so seeking counsel from a wise elder is time well spent. You will both appreciate the effort.

2. Call them. If you live too far from your elderly loved one to see them on a regular basis, be sure to pick up the phone and call them. In our busy lives, it's easy to forget just how much it will mean to an elderly relative if we take time out of our day to say *"hello."* Phone calls are a personal way of both saying and showing that you thinking of them and care.

3. Discuss family heritage, history and traditions. There's an undeniable strength in family stories. In fact, putting together an oral family history can not only bring family members together and strengthen the ties between generations, but they can also educate about family genetics, personalities and more. Family history translates into stronger family bonds and life successes. In fact, recent studies have shown that children who have more knowledge of their family history also tend to show greater emotional resilience, facing challenges and stress more effectively as they have a stronger sense of where they come from and who they are.

A survey conducted by Harris Poll and commissioned by *A Place for Mom* revealed the following topics were what U.S. adults wanted to know about their elderly family members, specifically their mothers:[57]

- Career highlights (e.g., significant work achievements, favorite job)
- Family history (e.g., genealogy, origins of the family)
- Life advice (e.g., view on aging, words of wisdom to share with children and grandchildren)
- Medical history (e.g. health issues common with family members, life-threatening disease diagnosis)
- Personal history (e.g., childhood memories, dating history)

Almost like a puzzle, heritage is many pieces that form a masterpiece to comprise an individual and their journey. Taking the time to visit aging loved ones during the holidays to no to not only reconnect, but also gather pieces of their heritage puzzle, can provide important info to pass on for posterity. After all, information about your family is lost in three generations if it is not written down.

4. Eat together. Eating together is one of the most universal social customs in almost all cultures. This is an opportunity to catch up, enjoy a good meal and have fun. Whether you venture to a favorite restaurant, pack a picnic or visit your senior loved one's home, try to eat together on a regular basis in your home.

5. Spend time with them (and listen intently). Many elders get lonely, whether they're retired and no longer have their social contacts at work, or they've lost their spouse and some of their friends. In either case, they still need frequent and meaningful social contacts for happiness as many can get isolated over time; which can lead to health decline. It's important to take time to visit elderly loved ones to not only spend precious time with them and learn from them; but also give them purpose, as relationships are key to healthy aging. When in the presence of an elder, make sure to listen as the senior's words come from a place with many decades of experience. The conversation can be beneficial to both of you.

6. Tell them how much you appreciate and respect them. Even if you demonstrate that you respect your elders through your actions, it's important to actually tell them how much you appreciate and respect them. Compliments and giving people purpose, especially older Americans, is a very positive message. If there is a senior who has positively impacted you, make sure to share this with them; it will probably bring a smile to their face.

7. Visit senior living communities. The world moves at a fast pace and people sometimes forget what's truly important. Seniors are sometimes forgotten, but are still very much alive. By visiting senior living communities, you communicate to seniors that you care. You give them purpose through social interaction. Visiting a senior living community, whether your loved one lives there or not, is an excellent way to reach out to the older community and show them you care.

8. Volunteer at a senior center. When we give, we feel better. Pay it forward is a good mantra to follow. It's the infinitely touching moments in our lives that make it all worthwhile, and often times these moments are the ones spent volunteering for seniors and giving to those in need. A little goes a long way in a nursing home or senior living community. Discover how the upcoming holidays are an excellent opportunity for volunteering in a senior living community as there are often activities and opportunities to help with festive gatherings and celebrations.

WHAT ARE THE ESSENTIAL TIPS FOR AGING WELL?

After searching through dozens of aging articles and studies, I found what I consider to be the top six things that wise elders can do to live a healthier and happier lives. Here is my list:

1. Stay Socially Engaged. Wise elders maintain connections with their community, family and friends. As we get older, our family relationships change and we also have opportune position of gaining a new perspective from their contacts with other friends, and they can learn from interactions with their children and grandchildren. Meanwhile, social isolation is the main predictor of depression, as well as having negative effects on their health.

2. Create A Plan for Your Later Years. Our ever-increasing life expectancy presents an amazing opportunity for personal growth and planning for a wise elder. Because people are living longer and with greater independence, they can plan their futures more actively. Of course, this means being proactive and not just sitting around and waiting to die, as we watch our bodies and minds deteriorate. Wise elders have an opportunity to think about what they might want to do, whether it's spending more time in the garden or learning a new creative skill. The best way to insure having a comfortable and interesting old age is to plan for one.

3. You Need to Rethink Your Ideas of Growing Old. Learning to accept the natural changes to our bodies and minds that occur as we age is a big part of combating the problems of aging. Whether it's the media or pharmaceutical companies, we are bombarded with messages about how we are falling apart, our body losing its vitality and our mind losing its acuity. This makes the prospect of getting older somewhat depressing; but with aging, as with anything else, there is such a thing as a self-fulfilling prophecy. If we look at getting older as an opportunity, or a chance to really focus on what is important to us, we can look forward to actually becoming healthier and happier as we age.

4. Stay Physically Active. We've all heard the saying: use it or lose it. If you want to remain healthy and vital well into your later years, exercise is a must. Regular physical exercise will help you maintain flexibility and muscle mass, sure, but it can also keep you feeling young. It's mentally empowering to be able to continue doing many of the physical activities you did when you were younger — some people, in fact, are more fit as older adults than they were as young adults. But perhaps the most compelling evidence of all for staying active comes from a study in the *Archives of Internal Medicine*: those who were more physically fit in midlife were less likely to develop chronic health conditions in old age, such as Alzheimer's disease or congestive heart failure.

5. Watch Your Stress Levels. Relax! Slow down! It's advice we're all used to in our increasingly hectic daily lives, but stress is a bit more complex than that. On the one hand, debilitating stress can have negative effects on our health later in life. On study found that adults who reported greater work stress in midlife were more likely to show disabilities and physical difficulties after retirement. Oddly enough, though, a little stress can also be good for us. If you never have to react to anything demanding, the mechanisms in your brain that help you deal with taxing situations will atrophy. Wise elders need to strike the right balance This is the key.

6. Heal your Emotional Wounds and Traumas. There is ample evidence to show the long-term-effects of childhood trauma and betrayal trauma. In Chapter Nine I present strategies for you to use to heal the emotional wounding you suffered other times in your life. The ACE research discussed in Chapter Six, clearly shows the long-term effects of adverse childhood experiences on both physical and mental health. This is something that does not go away just because you don't think about it. The only way to heal these emotional wounds is to do the conscious work needed to eliminate them from your life. Chapter Nine presents strategies for doing just that. It could lower your risk of getting a degenerative disease and add as much as 20 years to your life.

CHAPTER NINE

WHAT ARE SOME STRATEGIES YOU CAN USE TO OVERCOME THE PERSONAL/PSYCHOLOGICAL BARRIERS TO BECOMING A WISE ELDER?

The wiser mind mourns less for what age
takes away than what it leaves behind.

—William Wordsworth

The quality of life that wise elders can enjoy is dependent upon how much they have healed their childhood wounds particularly, their mother and father wounds. This chapter presents strategies for healing these wounds. At its core, the task of healing one's mother wound is ultimately one of de-coupling one's inner and outer life from the projections of your inner feminine on women, so that your full potential as a wise elder be actualized. The same is true of your father complex. Here it involves de-coupling your outer projections of your inner masculine on men. This father projection process causes you to compete with and do battle with father figures in your life that remind you in some way of your actual father.

HOW DO YOU KNOW IF YOU HAVE MOTHER OR FATHER WOUNDS?

Jungian analyst, James Hollis, says this about what he calls *"the mother complex:"* *"When we remember that patriarchy is a cultural contrivance, an invention to compensate for powerlessness, we realize that men, contrary to widespread opinions, are more often the more dependent sex. The Marlboro man, the rugged individualist, is most often ambushed by his inner feminine, for he is mostly in denial. Whenever a man is obliged to be a good boy, or conversely, he feels he must be a bad boy, or a wild man, he is still compensating for the power of the mother complex. I do not say it is a man's fault that he is so vulnerable, so dependent; that he is merely human."*

He adds, *"He may pretend to adult empowerment, hold the reins of government or the purse, but the lines of stress reach deep down into his relationship with his mother. Men must grasp and accept this fact, and then take responsibility for it, or they will continue to play out infantile patterns forever."* [58]

The way that wise elders try to heal their mother wounds is important. They need to do the following inner work to heal their mother wounds:

- Take responsibility for their emotions, feeling them and processing them. Getting support for them.
- Use sex as a way to connect, not a way to dominate or feel powerful.
- Provide comfort to the little boy within them when they are triggered by memories of unhealed childhood traumas.
- Differentiate between the pain of the past from what's happening in the present. Connect the dots between what happened to them as a child and what is currently happening to them.
- Become aware of their projections and begin seeing the women in their lives as people, not as objects
- Amplify the voices of those who feel marginalized, while listening and learning from them.

Healing Your Father Wounds. Men healing their father wounds involves some of the same strategies that wise elders use for healing their mother wounds, with a few exceptions. Men unconsciously or consciously deny any resemblance to their father. Under that denial is deeply-rooted hurt and anger that they carry on their shoulders, because they became adults silently carrying resentments about not getting their needs met in their father-son relationship. When men can accept any comparison with their father, they begin to open the door to positive change. Here are some *"warning signs"* of silent resentments toward your father:

1. **You're aloof.** You focus your mind on things other than what's going on in your relationships. You miss cues from those around you that your relationships need your attention. This is also called dissociation.
2. **You're unconcerned.** It's difficult for you to walk a mile in someone else's shoes if you're not comfortable in your own. You find it impossible to relate to others experiences emotionally. What concerns you the most is how something impacts you. You are less aware of how your behavior

affects others. This is the result of your narcissistic wounds, often inflicted on you by your father.

3. **You're disrespectful.** It's not on purpose. You just don't have a clue how to show respect.

4. **You're commitment-phobic.** You learned early in life not to rely on people. They turned out to be not trust-worthy. They always disappointed you, and that hurt. To avoid being hurt again, you avoid making commitments to others.

5. **You're irresponsible.** You were never able to figure out how to do things right. It seemed like the rules always were changing. Rather than be blamed for things going wrong when you do everything to try to get them right, it's easier just say, *"Hey, it wasn't my fault!"* The worst kind of shame is to have your father criticize you when you were doing the best that you could in that situation. This often leads you to conclude that there must be something wrong with you.

How Prevalent Are Your Mother and Father Wounds? One of the ways I help my clients to identify their mother and father wounds and how prevalent they are, is by asking them to complete *"The Two Lists"* writing exercise below. Think about your experiences as a child and follow the instructions.

Self-Awareness Writing Exercise: The Two Lists.[59] Use this exercise to identify any aspects of unhealed developmental traumas you may have.

Directions:
Write out two lists below using information from your childhood that are related to experiences you had with your mother and father or an adult caregiver who filled one of these roles when you were a child.

List #1: Look back at your childhood prior to age 18, and list of all the things that you wish your mother or father had done for you or said to you while you were growing up. These are the things that you believe, had you gotten them, your life as an adult would now be easier today. These are the things you feel that may have held you back. For example, *"I wish they had told me directly that they loved me"* or *"I wish they had given me birthday parties and helped me celebrate my birthday."* **Write a few words below to identify relevant experiences with each parent.** Place these items on the mother or father list, as appropriate, under List #1 in the first column: *"What I Wanted That I Did Not Get."*

List #2: Look back at your childhood prior to age 18, and list all of the things that you wish each parent had not said or did to you while you were growing up. These things hurt or damaged you in some important way and have interfered with your adult life. For example, *"I wish they hadn't humiliated me when I got pregnant in high school"* or *"I wish they hadn't called me names and hit me."* Place these items on either the mother or father list, as appropriate, under *"What I Got That I Did Not Want."* If you had a caregiver person in addition to or in place of one or both of your parents, use these experiences instead. **Write a few words below to identify relevant experiences with each parent**, such as, *"The time my mother yelled at me when I got hurt in the second grade."* At the end of this exercise, you will find an explanation about the meaning of each list.

MOTHER

List #1 "What I Wanted That I Did Not Get"	List #2 "What I Got That I Did Not Want"

FATHER

List #1 "What I Wanted That I Did Not Get"	List #2 "What I Got That I Did Not Want"

SCORING AND INTERPRETATION:

List #1: "What I Wanted That I Did Not Get." These items relate to unhealed childhood traumas during the codependent stage between birth to 8 or 9 months, and indicate unmet needs from your early childhood development. These unmet needs are usually caused by a lack of emotional support and unmet needs for bonding. The items on this list cause you to unconsciously fantasize about getting these needs met in your adult relationships without having to ask for them. You may try to manipulate or control others in order to get them. This kind of unconscious passive behavior is at the heart of codependency. It is often visible in people's victim body language that will attract rescuers to meet these bonding needs need.

Beside each item on List #1 to help identify where you can get each need met, place the name of a person who could help you meet this need. Perhaps you still feel angry and resentful toward your mother or father and fantasizing they will offer you what you need without your requesting it. Grudges and illusions cause stuckness, which is defined as waiting for somebody else to change so you can feel better. Maybe you fear asking for what you want because you might get refused or rejected. Indirect strategies usually don't work. They just keep you locked in anger, resentment, and rejection and feeling hopeless, helpless, and victimized. You need to be willing to ask for what you want and need 100% of the time in order to heal the lingering effects of these early traumas.

List #2: "What I Got That I Did Not Want." These items are related to unhealed childhood traumas that occurred during the counter-dependent stage of development. They involve experiences that were hurtful and/or harmful to you while you were growing, and particularly involve a lack of support for your feelings. These items make intimacy difficult, as they make you see yourself as different from others. A common belief is, *"I'm not going to let you get close to me because I don't want to get hurt again."* Or you engage in defensive behaviors that hide your vulnerability. The dilemma is that you must face the risk of being hurt again in order to get your needs met. Many people just stay stuck and angry.

If you have a lot of items in List #2, you may have erected barriers to protect yourself from being hurt. This puts you in a bind, because you want to get close to get your needs for intimacy met, yet it is hard to take the risk. The first step in breaking through this is admitting to yourself that you have unmet needs. The next step is taking the risk to ask someone to help you meet these needs. These steps will move you out of counterdependent behaviors and help you complete the psychological birth.

WHAT ARE SOME OTHER WAYS TO ACCESS CHILDHOOD TRAUMAS?

There are other ways to identify your childhood wounds. Below is a list of way that people typically use to connect the dots between their childhood wounds and the long-term effect of childhood wounds.

1. **Interpersonal Conflicts.** People get triggered by memories of unhealed childhood traumas in their close, intimate relationships. The closer the relationship, the more likely their relationship will help surface any unhealed childhood traumas. My book, *Conflict Resolution: The Partnership Way* also contains lots of information about how to use relationship conflicts to heal trauma.

2. **Chronic or Acute Body Symptoms.** Working with a body symptom is often a great way to help identify any hidden childhood trauma contained in it. The body keeps score. This does require special skills for following a body symptom process. I recommend that hire you a good body worker to do this kind of work.

3. **Symptoms like OCD, depression or anxiety disorders.** These usually contain hidden and unhealed developmental traumas that are the underlying causes of these symptoms. If you suffer from what I call *"premature hardening of the categories"* in your thinking, it is likely that you are suffering from unhealed childhood wounds.

4. **Addictions to Substances or Activities.** Almost all addictions are any attempt to avoid unwanted feeling stemming from as hidden and unhealed childhood trauma. Look at what the purpose of each of your addictions and you will find it is to self-medicate or avoid unwanted feelings. Generally, all addictions are ritualized, compulsive comfort-seeking behaviors. This means that if you are unable to get out of your *"comfort zone,"* it is likely you have become addicted to this lifestyle.

5. **Living an Adrenalized Lifestyle.** The addiction to our own adrenaline cause us to crave more activities that are adrenaline producing, this includes watching scary movies or TV shows or being involved in high risk activities. I include a self-quiz below to determine how addicted you are to your own adrenaline.

6. **Family Patterns.** Anything unhealed from your childhood will show up in addictive patterns of behavior in your present relationships. My book, *Breaking Free: How to Identify and Change Addictive Family Patterns* is a great resource to help understand and break free of this process.

7. **The Drama Triangle Dynamics.** If you are engaging in Victim, Persecutor or Rescuer behavior, you can be sure there is hidden childhood trauma present. All these are dysfunctional ways to try to get needs met. Look for what childhood traumas, usually relating to neglect, are motivating these behaviors. I include a self-quiz below to help you identify how much you play on the Drama Triangle

8. **Use of Self-Assessment Inventories.** Since unhealed childhood traumas are disrupting other people's lives in some important ways, asking them to assess their current problems will help you see what unhealed childhood traumas are still active in their lives. You can then work backwards with them to see if you can identify the source of their current problems. I have included several self-quizzes below to help you identify your unhealed childhood traumas.

HOW MUCH CHILDHOOD TRAUMA DID YOU EXPERIENCE?

Another way to determine how much childhood trauma you have to heal is by taking the self-quiz below and scoring it. There is a scale to help you determine the impact of your score.

SELF-QUIZ: HOW MUCH CHILDHOOD TRAUMA DID YOU EXPERIENCE?

Directions: Read the statements below and use 1-4 to make your self-assessment of each item. Key: 1= mostly not true, 2=occasionally true, 3= usually true and 4=almost always true.

_____ 1. I have trouble feeling close to the people I care about.

_____ 2. I feel like other people are more in charge of my life than I am.

_____ 3. I seem reluctant to try new things.

_____ 4. I have trouble keeping my weight down.

_____ 5. I am easily bored with what I am doing.

_____ 6. I have trouble accepting help from others even when I need it.

_____ 7. I work best when I am under a lot of pressure.

_____ 8. I have trouble admitting my mistakes.

_____ 9. I tend to forget or not keep agreements I make.

_____ 10. I have trouble handling my time and money effectively.

_____ 11. I use intimidation or manipulation to settle my conflicts.

_____ 12. I feel personally attacked when someone has a conflict with me.

_____ 13. I have a difficult time giving and receiving compliments.

_____ 14. I have a short fuse when I feel frustrated with myself or others.

_____ 15. I tend to blame others for causing the problems I have.

_____ 16. I feel like I have a huge empty place inside of me.

_____ 17. It is hard for me to have positive thoughts about my future.

_____ 18. Inside I feel like a tightly coiled spring.

_____ 19. When I get anxious I tend to eat or drink too much.

_____ 20. I feel empty and alone.

_____ 21. I tend to question the motives of others.

_____ 22. I feel unloved by others.

_____ 23. I have a hard time defining what I want of need.

_____ 24. When I get into a conflict somebody else gets their way.

_____ 25. I tend to overreact to certain people and/or situations that bug me.

_____ 26. I feel like I am on an emotional roller coaster.

_____ 27. I have trouble sticking with any spiritual practices I start.

_____ 28. Important people in my life have abandoned me emotionally or physically.

_____ 29. I have trouble concentrating on what I am doing.

_____ 30. When I think about my childhood, I draw a big blank.

_____ 31. I have trouble experiencing the intimacy I want in my relationships

_____ 32. I have trouble falling asleep and staying asleep.

_____ 33. I tend to *"walk on eggs"* around certain people or situations.

_____ 34. I avoid places or situations that remind me of experiences from my past.

_____ 35. I have recurring bad dreams about what happened to me in the past.

_____ 36. My thoughts seem to have a life of their own.

_____ 37. I have trouble paying attention to what others are saying.

_____ 38. I tend to avoid situations and people that could cause me conflicts.

_____ 39. I experience big gaps in my memory about my childhood.

_____ 40. I have a hard time knowing what I am feeling inside.

_____ **Total Score**

Interpretation:

If your score was between:

40 - 82 = Some evidence of childhood trauma.

83 –120 = Moderate evidence of childhood trauma.

121-160 = Strong evidence of childhood trauma.

Further analysis:

Identify the items where you scored 3-4 to learn more about your unhealed childhood traumas.

ARE YOU ADDICTED YOU TO YOUR OWN ADRENALINE?

Your own adrenaline is the most addictive substance that you will ever encounter. Take the Self-Quiz below and score it to determine how addicted you are to your own adrenaline.

SELF-QUIZ: THE ADDICTION TO ADRENALINE INVENTORY[60]

Directions: Place a number before each question that best indicates the degree to which this is true in your life. (1 = Almost Never, 2 = Occasionally, 3 - Usually, 4 = Almost Always).

_____ 1. I talk fast.

_____ 2. I drive fast.

_____ 3. I eat fast.

_____ 4. I read while I eat.

_____ 5. I read in the bathroom.

_____ 6. I believe that doing one thing at a time is inefficient.

_____ 7. I drink more than three cups of coffee a day.

_____ 8. I talk on the phone while preparing meals.

_____ 9. I love time efficiency devices such as cell phones, computers, instant messaging microwaves, and food processors.

_____ 10. I am better at starting relationships than making them work.

_____ 11. I work more than 60 hours a week.

_____ 12. I find it difficult to leave work at the office.

_____ 13. I smoke cigarettes.

_____ 14. I feel anxious when I am out of touch with my work setting.

_____ 15. I feel that sleeping is time wasted.

_____ 16. I find it difficult to relax when the workday is done.

_____ 17. Lying on the beach doing nothing seems more like torture than relaxation.

_____ 18. I find accomplishing many things at once (multi-tasking) immensely satisfying.

_____ 19. I don't spend as much time as I'd like with my family.

_____ 20. I don't spend as much time alone as I'd like.

_____ 21. I feel driven to get more done.

_____ 22. I schedule my time so tightly I am frustrated by the inevitable interruptions.

_____ 23. I get upset when others are late.

_____ 24. I have difficulty waiting in line.

_____ 25. I get angry when the traffic light changes and the person in front of me takes too much time getting moving.

_____ 26. I get frustrated with slow drivers.

_____ 27. I skip meals because I get busy with more important things.

_____ 28. I eat on the run.

_____ 29. I hurry my children because they aren't moving fast enough.

_____ 30. I love computers because they are fast, efficient, and accurate.

_____ 31. I have trouble with people who are slow, inefficient, and talk too much.

_____ 32. I believe that living faster means living better.

_____ 33. I hate to make two trips carrying in the groceries.

_____ 34. I do things in a hurry, even though doing it quickly may mean I may have to do it again.

_____ 35. I seek out high intensity experiences.

_____ 36. I resist reading directions, preferring to jump in and get started.

_____ 37. I find that a level of danger is a necessary ingredient for feeling fully alive.

_____ 38. I have trouble slowing down because I fear that something or someone might gain on me.

_____ 39. I feel I must keep myself *"revved up"* to keep from becoming bored or depressed.

_____ 40. I find people boring if they don't live high intensity lives.

_____ 41. I find it difficult to take time to just think and dream.

_____ 42. I find it difficult to *"shut down"* my mind, even away from work.

_____ 43. I keep a notepad or recording machine with me to jot down important thoughts.

_____ 44. I panic just thinking about the possibility that my computer may crash.

_____ 45. My fear of computer viruses rivals or surpasses my fear of AIDS.

_____ 46. I miss taking time to *"enjoy the sunsets and smell the flowers."*

_____ 47. I like the multiplex theaters because I can check out another movie if I get bored with the first.

_____ 48. I like reading USA Today because it is quick and easy to learn a little about a lot of things.

_____ 49. I find it difficult to read a book from cover to cover, even when I am enjoying it.

_____ 50. I have many partially read books lying around.

_____ 51. I read mostly business related material and feel slightly guilty if I read just for pleasure.

_____ 52. I feel dependent on the constant stimulation, pressure, and excitement I get in life.

_____ 53. I find myself accepting civic and business obligations even after I feel overloaded.

_____ 54. I am missing important times with my children, partner, or family because I am too busy.

_____ 55. My preferred forms of exercise or recreation are demanding and/or competitive.

_____ 56. I become anxious or depressed when I can't work out.

_____ 57. I feel my life is moving too fast.

_____ 58. I have had stress-related illnesses such as back problems, high blood pressure, ulcers, or *"nervous stomach."*

_____ 59. I dream of hitting the jackpot via lottery tickets, sports betting (horse or dog racing, weekly football pools, fantasy sports betting, etc.) or playing slots.

_____ 60. I like to watch scary movies and TV shows.

_____ **Total Score**

Scoring: Add the numbers in the left-hand column and record your total score. See the interpretation below to determine what your score might mean.

Interpretation:
Each person must decide the meaning of the scores when analyzing personal lifestyle. For one person, missing their child's first concert may be enough to make a change. For another, it may require a serious heart attack. The following interpretation guidelines will help you in your lifestyle analysis.

60–90   = Low risk of adrenaline addiction
91–120 = Some risk of adrenaline addiction
121–150 = High risk of adrenaline addiction
151–180 = Very high risk of adrenaline addiction
181–240 = Danger; extremely high risk of adrenaline addiction

If your score was more than 120 on the scale above, it indicates not only a risk of addiction to adrenaline, but also a strong likelihood of experiences involving childhood shock, trauma, or stress. Knowing that these behaviors are related to childhood trauma may motivate you to change some of your small daily habits that could be doing long-term damage to your mind/body.

WHAT IF THE SELF-QUIZZES SHOW THAT YOU DON'T HAVE MUCH CHILDHOOD TRAUMA?

If you had a low score on the ACE Questionnaire you filled out earlier in this book and/or you scored low on most of the above self-quizzes, you may still have had unhealed childhood wounds. First, the ACE Questionnaire is heavily weighed on abuse rather than neglect. Only two of the questions address neglect rather than abuse. My research shows that most childhood wounds are caused by neglect. They are just as painful and significant as those caused by abuse of some kind. The problem is since *"nothing happened"* so it is harder to remember what happened. To help people connect with their childhood wounding caused by neglect, I created the Adverse Childhood Neglect Inventory which is available below. Take it and score it to see how much adverse childhood neglect you experienced.

SELF-QUIZ: THE ADVERSE CHILDHOOD NEGLECT INVENTORY (ADULT FORM)[61]

In the first year of your life specifically and generally prior to your 18th birthday:

1. Were you placed in childcare or with someone other than a primary caregiver before you were one month old?
    Not Applicable__ If Yes, enter 1 __

2. Did you spend less than 20 hours a week being cared for by your mother during your first year of life?
    Not Applicable__ If Yes, enter 1 __

3. As an infant, were you allowed to cry yourself asleep at night without your parent(s) attempting to comfort you?
    Not Applicable__ If Yes, enter 1 __

4. Did you feel afraid of your mother or other adult caregivers?
    Not Applicable__ If Yes, enter 1 __

5. Was your mother or another primary caregiver chronically depressed?
    Not Applicable__ If Yes, enter 1 __

6. Did your mother or other primary adult caregiver suffer from substance abuse?
    Not Applicable__ If Yes, enter 1 __

7. Did your mother or any other primary caregiver fail to tell you that they loved you?
    Not Applicable__ If Yes, enter 1 __

8. Did your mother or other primary adult caregiver avoid hugging you, picking you up or making eye contact with you?
    Not Applicable__ If Yes, enter 1 __

9. Were you separated from your mother for more than a week for any reason in your first year of life?
    Not Applicable__ If Yes, enter 1 __

10. Did your primary caregivers leave you with strangers or other non-bonded caregivers for more than one week before your first birthday?
Not Applicable___ If Yes, enter 1 ___

11. Were you told directly or indirectly that your parents were too overwhelmed to care for you?
Not Applicable___ If Yes, enter 1 ___

12. Did your parents fail to make your home environment safe leading to accidents?
Not Applicable___ If Yes, enter 1 ___

13. Were you told or treated by either of your parents to *"be seen and not heard?"*
Not Applicable___ If Yes, enter 1 ___

14. Did you move frequently when you were very young?
Not Applicable___ If Yes, enter 1 ___

15. Was your mother cold toward you when you were a child?
Not Applicable___ If Yes, enter 1 ___

16. As a child, did you feel your parents didn't understand your needs?
Not Applicable___ If Yes, enter 1 ___

17. Did you feel unwanted by your parents?
Not Applicable___ If Yes, enter 1 ___

18. Were you unplanned by your parents?
Not Applicable___ If Yes, enter 1 ___

19. Did you have frequent illnesses when you were under a year of age (colic, ear infections, etc.)?
Not Applicable___ If Yes, enter 1 ___

20. Even though you weren't adopted, did you feel you were *"adopted"* when you were growing up in your family?
Not Applicable___ If Yes, enter 1 ___

21. Was your mother under 19 years of age when you were born?
Not Applicable___ If Yes, enter 1 ___

22. Were you a *"play-pen"* baby?
Not Applicable___ If Yes, enter 1 ___

23. Did you believe that there was something fundamentally wrong with you because of the way you thought or behaved?
Not Applicable__ If Yes, enter 1 __

24. Were you *"parentized"* or put in an inappropriate parenting role when you were very young?
Not Applicable__ If Yes, enter 1 __

25. Did your parents fail to provide proper medical care for you?
Not Applicable__ If Yes, enter 1 __

26. Did your parents fail to teach you or require you to develop proper personal hygiene habits?
Not Applicable__ If Yes, enter 1 __

27. Were you left unsupervised for long periods of time?
Not Applicable__ If Yes, enter 1 __

28. Were you left in the care of someone who was significantly impaired or of questionable character?
Not Applicable__ If Yes, enter 1 __

29. Were you placed in dangerous situations or with dangerous people?
Not Applicable__ If Yes, enter 1 __

30. Were you verbally abused and your parent(s) did nothing to protect you?
Not Applicable__ If Yes, enter 1 __

31. Were you sexually abused and your parent(s) did nothing to protect you?
Not Applicable__ If Yes, enter 1 __

32. Were you physically abused and your parent(s) did nothing to protect you?
Not Applicable__ If Yes, enter 1 __

33. Were you emotionally abused and your parent(s) did nothing to protect you.
Not Applicable__ If Yes, enter 1 __

34. Did your parents fail to make sure you got to school on time?
Not Applicable__ If Yes, enter 1 __

35. Did your parents fail to make sure you completed your homework?
Not Applicable__ If Yes, enter 1 __

36. Did my parents fail to provide proper nutrition for me?
    Not Applicable___ If Yes, enter 1 ___

37. Did your parents fail to provide proper or clean clothing for you?
    Not Applicable___ If Yes, enter 1 ___

38. Did you have siblings who were less than one year older than you?
    Not Applicable___ If Yes, enter 1 ___

39. Were you a *"latch key"* child who had no one there when you came
    home from school?
    Not Applicable___ If Yes, enter 1 ___

40. Did your parents compare you unfavorably to your siblings?
    Not Applicable___ If Yes, enter 1 ___

___**Total Score:** Count the number of items where you answered, *"Yes."*

Interpretation:

If you had five or more *"yeses,"* you likely had developmental traumas in your childhood caused by neglect. The higher number of *"yeses,"* the more severe the developmental traumas were in your childhood and the likelihood they could cause mental and physical health problems in your adult years. If you answered *"yes"* to 20 or more of the questions, we would define that as *"severe neglect."*

There are no national norms when it comes to incidences of childhood neglect. Almost all research into adverse childhood experiences lumps abuse and neglect together. Some leading researchers say, however, that neglect contributes more to long-term health effects than does abuse. Since abuse is easily identified and neglect is not, the symptoms of neglect are rarely treated unless there is obvious severe neglect.

HOW MUCH DOES THE DRAMA TRIANGLE RULE YOUR LIFE?

As I discussed in Chapter Seven, the Drama Triangle is a big obstacle for wise elders to overcome. Below is a Self-Quiz that helps you determine how your beliefs may contribute to Drama Triangle behaviors that may be present in your life. Take it and score it.

SELF-QUIZ: THE DRAMA TRIANGLE[62]

Directions: Please indicate how much these beliefs are true of how you think about yourself and others. Place a number in the blank in front of each item that indicates what is true for you. Key: 1= Hardly Ever; 2= Sometimes; 3= Frequently; and 4 = Almost Always.

_____ 1. It is my fault when someone gets angry with me.

_____ 2. Other people's feelings/needs are more important than mine.

_____ 3. People will think I am too aggressive if I express my feelings/ needs directly.

_____ 4. I worry about how others may respond when I state my feelings or needs.

_____ 5. I have to walk on eggs so I don't do something that causes people to get angry with me or abandon me.

_____ 6. I have to give up my needs in my relationships so people will want to be with me.

_____ 7. I must be perfect so that others will love me and not abandon me.

_____ 8. I need to rely on others to make important decisions.

_____ 9. I must to hold back when reacting to what others say and do, rather than saying what I believe.

_____ 10. How I feel about myself depends on other people's opinions of me.

_____ 11. It's dangerous for me to ask directly for what I want or need from others.

_____ 12. I avoid assuming a position of responsibility.

_____ 13. When faced with a problem, I can only think of two conflicting solutions to the problem.

_____ 14. I need to make sure I meet other people's needs so they will like me and want to be with me.

_____ 15. It's best to seek out relationships where I can meet the needs of others and make them happy.

_____ 16. If I have to ask for what I want or need from loved-ones, it means they do not love me enough to know what I need.

_____ 17. I have a difficult time knowing what I want or need.

_____ 18. I can't let others get too close to me or I my life will be consumed by their needs.

_____ 19. I have difficulty in knowing how I really feel.

_____ 20. I exaggerate my accomplishments when I meet someone new, so they will like me.

_____ 21. If people knew who I really am, they would not want to be with me.

_____ 22. I'm afraid people will find out that I'm not who they think I am.

_____ 23. I can't ask other people for help, even when I need it because they will think I am too needy.

_____ 24. I feel controlled by what others expect of me.

_____ 25. I feel it is really important for me to have the *"right answers"* or others will think I am stupid.

_____ 26. I can't admit to a mistake because I am afraid people might reject me if I did.

_____ 27. I reject offers of help from others, even when I need them.

_____ 28. I compare myself to others, because I feel either one-up or one-down in relationship to them.

_____ 29. I feel hurt when others don't recognize my accomplishments.

_____ 30. I don't deserve to be loved by others.

____ **Total Score**

Interpretation of Scores:

30-50 = Few beliefs that might contribute to the Drama Triangle in your life.

51-80 = Some beliefs that might contribute to the Drama Triangle in your life.

81 + = Many beliefs that might contribute to the Drama Triangle in your life.

Note: Look at those beliefs where you answered *"3 or 4."* These are the ones that have the most control over you.

WHAT ARE SOME OTHER STRATEGIES FOR HEALING CHILDHOOD TRAUMA?[63]

This tool was developed by Janae Weinhold. It is very useful if you find your-self getting triggered or emotionally dysregulated by memories of unhealed childhood traumas. She says this about why she developed this tool: *"In all my years of work in clearing trauma in myself and with my clients validated that it is possible truly to clear trauma from your nervous system, brain and behavioral responses.* **The Trauma Elimination Technique (TET)** *is not only the most effective tool I've ever used, it also allows you to really take charge of your own healing process. I also like it because you can use it yourself when you really need it. This empowering aspect is really important to me, for most people who have been traumatized, feel disempowered, helpless and powerless.*

"I developed TET by synthesizing the best of a number trauma healing modalities: The Tapas Acupressure Technique (TAT), EMDR (Eye Movement Desensitization and Reprocessing) and Thought Field Therapy (TFT). In the extensive use of TET on ourselves and with our clients, we discovered that it will not only clear trauma from present-life experiences, but also from other dimensions of realities, such as past lives.

"If you wish to use TET to clear traumas held in other realities, just set this intention before you begin to use it. If this idea intimidates you, set you intention to only clear your present-life trauma. You are always in charge when using TET. Here is the procedure."

Step 1: Learn the TAT holding pose.

- Use one hand to hold three points on your face. Touch the points lightly.
- Touch thumb lightly just above and adjacent to the inner corner of one eye
- Place the end of your ring (4th) finger just above and adjacent to the in-ner corner of the other eye
- Place the end of your middle finger on an indentation in the middle of your forehead about 1/2" higher than your eyebrows
- Place your other hand palm down at the back of your head just below the bump at the bottom of your skull (the occipital ridge), centering it at the midline.
- Once you have learned this pose, go directly to Step 2.

Step 2: Identify the trauma you want to work on. This should be one par-ticular trauma, not one that is long-term or recurring.

a. Focus your attention on a picture about this trauma.

b. Notice what thoughts go with this picture.

c. Identify the belief about yourself that goes with this picture.

d. Notice what emotion you feel when you see this picture, think these thoughts, and believe this belief.

Step 3: Simultaneously hold the picture, thoughts, belief and the feelings while doing the TAT holding pose. Remain in this pose until you feel something happen internally (different for each person: a subtle shift of energy, a feeling of relaxation, a deep sigh or for one minute, whichever comes first).

Step 4: Notice where you have been holding tension in your body related to the picture/thoughts/belief/feelings and focus your attention in this place while continuing to hold the TAT pose. Remain in this pose until you feel the shift or for one minute.

Step 5: Return to your picture of the trauma you began with and zoom in close to review it with a *"magnifying glass,"* looking for *"hot spots"* or things that still upset you.

Step 6: Zero in on a "hot spot."

a. Focus on the picture/thought/belief/feeling.

b. Do the TAT holding technique until you feel a shift.

c. Focus on the *"storage place"* in your body where you hold tension related to this memory while using the TAT holding technique until you feel a shift.

Step 7: Continue returning to the original picture and reviewing it until there are no more hot spots.

Step 8: Drink a glass of water immediately after completing a session. Be sure to drink another eight glasses in the next 24 hours to help the toxins released by the TET procedure to leave your body.

PERSONAL NARRATIVE PAPER.

Research shows that when people can write a paper that shows they understand their childhood wounds and the effects of those wounds in their current problems that is coherent and concise, it literally begins to rewire your brain. It helps you build new neural connections between the hippocampus and the pre-frontal cortex.

Directions: Write a 6-page maximum narrative that makes sense of your childhood history from a *"victor"* vs. *"victim"* perspective.

Please include the following:

1. Your mother and father wounds.
    *   What wounds did you get from your childhood that relate to your relationship with your mother and your father?
    *   How have those wounds affected your life?

2. What traumas have you identified in your childhood?
    *   Which were caused by abuse or by neglect?
    *   Which parent was involved with each?

3. Identify the *"triggers"* you commonly experience in your close relationships.
    *   What are they?
    *   How do they relate to what happened to you as a child?
    *   How do you typically respond when you get triggered?
    *   Are you aware of any splitting against someone when you get triggered?

4. How much do you see the Drama Triangle operating in your life?
    *   Can you connect the Drama Triangle to what happened to you as a child?
    *   What do you do to break free of the Drama Triangle?

5. What aspects of your childhood abuse or neglect hold you back the most in your life?
    *   What are these issues?
    *   How do you see yourself working to heal them?

WHAT ARE SOME OTHER STRATEGIES THAT A WISE ELDER MIGHT USE?

Meditation has been shown to possibly take years off your actual age. One study showed that meditation slows down the aging process. Bernie Siegel says this about meditation, *"The physical benefits of meditation have recently been well documented by Western medical researchers."* Dr. Siegel added, *"Meditation also raises the pain threshold and reduces one's biological age... In short, it reduces wear and tear on both body and mind, helping people live longer and better.*[64] Experts say that regular meditation can significantly increase your life expectancy.

How Can You Heal Your Betrayal Traumas? Healing your betrayals is another way to increase your well-being as a wise elder. Our book, *Betrayal and the Path of the Heart,*[65] is an excellent resource to help you heal your betrayal traumas. However, the simplest and most direct way to heal your betrayals is to be able to forgive or *"give-back"* any misperceptions you had of yourself and the other person or persons who betrayed you. This may involve giving back to your betrayers all the misperceptions you had about them that contributed to the betrayal and being willing to see them as they really are not as you hoped or fantasized they would be. It also means giving back to yourself all the new awarenesses you gained about yourself as a result of the betrayal and the way you really are not what you thought you are.

Often you have a positive projection on the betrayer that contributed to the betrayal that you will now have to take back. You may have projected some fantasy of them by seeing them as 100% trust-worthy, when in fact they were just ordinary people who were doing the best they could do, but certainly were not perfect people.

This need to project perfection on another person is related to a childish belief that your parents were supposed to be perfect and the feelings of disappointment that they turned out not to be 100% perfect. If you carry anger about them not being perfect parents, you may wish to punish them by finding other *"parental"* figures who truly are perfect. At least this would validate your anger that your parents disappointed you by not meeting all your needs. If you maintain this fantasy as an adult and project it on others who are close to you, you are likely going to get betrayed again and again when you learn that these people too are not perfect, just like your parents were. The original betrayal in this case is the result of your fantasy that your parents were going to be perfect and take care you of all your needs. In order to avoid a series of betrayals as an adult, you will have to change this infantile belief that people who are close to you are going to be perfect.

SELF-QUIZ: WHAT ARE YOUR PATTERNS OF BETRAYAL?

Directions: Make a list of the significant betrayals in your life. You can make the list chronological, starting with the earliest one you can remember, or you can arrange your list from the most significant down to the least significant. After you have listed all these events (you only need a few words to describe the event: *"The time when _____ happened"*), go back and examine each betrayal using the following questions. Write down what you find.

- What were the predominant feelings you had then and have now?
- How did you handle this betrayal?
- What illusions, misperceptions, or expectations contributed to the betrayal?
- What other choices could you have made in this betrayal situation?
- What new choices still exist for you in this betrayal situation?
- What lessons did you learn as a result of this betrayal?
- What, if any, important benefits came out of this betrayal experience?
- Have you had similar kinds of betrayals?
- What were the common elements in all these betrayals? How do they form a pattern?
- Which betrayals do you feel you have successfully healed? How did you do that?
- Which betrayals have you not healed? What opportunities still exist to heal or heal these?
- After you have answered the above questions, make a second list of the times when you were the betrayer. Answer the following questions as honestly as possible.
- What were the most prevalent feelings involved in your betrayals?
- How did you deal with each betrayal?
- What were the short-term and long-term effects of the betrayal on you?
- What were the short-term and long-term effects of the betrayal on the other person(s) involved?
- What could you have done instead of betraying the other person?
- What, if any, benefits did you receive as a result of the betrayal?
- What, if any, unfinished business do you think still exists with each of your betrayals?
- What actions do you still need to take to clear any unfinished business left over from any of your betrayals?

CHAPTER TEN

WHAT STRATEGIES CAN BE USED TO OVERCOME THE SOCIAL/ CULTURAL BARRIERS TO BECOMING A WISE ELDER?

It is easier to build strong children
than to repair broken men.

—Frederick Douglass

It seems to me there are ample opportunities for wise elders to contribute in meaningful ways to the well-being of society despite the social/cultural barriers that currently exist. This chapter highlights some of the ways that wise elders already are contributing to the well-being of society and these will continue to increase. Some oft the opportunities that I include in this chapter may be new to you and I urge you to take advantage of all the opportunities that currently exist to serve.

As wise elder contributor, **Aric Rohrer**, mentioned, the lack of recognition of the contributions of elders may be a marketing problem. He writes the following: *"Popular opinion suggests that the fate of our Elders is to be isolated and lonely victims of circumstances — doomed to declining health, mental capacity, and relevance — who will finally die alone, forgotten, and meaningless. But I'd like to suggest that what we actually have here is faulty expectations, a failure of responsibility and imagination, and a marketing problem.*

"We are the ones who know what we know. It's silly to expect other people to know what they don't know. And it's even sillier to expect them first to value what they don't know about and then expect them to take action to search for it, particularly since they would have a massive 'needle in a haystack' problem.

There are millions of elders. Which of them would be willing, available, and a good match?

"If we want to be useful, it is our own responsibility to become useful. If we want not to be lonely, it is our responsibility to connect. In our wisdom, let's band together and figure out how. There are even some working examples out there. For example, institutions like the Service Corps of Retired Executives (SCORE), whose members counsel business owners and aspiring entrepreneurs.

"And then, once we've figured out some value we can provide, it is up to us to get the word out. If nobody knows about the value we can provide, then they can't find us to get it. That's where good old internet marketing techniques come into play. And even if we don't have the skill to do the marketing ourselves, we can certainly find people (perhaps other Elders) who do have the skill. Let's not play the victim here. It's not pretty and it doesn't work."

STRATEGIES FOR OVERCOMING CULTURAL BARRIERS

What are their secrets to aging well? We have centuries of wisdom that should not be overlooked. So that's what researchers are now doing—mining the minds of centenarians for nuggets of wisdom. Regardless of which interviews you read, this is where patterns really DO emerge. In interviews and surveys with centenarians, the following themes come up time and time again when asked to explain why they've lived so long:

- Keeping a positive attitude
- Eating healthy food
- Exercising moderately (do things like walking, biking, gardening, swimming, etc.)
- Clean living (not smoking or drinking excessively)
- Living independently for as long as you can
- Having close contact with your family
- Having *"good genes"*
- Good friends that you see or communicate with on a regular basis
- Staying mentally active and always learning something new
- Faith/spirituality
- Heal your childhood traumas
- Live an authentic life

Some elders jokingly said they attribute their longevity to their ability to *"avoid dying."* Others say it is their life philosophy that keeps them feeling and acting young, such as *"Find your passion and live it,"* *"Take time to cry,"* and *"Practice forgiveness."* Centenarians overwhelmingly cite keeping their stress levels low as the most important thing to do to increase their longevity. Even if your life is marked by as many stressful events as the rest of us, how well you manage your stress makes the difference. Rather than dwelling on the things that are stressing them out, they let go of them. And they are *very happy people!*

What Is the Prescription for Happiness? Research shows that happy people live longer—by 35 percent. Another study found that happiness and contentment increases your health and longevity. Other studies show that people who hold optimistic attitudes live longer than people who are pessimistic. So it's no surprise that centenarians generally are happy and optimistic campers. Positive thoughts and attitudes seem to have a positive effect on your body that strengthens your immune system, boosts your positive emotions, decreases your pain, and provides you with stress relief. In fact, it's been scientifically shown that happiness can alter your genes!

Another study showed that people with a deep sense of happiness and well-being had lower levels of inflammatory gene expression and stronger antiviral and antibody responses. This falls into the realm of .changing the way your genes function by turning them off and on.

Part of your longevity may depend on the DNA you were born with, but an even larger part depends on epigenetics. You have control over which genes are switched on or off. Your thoughts, feeling, emotions, diet, and other lifestyle factors such as whether or not you have identified and healed your childhood traumas, exert epigenetic influences every minute of the day, playing a central role in aging and disease. Perhaps it's not as important to avoid that bowl of ice cream as it is to feel sheer bliss when eating it... at least, on occasion!

Four Nutrients That Will Help You Reach the Century Mark. The fact that you can manipulate your genes with happiness doesn't mean you can completely disregard lifestyle choices, as that would be foolhardy. The basics are still important—diet, exercise, sleep, etc. Research suggests the modern American diet is increasingly low in four important nutrients that have a direct bearing on aging, and our brains are suffering for it. If you hope to one day become a healthy, happy centenarian, you must address the following: Vitamin D, DHA, Folate & Magnesium.

WHAT ARE SOME WAYS THAT WISE ELDERS CAN CONTRIBUTE IN MEANINGFUL WAYS?

Beyond just volunteering, which isn't always the most meaningful way to contribute, there are a myriad of ways to contribute in meaningful ways to society. I describe some of those below. It may be up to you as a wise elder to create your own ways that you can contribute to others and pass on your wisdom to your children or grandchildren.

What Are Ethical Wills or Legacy Letters? Ethical wills or legacy letters are documents designed to pass wisdom from one generation to the next. The goal of writing an ethical will is to link a person to both your family and your cultural history, clarify your ethical and spiritual values, and communicate a legacy to future generations; it addresses people's *"universal needs."* Writing an ethical will clarify your identity and focuses life purpose. It helps you answer questions like: *"Who am I?" "What was my purpose for being on this planet?"* and *"What can I pass on to my children and grandchildren that would possibly help them have an even better life than I did?"*

Writing an ethical will addresses people's needs to belong, to be known, to be remembered, to have one's life make a difference, to bless and be blessed. The content may not differ from writers of spiritual autobiographies or memoirs, but the intent makes an ethical will unique. The generic purpose of the ethical will is to pass on wisdom and love to future generations. It can include a family history and cultural and spiritual values; blessings and expressions of love for, pride in, hopes and dreams for children and grandchildren; life-lessons and wisdom of life experience; requests for forgiveness for regretted actions; the rationale for philanthropic and personal financial decisions; stories about the meaningful *"stuff"* for heirs to receive; clarification about and personalization of advance health directives; and requests for ways to be remembered after death. It can also include instructions for a memorial service or burial preferences.

Some years ago, I decided to create an Ethical Will for my 93-year-old Dad. So I interviewed him and wrote down his stories. It was a delightful experience for both my Dad and I. We got so much closer in the process of me interviewing him and writing down the important stories of his life. I made copies of the final product and gave it to all his children, grandchildren and great grandchildren when he died.

Below is an excerpt of his Ethical Will about his childhood memories: *"I went fishing and hunting for fun. I raised fancy pigeons in the old barn in* back of our house. I had high flyers and fantails. I noticed that the fantails kept disappearing and then one day I caught the neighbor's cat carrying off one of the fantails. I got my dad's 12-gauge shotgun and I shot the cat. I was only 12 years old and the police came right away, but my dad got me out of trouble.

"I was always scared when I went rabbit and pheasant hunting with my dad because he was ambidextrous and I never knew which way he was going to shoot. My dad would come home from work for dinner and go out back and shoot a rabbit. My friend and I stuffed a rabbit skin with newspaper and set it out back and when my dad came home he saw it and got his gun and shot it. He laughed when he found out what we had done.

"I had a little dog, Sally, a beagle that I hooked up to a little wagon and had her haul me around. I had another dog, Sport, who was also a beagle. I took him with me when I went trapping; once he fell on the ice and broke his leg. I had to carry him back home and he bit me many times before I got home. I took him to the vet and had his leg set and then kept him up in the barn in the hay mount until his leg healed.

"I caught skunks by shining a light in their face and grabbing them by the tail and putting them in a bag. I sold them for their furs. I got sprayed many times and once I went to school and the teacher came down the aisle sniffing until she came to my seat and she sent me home. I also trapped for muskrats and sold them. I made a lot of money off the muskrats because their fur was in great demand.

"When I was about 13, I decided to raise guinea pigs and sell them. I bought them for $.50 apiece and planned to sell them for $3.00. I had hundreds of them, but they all died in the winter. I had them out in the barn. I took a financial loss on that venture.

"As a child I wanted a pony and a saxophone instead of an education. The neighbor played a saxophone and I loved to listen to him play his sax. I never got either of them.

"My mother grew up on a farm near the town of Red Run with her three sisters and a brother. Her sister died when she was a child. So my mother became the Postmistress at age 16. They had a store and Post Office at Red Run. Grandpa Kern was a notary and helped people with their wills. He was one of the founders of the Denver Bank. He sent my mother and her sister to college and bought her brother a car. My mother graduated from Selinsgrove Music School that later became Susquehanna University.

"My Grandpa Kern was a cooper and made whiskey barrels. He wanted me to be a preacher so he would have me stand on a stump and he would tell *me what to say. He died when I was 10 years old. He founded the Lutheran Church in Reamstown. My Grandpa Weinhold was 80 when he died. He was a very tall man with a long white beard. He would give a blessing at all meals, sometimes ten minutes long. He didn't speak much English, so his meal blessings were always in German. Us kids were very impatient. Grandma Weinhold only had one eye and wore a patch. Her sister was a pow-wow doctor. They never went to a regular doctor. I don't know how she lost her eye.*

"*I went to work at Grandpa Kern's farm from the time I was 8. I worked there in the summers and got paid $1.00 a week. It was hard work and I hated it. I would never get back from the farm in time to go to the Saturday movie.*"

"*I remember hoeing the cornrows behind a horse when a car backfired and spooked the horse. He took off and knocked down several rows of corn. Uncle Clarence was really mad at me. Another time I was raking hay and uncovered a big black snake. I killed it and took it to show my uncle and he got mad at me because he said the snake kept the mice away.*"

"*My best friend was Julies Bernstein who was Jewish and I remember when we ate hot dogs at his place and after eating he would throw away the pan where he cooked the hot dogs afterward. I guess that was part of the Jewish tradition to not eat pork products. He was a good friend. I worked at his Dad's tailor shop when I was a teenager. His family were all asthmatics and I remember when we were 14 we would buy Q-Pebs at the drug store for a nickel a pack. Then we would go up to the Mountain Springs Hotel and swing on the swings and smoke them. We thought we were really cool.*"

"*We used to go back to Red Run just about every Saturday. We would take the trolley to Reamstown and then walk from there to Red Run, a distance of about 4-5 miles. My mother was scared to ride with her brother in his new car when he came to pick us up, so we walked. When we left, however, we would get a ride back to Reamstown by horse and buggy and then take the trolley back home.*"

"*Once when I was at Red Run, my dad and I went up into the apple orchard and he stuck his stick into a tree and accidentally hit a hornet's nest. They swarmed all over me and stung me. I almost died. All they did for me was to put mud all over me where I was stung to draw the stingers out.*"

"*When I was 17, I did my first solo flight in an airplane. It was the biggest thrill of my life. I was required to do two tailspins where you stall the airplane letting it spin backwards and pulling it out and starting the engine again. My dad was there and he almost had a heart attack when he saw me do that.*"

"Later at the beginning of the war, I belonged to a flying club of seventeen guys who each put in $100 to buy a Taylor Craft single engine airplane. When I left the club after 10 years, I got all my $100 back. I would fly when I had enough money. It cost $6.50 an hour for the dual instruction, plus the gasoline.

"When I was a senior in high school I got into trouble for rolling a bowling ball down the hallway. I got suspended and when my dad found out about it he was really mad at me. He told me if I was going to do those kinds of things at school, I might as well quit school, so I did. I was hurt that he didn't see the humor in what I had done. So I quit to spite him. I wished later that I hadn't quit school and my lack of a degree held me back in life.

As you can see from this excerpt from my Dad's Ethical Will, that there are a lot of stories that wise elders can pass on to their children and grandchildren, and in my Dad's case, also to his great grandchildren. In addition to his childhood memories, he shared how he met my Mom and some about their married life together. He also shared extensively about his work history. Lots of other topics can be included in an Ethical Will such as advice a father would pass on to his children and grandchildren or his biggest regrets and biggest triumphs. A wise elder can write it himself, but I chose to interview my Dad and write it up myself. I think this method is preferable for lots of reasons, including the closeness it produces between you and the wise elder that you are interviewing.

WHAT OPPORTUNITIES EXIST FOR WISE ELDERS TO MENTOR YOUNG MEN?

I believe, if possible, your mentoring should begin with your own children and grandchildren. This can be tricky, depending on the relationship you have with them. There are no norms here. You will have to figure out a way that works to mentor your own children and/or grandchildren. They may not ask you directly for advice, even when they may need it. You may have to be proactive and tell your children and grandchildren that you are willing to share with them what you have learned in order to save them some grief or hardship. You may choose to write an Ethical Will like the one described above. In this way you have written what you want to pass on and it is left up to them to read it and follow any of your advice. Some wise elder contributors to this book did pretty much just that.

Wise elder contributor, **Michael Lightweaver**, did it with great clarity and purpose in writing his Ethical Will to his children and grandchildren. Excerpts of his Ethical Will appear in other chapters. He called it *The World*

According to Michael and here is what he wrote in the Preface: *"This book is really being written for my great, great, great grandchildren who will be living into the 22nd century and whom I may never know. I remember as a child hearing scattered stories of my great grandfather, Anderson Hewitt: of how he fought in the civil war, how he was educated for his time in a world of peasant farmers in Kentucky. How he used to go out in the fields and 'make speeches to the Black folks.' From the little I could piece together, he was apparently an abolitionist, which said to me that he marched to the tune of a different drummer than most of his peers and family in southern Kentucky... So this is why I am writing this book; as a gift to you, my descendants; a gift that I would have loved to have received from my own ancestors. It is my attempt to give you a window into my world, back in 2014 and let you see what I thought and what made me tick."* Incidentally, Michael is still alive and well and he may continue to update his life experiences in his book.

If you want to venture out and mentor someone outside your family, below are some suggestions of organizations that make it easier to mentor other younger men.

What Is the Boys to Men Program? Boys to Men Mentoring is a nonprofit organization that is committed to creating communities of dedicated men who are able to guide and support at-risk, often fatherless, boys on their journey to manhood.

They have a proven approach to producing real change within young men, and they lead the charge in a much overdue movement. The circumstances and daily environment that many of our nation's youth experience is absolutely heart breaking. Despite this reality, Boys to Men can't help but remain passionate and optimistic for we have found a real answer that produces *REAL* change.

What Do They Do As Mentors? Every week, their mentors show up at middle schools, high schools, and community centers to give teenage boys a community of men who listen, encourage, and empower them. They hold 2-hour group sessions where boys and elders can connect. Over 75% of the boys currently in the program are growing up without a father.

Their community based mentoring approach gives boys a variety of positive male role models who show up consistently, tell the truth about their struggles as men, ask the boys what kind of man they want to be, praise them for their gifts, support them when they mess up, and encourage them to become the man they want to be. They are dedicated to providing this opportunity to every boy in need.

The Location of Boys to Men Programs. Their U. S. headquarters is in San Diego, California and they have started Centers in the following U. S. cities: In Arizona (Phoenix, Tucson and Prescott), California (Southern California), Colorado (Littleton), Hawaii (Kamuela), Iowa (Central Plains and Sioux City), Minnesota (St. Louis Park), New England, North Carolina (Asheville), Oregon (Southern Oregon), Texas (Houston) and Virginia (Richmond). They also have Centers in Canada (Montreal, Toronto and Vancouver), South Africa (Cape Town and Johannesburg), Switzerland (Schweiz) and in the United Kingdom (Bristol and Stroud).

Journeymen Mentoring Program. I am familiar with one of the Boys to Men Programs located in Asheville, North Carolina. It is called the Journeymen Mentoring Program and is a nonsectarian, non-partisan, non-profit organization created by elder men for the specific purpose of mentoring boys 12-18 years of age through their passage into manhood. The Journeymen Organization is staffed by dozens of committed and trained volunteers and professionals who have undertaken their own journeys of personal development.

Their staff creates a safe and stimulating environment that supports and challenges the boy in his epic transition to adulthood. They model what it's like to be a man of integrity and authenticity, and they teach specific processes that help the boy become the man he wants to be.

What Are JGroups? The mentoring program at Journeymen uses group meetings, called JGroups, for mentors and Journeymen to interact on a regular basis. The JGroup schedule involves meeting regularly every other week for a two-hour period. Journeymen specializes in creating safe circles where boys can talk about the events, emotions, and experiences of their lives. It is a place where Journeymen get to practice being a fully alive and communicative man among men.

Their groups meetings are structured opportunities to explore aspects of healthy masculinity. Participants learn about accountability, integrity, personal responsibility, honest communication, emotional literacy, and the importance of discovering and articulating a sense of personal mission in the world.

Additionally, once a month they schedule an outdoor activity. These activities are focused on continuing to develop the bond of trust between the JMen and the Mentors and take place in nature. Their stated goal is to reintroduce the boys to the wonder of the outdoors, while reinforcing their regular team building initiatives.

The mentoring model they follow assigns a man to be the primary contact person for the boy. This may blossom into a mentoring relationship; however, it is within the group environment that these relationships develop. They have found that one-to-one pairings initiated by the boys is more effective and longer lasting. All Mentors have been subjected to state and national criminal background checks and must go through a probationary period before being paired with a boy.

What Is Their Mentor Training? Journeymen has developed its own Inner Mentor Awakening Opportunity for their Mentors. The men who take this special training learn at a deep level how to listen, accept, admire and bless the young men and to be there for them.

The training is designed to:

- Teach mentors better listening, empathy, and attending skills.
- Raise the mentor's consciousness around his own issues during adolescence and how those issues have affected a young man's life.
- Create a bond among the mentors and mentees through group discussions and team building exercises.
- Teach mentors their roles and responsibilities in the lives of these young men.
- They require the following commitment from their mentors:
- Examine your life and be ready to live your mission.
- To better connect with his own children.
- Have a passion to mentor a boy in the Journeymen Mentoring Program.

As a result of the training they get, their mentors form a community that meets quarterly to discuss their lives, share best practices, attend personal growth workshops, and provide feedback for organizational growth. Their mentors also have the opportunity to continually work on themselves within the program structure, which is a unique aspect of their program.

What Are Rites of Passage? Rites of passage for young men have played an important role in many cultures for thousands of years. A primary function of any rite of passage is to allow young men to choose a new adult identity in their community. Adult men help to facilitate this process, and help them gain the skills and understandings that they will need to fulfill their potential role as members of the community.

The isolation in a primitive setting removes these young men from the routines and patterns of their lives so that they can *"re-create"* themselves. They are given the opportunity to let go of old behavior patterns that might no longer serve them.

The weekend incorporates physical, mental, and emotional tests. These tests help the boy discover inner resources that he was previously unaware of to help him gain new self-respect and confidence. In the weekend events, the tests are challenging, but do not involve winning and losing, which they believe create the potential for shame. Each boy has the opportunity to test himself in ways that build self-esteem and facilitate growth.

The specific processes used at a rite of passage are kept confidential, so that, younger members of the community do not receive the adult information before they are ready for it, as a rite of passage is considered sacred and personal and should not be treated casually. Also, it relies on a degree of theater, surprise, and spontaneous response that would be lost if participants knew in advance what was going to happen. (They do share all information ahead of time with the parents/guardian of the boy, asking that this information be kept in confidence).

Following a traditional rite of passage, a young man's family and community celebrate his change of status with a welcome home ceremony, which usually involves some form of sharing food together. At these weekend events, boys and young men who participate are honored for their accomplishments with a homecoming feast. I participated in one of their homecoming ceremonies and feasts while living in Asheville and it was an inspiring event. They conduct two Rites of Passage Adventure Weekends a year, one in the Spring and one in the Fall.

One of the Journeymen Mentors shared this account of what he personally got out of being a Mentor: *"When I left the weekend I was full of awe, excitement, love, and in an altered state. I have been part of conscious initiatory experiences going on 18 years and I found this one to be one of the most potent, powerful, and loving. I stepped into my elder and the elder role in a new way and am thankful for the opportunity to figure out what this is for me and how to share it. On my journey through life I have been mostly void of teachers and mentors to guide me along the journey."*

"That scenario I believe is both due to myself and our culture at large. I grew up not trusting men so I did not seek out the mentors for fear of being con-

trolled and shaped the way they wanted me to be rather than guided, coaxed, and encouraged into finding my creative expression in the world. And I believe our culture let me down as well. Where were these men I needed? Once again I find myself out there piecing together the place of the elder and who I am as an elder. Where are the mentors? I find myself relating to these boys."

Another Journeymen Mentor shared this account: *"For me, I have little connection with my dad and grandfathers and don't know any ancestors past that. So the consciousness that was raised in me to imagine the men on whose shoulders I now stand and whose shoulders my sons now stand as well, is inspiring and brings tears to my eyes as I think about my own mortality and what kind of world I am creating and will ultimately leave behind for the next generation."*

Each community where this program exists has its own ways to sign up to become a Mentor. I suggest you use Google to determine if there is a similar program in your community and then follow their instructions on how to become a Mentor. If there is no *"Boys to Men Program"* in your community, then Google *"Boys to Men USA"* and follow their instructions. They will help you start one.

Experience Corps. Experience Corps is a high-impact, social model for senior volunteering that has been adopted by AARP. The program is now operating in 23 cities and several countries and has over 2,000 trained volunteers and currently is serving over 30,000 students every year in high need elementary schools. Its lessons contain clues to help us challenge the assumptions we make about the role of older adults, and to stimulate innovation in envisioning this new stage of life.

The founders designed and implemented this program that could achieve three simultaneous objectives:

- Use the abilities of older adults to effect significant and positive social impact in a critically needed area, with impact well beyond what any one person could do alone—and in so doing realize the potential for our longer lives
- Improve the physical and cognitive health and social well-being of older participants
- Meet the need of many older adults to contribute in a meaningful way

They use volunteer mentors to try to improve the academic achievement of young children, as a key social need. They focus on children in kindergarten, first, second, and third grades, because of strong evidence indicating that children who succeed by third grade are positioned for successfully completing school, rather than failing or dropping out.

We scientifically designed a model for a volunteer program for older adults, requiring a commitment of at least 15 hours per week for the full school year to create the conditions for high impact for children and high benefits for health, including being more physically active. The volunteers perform specific duties selected by the school principals to fill their greatest unmet needs, whether in literacy, math, computing, or other areas.

Currently, Experience Corps operates in the following areas: Baltimore, MD; Beaumont & Port Arthur, TX; Boston, MA; Chicago, IL; Cleveland, OH; Evansville, IN; Macon, GA; Marin County, CA; Minneapolis/St. Paul, MN; Oakland/Bay Area, CA; Orange County, CA; Philadelphia, PA; Portland, OR; Sacramento County. CA; Yolo County, CA; City of Sacramento, CA; San Francisco, CA; Tempe, AZ and Washington D.C. Metro. If you do not live in any of these locations and want to bring an Experience Corps Program to your town or city use this link to get further information: https://www.aarp.org/experience-corps/affiliates/

WHAT ARE SOME OTHER WELL-KNOWN MENTORING PROGRAMS?

There are three established programs that together involve over 360,000 older Americans who are 55 and older in volunteer community service programs. These three programs are Foster Grandparents, Senior Companions and RSVP or Retired and Senior Volunteer Program. Below is a brief description of each of these three volunteer/mentoring programs. Described below are many more other well-known volunteer/mentoring programs.

Foster Grandparents. Foster Grandparents is part of the Senior Corps. They tutor children, mentor troubled teens and young mothers, care for premature infants and children with disabilities, and help children who have been abused or neglected. The requirements are that you have to volunteer 15-20 hours per week and have an annual income of $22,000 or less. Foster Grandparents earn a tax-free stipend while serving as volunteer mentors and tutors to disadvantaged children and youth in schools, Head Start Centers and other agencies. Join a popular and respected national program that's been active in your community for over thirty years. Here are the benefits to anyone who becomes a foster grandparent:

- A tax-free stipend averaging $220 per month. It is not income and cannot be used to calculate eligibility for federal and state entitlements like Social Security, SSI, MediCare, MediCal, HUD housing, etc.
- Monthly training session including all-you-can-eat lunch
- Reimbursement for transportation – mileage or bus pass;
- A hot meal each day at the work site or a cash lunch subsidy
- Paid Time Off
- Accident and liability insurance while on duty
- Annual Recognition Luncheon and Gifts

This program has proven highly effective in helping wise elders find a purpose in their lives. Seventy-one percent of Foster Grandparents, for instance, reported never feeling lonely. For information on a similar program in your city or town, go online and type in *"foster grandparents."* To learn about a Foster Grandparents program in your area, use the following link: https://www.nationalservice.gov/programs/senior-corps/get-involved.

Senior Companions. Senior Companions provide assistance and friendship to adults who have difficulty with daily living tasks and help them remain independent in their homes. The program aims to keep seniors independent longer, and provide assistance to family caregivers. Senior Companions serve 15 to 40 hours per week helping an average of two to four adult clients live independently in their own homes. Volunteers receive pre-service orientation, training from the organization where they serve, supplemental insurance while on duty, and may qualify to earn a tax-free hourly stipend. To find similar programs in your area use this link: https://www.nationalservice.gov/programs/senior-corps/get-involved

RSVP (Retired and Senior Volunteer Program). RSVP gives volunteers a chance to use their skills and talents in service to their communities, typically organizing neighborhood watch programs, tutoring and mentoring youth, renovating homes, teaching English, and assisting disaster victims. RSVP volunteers reported having improved self-perception and satisfaction towards life. Again, to find out about RSVP in your area, use the following link: https://www.nationalservice.gov/programs/senior-corps/senior-corps-programs/rsvp.

OASIS International Tutoring Program. OASIS puts into practice the landmark MacArthur Foundation study of successful aging, in which found that the key ingredients for a high quality of life are maintaining a low risk for disease, a high level of engagement with the community, and high physical and cognitive function. This program enables volunteers to work one-on-one with children at schools to increase reading skills and esteem; and the which pairs older volunteers with young adolescents to reduce health risk behaviors. OASIS volunteers reported improved wellbeing. Information on how you can get involved with this program can be found at https://www.oasisnet.org/National-Programs/Intergenerational-Tutoring.

Across Ages. This organization pairs older volunteers with young adolescents to reduce health risk behaviors. This is a mentoring initiative designed to delay or reduce substance use of at-risk middle school youth through a comprehensive intergenerational approach. It pairs older adult mentors (55 years and older) with young adolescents, specifically those making the transition to middle school. The overall goal of the program is to increase protective factors for high-risk students to prevent, reduce, or delay the use of alcohol, tobacco, and other drugs and the problems associated with substance use.

In a follow-up study, the program significantly reduced school absences and had a positive effect on measures of youths' reactions to situations involving drug use and attitudes toward school, the future, and elders. However, the program did not significantly impact youths' frequency of substance use or well-being. If you are interested in this program go to their website for more information at http://www.cebc4cw.org/program/across-ages/.

ReServe. ReServe matches this talent with the expressed needs of government and social services agencies to help fill critical gaps such as support for strategic planning, foundation outreach, administrative support, event planning, IT administration, and so much more. ReServists, age 50+, hit the ground running and bring to organizations a tremendous work ethic, a *"no-drama"* attitude, and an amazing wealth of problem solving experience.

In addition to general capacity building, ReServe works with agencies to develop proposals to the government and foundations building in ReServists as a practical and cost effective part of the solution. ReServists bring tremendous skills in the areas of health care through their Health Care Navigator and Dementia Care Coaching products, education through their truancy fighting and college readiness programs and poverty fighting through their efforts to assist people obtain critical supports such as nutrition assistance and help applying for health care.

ReServe has over a decade of experience in leveraging this workforce for the good of communities. ReServe is creating new paid roles for older adults in high-need areas. The impact of this program has yet to be evaluated formally.

People join ReServe for its variety of personal options: to give back, try new things, challenge themselves, learn new skills, and/or connect with a cause that is important to them. The vast majority of ReServists – 84 % – find fulfillment with part-time assignments.

ReServe is not only about doing good it is about feeling good. When you dedicate your time and talent to social change, reinvest your skills and play a critical role in helping nonprofits, public institutions and city agencies stay on mission your life takes on new meaning. Working 10-15-20 hours a week you can change the life of a young person, help a family navigate the health care system, lift a person out of poverty. Earn a stipend while serving your community! For information go to: http://www.reserveinc.org/become-a-reservist.

Boys & Girls Clubs. Since 2008, Boys & Girls Clubs and the at-risk youth they serve have benefited from grant funding provided by the Department of Justice (DOJ), Office of Juvenile Justice and Delinquency Prevention (OJJDP). As a result, Club mentoring programs in underserved communities have been expanded and enhanced exponentially. Grant funding from OJJDP, will provide local Clubs with the resources to effectively mentor more 32,000 youth at 1,450 Club sites in all 50 states, plus American Samoa, Puerto Rico, and the U.S. Virgin Islands.

The Mentoring at Boys & Girls Clubs (MBGC) approach unites the powerful mentoring elements present in Clubs with formal mentoring practices and research/evidence-based prevention programs. MBGC provides a combination of one-on-one, group, and peer mentoring services. Mentoring is site-based and provided by Club staff, volunteers, and peers, with ongoing efforts to recruit minority male mentors.

MBGC incorporates each of the elements of effective practice for mentoring, including screening, training, matching, monitoring and support, and closure. MENTOR, the National Mentoring Resource Center and the *Elements of Effective Practice for Mentoring*™ have been invaluable resources guiding the development of MBGC mentoring programs and services. MBGC training resources updated this year integrate new research and evidence-informed training topics included in the 4th Edition of the Elements of *Effective Practice for Mentoring*™, as well as research-informed training regarding the effective assessment and usage of mentee risk data. More information can be found at: https://nationalmentoringresourcecenter.org/index. php/31-featured-grantees/185-mentoring-at-boys-girls-clubs-shaping-the-dialogue-with-law-enforcement.html.

The YMCA Mentoring Program. The resource office for the nation's 2,700 YMCAs has expanded the YMCA's Reach & Rise™ program, which connects kids and teens with adult mentors for 12-18 months. Through a $4 million grant from the Office of Juvenile Justice and Delinquency Prevention (OJJ-DP), the Y expanded the service area of their mentoring program from six to 38 states by the end of 2013.

Nearly one in five youth live in poverty1 and are at risk of falling prey to crime, drugs and other hurdles that could keep them from reaching productive adulthood, obtaining an education and successfully entering the workforce. Research shows that youth are more likely to succeed with the support of a caring adult. The YMCA's Reach & Rise program, led initially by the YMCA of San Francisco, is designed for youth ages 6 to 17 who lack role models and are in communities challenged by poverty, crime, truancy and single parent households, among other social issues.

At the following link here is a list of YMCAs that offer the Reach & Rise program: https://s3.amazonaws.com/ymca-ynet-prod/files/news-media/ Reach-and-Rise-Program-Locations.pdf

The National Mentoring Resource Center. Their program is called MENTOR. Their vision is to make sure that every young person has the supportive relationships they need to grow and develop into thriving, productive and engaged adults. MENTOR's mission is to fuel the quality and quantity of mentoring relationships for America's young people and to close the mentoring gap for the one in three young people growing up without this critical support. For over 25 years this organization has provided a public voice, developed and delivered resources to mentoring programs nationwide. In addition, they have improved the quality of mentoring based service through the establishment of evidence-based standards, innovative research and essential tools.

They have created a national network of affiliates. They have created structured mentoring programs for an estimated 300,000 at-risk youth. Their research indicates that 4.5 million at-risk youth have a structured mentoring relationship. However, their research also shows that one in three young people reach adulthood without the benefit of a mentor. There is still a lot of work to do. You can apply to become a mentor by using the following link: https://www.mentoring.org/our-work/about-mentor/

Silver Key. Silver Key operates primarily in Colorado Springs where I live. It serves in partnership with their stakeholders to support quality of life for seniors - allowing them the choice of safely aging in place with dignity and independence. Their services include home delivery of meals to shut-ins, Transportation of seniors to the grocery store, medical and dental appointments, social & recreational events, worship services, employment, to the military bases for their veteran services, education and volunteer sites, a free or low cost café, a food pantry, legal services, short-term case management services and a thrift store. Here are the many ways volunteers are utilized: Clerical/Data Entry, Committee/Events, Delivering Meals, Errand Running/Companionship, Food Pantry Sorting, Kitchen Aide, Receptionist, Thrift Store Staff & Reserve & Ride Van Driver. This program should be implemented in other cities and for information on the program use this link: https://www.silverkey.org/volunteer/.

Meals on Wheels. Meals on Wheels has volunteer drivers delivering meals to shut-ins in virtually every community in America through our network of more than 5,000 independently-run local programs. While the diversity of each program's services and operations may vary based on the needs and resources of their communities, they are all committed to supporting their senior neighbors to live healthier and more nourished lives in their own homes. You can go to this link for information about the program in your area: https://www.mealsonwheelsamerica.org/find-meals.

SCORE. This is the nation's largest network of volunteer, expert business mentors, with more than 10,000 volunteers in 300 chapters. As a resource partner of the U.S. Small Business Administration (SBA), SCORE has helped more than 10 million entrepreneurs through mentoring, workshops and educational resources since 1964. SCORE volunteers provide confidential business mentoring services, both in person and online. They lead seminars and workshops to help small business owners meet their goals and achieve success. They help expand outreach of SCORE through marketing and alliance building in our local communities. Volunteering at SCORE is a way for you to give back to your community, connect with fellow business owners, and pass on your knowledge to the next generation of entrepreneurs in your community. To volunteer go to: https://www.score.org/vo

lunteer?gclid=Cj0KCQiA597fBRCzARIsAHWby0E07heBzKwUNo9RPlsel
if-TfaZUFdW7bugAfle0sGsbS6-EwlFbN8aAgg2EALw_wcB.

Project SCOUT (Senior Citizen Outreach). This program offers volunteer income tax assistance and tax counseling for local residents during tax season. They train their volunteers using Internal Revenue Service and Franchise Tax Board personnel to assist senior, blind, disabled and low income persons to prepare their tax returns. For disabled individuals unable to get to the tax sites, we have trained volunteers who can do in-home tax preparation. They also have help available on an appointment basis after the tax season is over for people who did not file during the tax season. Anyone over the age of 60, individuals with a disability and low-income residents is eligible to receive SCOUT's assistance programs. Donations are gladly accepted. I could only find information on programs in Santa Cruz and San Benito Counties in California. Perhaps they exist in other communities under other names. Do an online search for other similar programs. Here is the contact information for this program: http://www.seniorscouncil.org/scout.html.

The Story Project. This program brings people together to record and share the stories of their lives. Family stories. Shared memories. Local history. Important events. It's a chance to ask the questions that matter, and to make sure stories aren't lost. These are public events that are usually recorded and played on local radio. It has other names across the country and is featured on the National Public Radio website where it is called StoryCorps. It is also featured weekly on NPRs Morning Edition. Here they record intergenerational stories.

Since 2003, StoryCorps has given a quarter of a million Americans the chance to record interviews about their lives, to pass wisdom from one generation to the next, and to leave a legacy for the future. It is the largest single collection of human voices ever gathered. These powerful stories illustrate our shared humanity and show how much more we share in common than divides us. They also have a Mobile Tour that travels to various cities across the country.

StoryCorps offers three options on how to capture the stories of your loved ones:

1. Head to one of their StoryBooths located in Atlanta (https://storycorps.org/atlanta/), or Chicago (https://storycorps.org/chicago/).
2. Schedule an appointment with one of their Mobile Tour booths located in 10 different cities each year: https://storycorps.org/mobile-tour/

3. Record your own session with a StoryCorps Do-It-Yourself interview kit: https://storycorps.org/participate/

For the first two options, they use a model of two people who know each other to come in together to interview each other, but if needed, they also will provide a facilitator to assist with the recording process and the interview as needed.

Participants receive a broadcast quality CD, and with permission, their story can get broadcasted in different areas. Additionally, there is no charge for participants since StoryCorps considers itself a public service, however, they do accept donations (at https://storycorps.org/other-ways-to-give/). Check their website for more information at: https://storycorps.org/mobile-tour/.

Big Brothers/Big Sisters Mentoring Program. Big Brothers Big Sisters seeks to change the lives of children facing adversity between 6 and 18 years of age. Our network of volunteers, donors and supporters comes from all walks of life, all backgrounds, all corners of the country. Their unique brand of one-to-one mentoring, in which a child facing adversity is carefully matched with a caring adult mentor in a relationship supported by professional Big Brothers Big Sisters staff members, changes lives for the better forever. For information on Big Brother/Big Sister Mentoring Programs in your area use this link: https://www.bbbs.org/become-a-big/.

The National Institute on Aging is a division of the U.S. National Institutes of Health, located in Bethesda, Maryland. The NIA itself is headquartered in Baltimore, Maryland. The NIA leads a broad scientific effort to understand the nature of aging and to extend the healthy, active years of life. NIA, one of the 27 Institutes and Centers of National Institute for Health, is the primary Federal agency supporting and conducting Alzheimer's disease research. They also convene the National Advisory Council on Aging that advises the Secretary of the U. S. Department of Health and Human Services. They meet three times a year to consider applications for research and training and to recommend funding for promising proposals. You can find out more about their programs at https://www.nia.nih.gov/about.

Wise Elders: Creating Family and Improving Health in the Latino Community. Juniper is a support program for elderly Latinos in Minneapolis. I am including it here because it provides a model of the kind of program that probably is needed in every city where there is a Latino population. The

Juniper Program is called *Tomando Control de su Salud (Taking Control of your Health.)* This means helping people live well with chronic conditions and reaches out to all Spanish-speaking persons in Minneapolis and across the state of Minnesota.

The evidence-based program helps people manage chronic conditions such as diabetes, arthritis, heart disease and anxiety. In the six-week class people learn how to manage pain and fatigue, improve nutrition and exercise and talk to doctors and families about treatment choices.

Opening New Doors for Engagement. The leaders of the Wise Elder group, work to motivate and engage others. One leader in the apartment building where she lives started a music group so she and her neighbors can enjoy music and socialize with each other.

Creating A Culturally Sensitive Environment. One participant said this, *"It makes a big difference to be surrounded by people who share your culture and speak your language,"* She said. *"Having the classes led by people from the community is so much more powerful than having a translator. Working with Juniper is a natural fit for us. We want to be proactive in helping people address concerns and the Juniper programs do that. They are preventative, use a holistic approach and are based on research."*

As far as I could tell, there are no other Juniper type programs in other places in the U. S., but you can contact them to see if they would help you start a similar program in your city or town. The link to contact them is: info@yourjuniper.org.

Mankind Project. I had planned to include the ManKind Project as a possible way to mentor young men. However, I decided there were too many red flags for me to fully recommend the ManKind Project. There are several reason for my reluctance. First, they do not allow informed consent. They keep the process they put men through on their weekend New Warrior training a secret. Second, from what I know of the program, (I had a close friend go through the weekend and he felt it was harmful to him) I see there is a real potential to do harm to men.

They use coercive and manipulative tactics to break down the defenses of the men who participate in their weekend. They also emphasize highly masculine behaviors and seem to suppress the feminine side of men. For all these reasons I cannot recommend the ManKind Project as a way to mentor younger men. You can go online and do your own research and then decide if this program is for you. Their URL is https://mankindproject.org/who-we-are/.

HOW DO YOU START YOUR OWN MENTORING PROGRAM?

I found several online resources to help you start your own mentoring program. One can be found at www.mentoring.org. They will walk you through the steps you need to take to create your own functioning mentoring program. There are several online resources to help you start as mentoring program. In general, the steps are these:

1. Define the youth population that will be served....
2. Identify who you will recruit as mentors.
3. Determine the type of mentoring relationships you would like to develop (e.g., who will be served, and how they will be served?).
4. Determine the focus of the mentoring relationships. ...
5. Determine where and how often the mentoring sessions will occur.

CHAPTER ELEVEN

WHAT WOULD THE WORLD BE LIKE IF IT WERE FILLED WITH WISE ELDERS?

What we have done for ourselves alone dies with us. What we have done for others and the world remains and is immortal.

—Albert Pike

Can you imagine a world where our elders are treated with respect and their wisdom is sought out? I remember the movie, *Being There,* with Peter Sellers. He played Chauncey Gardener who was a simple-minded actual gardener for a wealthy patron. However, because he spoke so simply that people began to believe he was the wisest man they had ever met. In the movie, he even gets to advise the President. In some ways when we are wise, we can speak the truth in a simple way that everybody can understand. Albert Einstein once said that the real geniuses are those people who can speak to others at their level. Wise elders often surprise people by their simple but direct truths.

WHAT HAS TO CHANGE?[66]

We have to change our attitudes about our elderly. Traditionally, our Native Americans are usually thought of as our best examples. Though traditions and ways of life vary from tribe to tribe, showing respect to our Native elders has been an example to follow in their culture. However, they too have some problems with their younger members not showing true respect or their elders. Here are 10 ways they suggest to show respect to their Native elders. These could also apply to elders of any cultural background.

1. **Listen More.** The old adage *"We have two ears and one mouth for a reason"* applies here. When in the presence of an elder, make sure to listen

more than you speak as an elder's words come from a place with many decades of experience.

2. **Be Polite.** Acting in a polite way to an elder is a demonstration of respect. If you are in the presence of an elder, be polite. This means if they are talking, listen, if they ask you a question, respond respectfully and with a calm tone. Do not interrupt them, and always ask if they need anything. Do not address them by their first name unless they have given you permission to do so. If you do not know their name, you may use sir or ma'am again unless they tell you different. If meeting an elder for the first time, do not sit down with them unless you ask permission.

3. **Ask for Advice.** It's a shame to think an elder, who has had a lifetime of experience, would ever be overlooked for their advice. If you are ever in need of advice about how to respond in a life situation, take some time out of your day to seek the counsel of a wise elder. Their advice may be better than what the doctor ordered.

4. **Visit with Them.** Sometimes our Native elders may spend time without the benefit of their communities because they may be at home, in an elder retirement facility or simply sitting alone during a powwow or other social gatherings. It is a great show of respect to visit with them and bring members of your community to them.

5. **Let Them Eat First.** In many tribal communities it goes without saying that at any social event, the elders always eat first. In any case, you can show an elder respect by offering to get them a plate before you serve yourself. This is especially true if they are not able to stand for a period of time or could use any sort of assistance.

6. **Ask Them About Their Traditions.** It's a great show of respect to ask the Native elders of the tribe to tell you about your traditions and culture. You can also learn from them in the process, which not only is respectful, but of benefit to learning the ways of your ancestors—a definite win-win.

7. **Speak Their Language, If Possible.** If they speak your tribe's traditional language—speak with them using their language. Whether you know the language of your tribe or not, offering to speak words, learn words and share their language is a nod of respect for the ways of your tribe. You will learn in the process no matter how well you speak their lan-

guage. Even if you don't speak the language it is a great way to start a conversation.

8. **Ask About Their Lives.** When you ask an elder about their life, you will hear some of the most amazing stories. It also shows that you are interested in them, and that you care. Something as simple as asking an elder to tell you their stories shows a great deal of respect and reverence for an elder who deserves it.

9. **Give Them a Call.** Sometimes we are not close enough to see an elder in person, but this certainly does not mean we cannot reach out to them in a personal way. In our busy lives it's easy to forget the amount of meaning an elder will experience if we take time out of our day just to say, *"Hello, I was thinking about you and I decided to call you."*

10. **Tell Them You Respect and Appreciate Them.** Though we may practice respect to our Native elders by listening, being polite or visiting, how often do we actually say, *"I respect you greatly and appreciate that you are here."* This may seem simple, but it can be overlooked. If possible, the next time you see an elder that has been a positive force in your life, tell them this message of respect.

These 10 suggestions are ones we need to use any time we have an opportunity to interact with a wise elder. In addition, here is an additional list of 8 suggestions on ways to serve as a wise elder:[67]

1. Ask for advice....
2. Call them....
3. Discuss their family heritage, history and traditions....
4. Eat together with them....
5. Spend time with them (and listen intently) ...
6. Tell them how much you appreciate and respect them....
7. Visit their senior living communities....
8. Volunteer at a senior center.

GET YOUR BUT OUT OF THE WAY

Wise elder contributor, **Rafa Flores**, writes that it is up to wise elders themselves to become the change agents. He suggests the following: *"Like you have said Barry, as an elder, the only way for us to show up and be available to those in need, and more/most importantly those who are not in need, is to be present. As an elder, advocate, mentor, teacher, leader, example, we as adults with life* *lessons and wisdom to share, must be proactive. If the mountain won't come to you, YOU must go to the mountain. This means, that youth in general doesn't know they need help and won't seek it. We as self-aware conscious beings (Wise Elders), must go to where the kids are. It is only then that they will have access to us, and we to them. This requires awareness of the need and also effort on our parts to make ourselves available."*

THE CALL TO AWAKEN.

Following what wise elder contributor, **Rafa Flores**, says above, He urges wise elders to heed a Call to Awaken, instead of waiting for society to change its view of the elderly. He writes: *"To make a difference in our lives and future lives, a Wise Elder will require innovation, and a combination of active participation, internet gaming, Apps, and to be proactive. Go where there is no demand. Go where there is demand. Volunteer. Engage. Enroll with the school district to be able to read to the students once a week. Volunteer to tutor. Volunteer to mentor. The potentials for involvement can be daunting and in the same breath can be easy. These are the ideas for engaging the Wise Elders more in our communities."*

THE LEGACY PROJECT

We do need organizations who can help us change society's attitudes toward our elders. One such organization is called *The Legacy Project*. The Legacy Project at www.legacyproject.org is an independent, big-picture research, learning, and social innovation non-profit organization that works across generations. Drawing on the natural and social sciences, their *YOU 177* global initiative is about building 7-Generation communities.

The Legacy Project has three banner programs, reflecting the three levels at which you develop your legacy through your lifetime: *LifeDreams* to develop your personal potential and *create* your own life; *Across Generations* to help you *connect* with others, particularly intergenerationally; and *Our World* to help each of us work together to *change* the world to address issues like building stronger communities and caring for the environment. Create, connect, change.

For over two decades, they have brought together research in areas ranging from community building, lifelong learning, and demographics to systems design, economic value structures, and sustainable development. Drawing on this multidisciplinary research to make interconnections, they use an intergenerational approach to big-picture problem solving. The intergenerational connections are valuable in themselves; more importantly, they're a means to a much bigger end catalyst for larger systems change, using systemic thinking. In our highly age-segregated society, if we can meaningfully reconnect generations in live, everyday experience, then we'll have more easy access a bigger perspective on how to create an integrated and sustainable community. Further, research also shows that bringing the generations together can also bridge gender, racial, socioeconomic, and ideological divides.

Increases in longevity are causing a historic demographic shift. Where once we may have personally known two or three generations in our family and community, we can now have relationships with at least seven generations – our own; parents, grandparents, great-grandparents; children, grandchildren, great-grandchildren.

Here are some problems and issues that *The Legacy Project* is addressing through its YOU177 initiative:

- The lack of a vision for what tens of millions of elders might do with their additional years.
- The lack of an educational system, that is based on an outdated industrial model, to meet the needs of our elders.
- Estimates are that about one-third of all elderly people have high levels of debt, little savings and no pension or inheritance. Poverty is a big issue among the elderly.
- Most people over 65 are white, while half of recent births are to minorities.
- There now is a need to connect families over seven generations not just three as in the past.
- 70% of those over 65 will need long-term care before they die. Most of this will be in their own homes or the homes of their children or relatives. They present both a problem and an opportunity for extended family, intergenerational connections.
- Community engagement contributes to longevity, life satisfaction and other indicators of psychological well-being for wise elders. We have to develop programs that increase community involvement of wise elders.
- Those currently over 65 have the highest volunteer rate of any age group. There needs to be better ways for the elderly to contribute to society than just volunteering.

- Technology is impacting our elders through changes in the way products and services are delivered, the way relationships are formed and maintained and the way elders interact with their surroundings. They also emphasize the *"new"* over the *"old"* and this accelerates the pace of change which emphasizes generational differences.
- There is a real need for cooperative, supportive communities and there still remains an over-emphasis on competition rather than cooperation.
- We need to make big-picture, long-range thinking to address these problems and issues, commonplace and accessible. This is still a rarity and we desperately need big-picture thinking, if we are going to build a sustainable world.

Their other related programs include the *Dream Bigger* program. They ask people, *"What's your dream for yourself and your community?"* That's a big question and it deserves careful consideration. Their goal is to get wise elders and others to discover – or perhaps rediscover – what really matters to them.

When you're building a physical infrastructure, like homes and roads, you need tools like backhoes and bulldozers. When you're building a psychosocial infrastructure, like greater connection and meaning between all generations that will help us thrive and innovate, you also need tools. But few exist. So they decided to invent one. It's called a *Dream*.

A *Dream* is a story for all ages to share about hopes and dreams across a lifetime, through our history, and into the future. It may look like a simple little book, but it's a transformational tool developed over five years by an international team that included educators, librarians, and social researchers. It's a small package with a big message. Stories inspire us, getting to the head through the heart. They enable us to discover and share what really matters. Too often we get stuck in little stories that fail to sustain us or effect real change. *YOU 177* is about discovering a bigger story, so we think it makes sense to start with a story.

They invite people of all ages to join in the community read program, *Generations Dream* using *Dream* (http://www.legacyproject.org/you177/1w1b.html), to connect us across communities, cultures, and generations. Self-discovery and real community begin in conversation. By participating in *Generations Dream*, you can help start a big-picture dialogue that inspires everybody to dream bigger. Each of your dreams may be different, but they can grow from a common experience and help build a more connected humanity.

7-GENERATION THINKING

As a part of the *Dream Bigger* program (http://www.legacyproject.org/you177/1w1b.html), which is a shared reading and intergenerational dialogue experience, they have developed 7-Generation resources and ideas that help people reframe and expand their life, school, organization, or community story. Bigger, better, longer-term thinking is rare and difficult in today's fast-paced world. *7-Generation Thinking* is a way to make bigger thinking more commonplace and accessible.

Generations are a way to get beyond yourself at this single moment in time. They are a way to touch Big Time. With increases in longevity, more of us than ever before in history will personally know 7 generations – our own generation; three generations before us (parents, grandparents, and great-grandparents); and three generations after us (our children, grandchildren, and great-grandchildren). Generations are a living big-picture time perspective.

7-Generation Thinking combines intellect and creativity, using the left and right brain; builds empathy and perspective-taking skills; looks for bigger patterns and new connections; allows for reflection to translate knowledge into wisdom; travels time, learning from the past and making informed predictions about the future; and reaches for a higher level. I call it systemic thinking or a developing a *metaperspective*.

People often talk about needing a new paradigm to solve complex, interconnected problems. A paradigm is essentially a mental model – for example, shifting from a flat-Earth to round-Earth understanding of this planet. But what we really need for transformation is a metaperspective – seeing the Earth not by itself, but as part of the universe and beyond *including all the stars*.

The *Create Legacy Project*. Another legacy project is called, *Create Legacy*. It has impact that matters and lasts. A legacy project involves two or more generations in some way, directly or indirectly. *Create Legacy* projects take advantage of intergenerativity. Intergenerativity is the big-picture, innovative spark that can happen when you bring together the perspectives of different generations. It's the power to multiply impact when you blend the beliefs of childhood, the power to do of youth, and the think of experience of the elderly. By using intergenerativity, you can expand your understanding of time and internalize the bigger flow of life as you build on what has come before and contribute to what comes after you.

Legacy Bridges in India involve generations working together; one generation passes the responsibility of caring for a bridge to the next generation. The entire community depends on each generation doing their part. Some of the bridges in the community are centuries old.

At the simplest level, a *Create Legacy* project involves a real or symbolic tree. The tree reminds us that everything we do is connected to the world around us. The legacy bridges directly involve a tree, cleverly coaxing the roots of a tree to grow to form the bridges. Trees play a critical role in the health of our global ecosystem.

More sophisticated legacy projects expand the simple tree metaphor to *Eco-Connection*. "Eco" stands for both ecology and economy, and the intersection between the two. Everything we do is connected to the world around us, and the value we take out we also put in. *Eco-Connection* also invites you to take advantage of biomimicry in your legacy project, using nature as a mentor, model, and measure.

You can register to tap into an extensive global network of resources, connect with others, and submit your legacy project to be recognized and use the *YOU 177* designation. Their team evaluates your legacy project proposal under a LEED-like rating system. Leadership in Energy and Environmental Design (LEED) was developed by the US Green Building Council. Instead of a rating system for buildings, *YOU 177* offers a rating system for thinking. Legacy projects can be certified as a silver, gold, or platinum project – platinum representing the best big-picture, high-level, long-term thinking.

Other Opportunities for Wise Elders in The Legacy Project. This isn't about *leaving* a legacy; it's about *living* a legacy. 70% of our older adults say they want to create a positive legacy. What if…we could meaningfully connect the young and the old – particularly the far ends of the age spectrum which are often the most vulnerable, least powerful, most marginalized – in strategic action to transform their own lives and the world? The *YOU* in *YOU 177* not only stands for the power you have as an individual to make a difference regardless of your age, but also stands for *Young and Old United*.

Research tells us that social isolation of elders can result in more health issues and a 50% higher mortality. When elders are vitally connected with the young, this can shift dramatically. We know frail elders and those with dementia are particularly isolated, as are their caregivers. What if we shift the way we see these elders – not as dependents, but as teachers, not as being *"at the end of the line"* of a lifetime, but as being part of helping to create a bigger circle of life?

Based on a decade of research in the social and natural sciences, *YOU 177* takes a systems approach that focuses on the life course and aging, intergenerational relationships, health, lifelong learning, community building, systems design, economics, and environmental studies.

YOU 177 is helping to give wise elders a real role in society. To create genuinely satisfying, realistic images of older adulthood, we have to better understand its complexities. As we create new life maps, there are no prescribed role models to follow, no guideposts, no rigid rules or obvious rewards. *"Aging"* is much more than a problem to be solved. It's about your vision of what it means to *live an authentic life*. You can find out how you can get involved in *The Legacy Project* initiatives at http://www.legacyproject.org.

VISITING THE ELDERLY IN ASSISTED LIVING OR NURSING HOMES.

German wise elder, **Franz Schlink**, reported that he is familiar with a program in his church. He writes: *"My parish has organized, together with other church congregations, a visiting service for people living alone or residents of retirement homes. The visitors are dedicated volunteers."*

MULTIGENERATIONAL HOUSING CREATES MORE CONTACT.

Another way to create more contact between the generations is arrange for them to live in proximity. German wise elder contributor, **Franz Schlink**, writes about housing projects like this in his country: *"In various cities in Germany, so-called multi-generational houses were founded in mostly charitably oriented houses. The idea here is that people of all generations can meet in these homes.*

"In Bensheim we also have a multi-generational house in the Franciscan house of Caritas. A multi-generation house is a new way and a timely response to the challenges of demographic change. The self-evident togetherness of young and old is the basis for passing on everyday skills and knowledge of experience. The house creates spaces and opportunities with the aim of strengthening the cohesion of generations - regardless of family ties. In a multigenerational house, the principles of the extended family are transformed into a modern form. The multigenerational house in Bensheim is a lively meeting place, in which people of different generations come together and spend time together, eat and play with each other, learn with and from each other, support each other and perceive offered services.

"In the Franciscan house, also a lunch is offered and they have their own café. Even without official events, this house brings together students, working people and the elderly. Here, events are organized together with parishes, kindergartens and retirement homes. For example, a worship service of the parish is moved to the garden of a retirement home. Also groups of kindergarteners regularly visit the elderly in the nursing home. Elders can also be enrolled in sponsorship programs for adolescents and homework help at school."

HOW CAN WISE ELDERS MAINTAIN THEIR HEALTH AND WELL-BEING?

This is a big problem because we have a health care system that is structured to handle acute health issues not chronic ones. There is very little medical research on how to prevent degenerative diseases or how to effectively treat degenerative diseases that may have been caused by what happened to them as a child.

The only research on the long-term effects of adverse childhood experiences on the physical and mental health of the elderly is the ACE research we mentioned earlier in this book. This research has the potential to change the whole way we treat patients, particularly the elderly.

The findings clearly help connect the dots between what happened to you as a child (before the age of 18) and the long-term effect on your physical and mental health 50 to 60 years later. All patients, particularly the elderly, need to be routinely screened to determine the effects of adverse childhood experiences on their later health problems.

In Chapter Four you filled out and scored your ACE Questionnaire and in Chapter Nine your filled out and scored your Adverse Childhood Neglect Inventory. Chapter Ten provides you with tools to help you heal your childhood wounds. It is never too late to do this work. The last piece is to fill out and score the ACE Resiliency Questionnaire that appears below.

ACE RESILIENCY QUESTIONNAIRE[68]

Directions: Please place the number that best represents your experience in the blank in front of each item below. Key: 1=Definitely Not True, 2= Probably Not True, Not Sure = 3, Probably True= 4, and Definitely True= 5.

_____ 1. I believe that my mother loved me when I was little.

_____ 2. I believe that my father loved me when I was little.

_____ 3. When I was little, other people helped my mother and father take care of me and they seemed to love me.

_____ 4. 've heard that when I was an infant someone in my family enjoyed playing with me, and I enjoyed it, too.

_____ 5. When I was a child, there were relatives in my family who made me feel better if I was sad or worried.

_____ 6. When I was a child, neighbors or my friends' parents seemed to like me.

_____ 7. When I was a child, teachers, coaches, youth leaders or ministers were there to help me.

_____ 8. Someone in my family cared about how I was doing in school.

_____ 9. My family, neighbors and friends talked often about making our lives better.

_____ 10. We had rules in our house and were expected to keep them.

_____ 11. When I felt really bad, I could almost always find someone I trusted to talk to.

_____ 12. As a youth, people noticed that I was capable and could get things done.

_____ 13. I was independent and a go-getter.

_____ 14. I believed that life is what you make it.

_____ **Total Score**

Interpretation of Results:

How many of these 14 protective factors did I have as a child and youth? (How many of the 14 items did you mark *"Definitely True"* or *"Probably True"*?) _____

Of these marked, how many are still true for me? _____

By completing his Self-Inventory, you should have a clear picture of the amount of adverse childhood experiences you might have had that can produce long-term effects on your physical and mental health and your overall well-being. A high resiliency score can indicate that there were *"protective factors"* that can mitigate against these long-term effects.

WHAT ARE SEVEN WAYS ADVERSE CHILDHOOD EXPERIENCES CAN CHANGE YOUR BRAIN?[69]

Here are some of the ways that ACE's can change your brain:

1. Epigenetic Shifts. When we experience repeated stress-inducing situation early in life, our brain adapts and we lose the ability to respond appropriately and effectively to future stressors – 10, 20 or 30 years later. The reason for this is known as gene methylation where small chemical markers, or methyl groups, adhere to the genes involved in regulating our response to stress and prevent these genes from doing their jobs. If the function of these genes is altered by adverse childhood experiences, the stress response is reset on *"high"* for life, promoting inflammation and disease.

This makes us more likely to over-react to everyday stressors such as an unexpected argument with your spouse or a car that swerves in front of you on the highway, thus creating even more inflammation. The new research on epigenetics shows that early emotional trauma breaks down longstanding delineations between *"physical disease"* and mental or emotional disorders.

2. Size and Shape of the Brain. Studies show that when the developing brain is chronically stressed, it releases a hormone that actually shrinks the size of the hippocampus, the part of the brain that processes emotions and regulates responses to stress. Recent (MRI) studies show the higher the individual's ACE score, the less gray matter he or she has in other key areas of the brain including the prefrontal cortex, where decision-making and self-regulation take place. The amygdule, or the fear-processing center of the brain is also smaller. People with high ACE scores become adults who find themselves over-reacting to even minor stressors.

3. Neural Pruning. Children naturally have an overbalance of neurons and synaptic connections to help them process their *"busy"* lives. It was once thought that you either *"use it or lose it"* when it comes to these brain functions, but recently it was learned non-neural brain cells known as *"microglia,"* make up one-tenth of all brain cells and are part of the immune system. These cells participate in a natural pruning process. However, when a child experiences unpredictable, chronic stress, these cells get activated and create neuro-inflammation, that can reset the brain for life. Kids who enter adolescence with experiences of chronic stress and who lack the presence of a consistent, loving adult are more likely to develop mood disorders or have poor executive functioning and decision-making skills.

4. Telomeres. Adults, who faced developmental trauma showed greater erosion of the protective caps on the ends of their DNA strands, like the caps on shoelaces that are known as *"telomeres."* As our telomeres erode, we are more likely to develop degenerative diseases and age prematurely.

5. Default Mode Network. Inside our brain is a network of neuro-circuitry known as *"default mode network."* It is always on stand-by, helping us to figure out what to do next. Children who faced early adversity are routinely thrust into a state of fight-or-flight. When this happens the default mode network goes *"off line."* It is no longer able to help us figure out what's relevant or what we need to do next. As a result, they have trouble reacting appropriately to the world around them.

6. Brain-Body Pathway. Until recently it was thought that the brain is separate from the body's immune system. Researchers have now found that an elusive pathway travels between the brain and the immune system via lymphatic vessels. They found that the relationship between mental and physical suffering is strong and inflammatory chemicals associated with early childhood trauma flood a person's body from head to toe.

7. Brain Connectivity. Researchers recently found that children and teens, who experienced chronic adversity, showed weaker neural connections between the prefrontal cortex and the hippocampus. This connection plays an essential role in determining how emotionally reactive we are on a day-to-day basis. Importantly, it also determines how likely we are to perceive these events as stressful or dangerous.

Summary. These scientific findings can seem overwhelming, especially to parents who want to do the right thing for their children. So, what can you do if you or your child has been affected by adverse childhood experiences? The good news is that this is reversible, if parents and other adults recognize the causes of these brain dysfunctions. First, you have to connect the dots and understand the core causes of the symptoms you are seeing. It is easy to miss these signals or misdiagnose the nature of the problem.

Just as we can regain our muscle tone though exercise, we can recover functions in under-connected areas of our brain. The brain and our DNA have *"neuroplasticity,"* which means it is open to change and is never static, unlike we thought only 20-30 years ago. Actually, by just connecting the dots, you begin to re-wire your brain and can reverse these symptoms.

WHAT ARE THE LIMITATIONS OF THE ACE RESEARCH?

These results are very important because they show correlations between the effects of childhood adverse experiences not only on adult mental health, but also on adult physical health as well. This research supports the movement toward an integrated model of physical and behavioral health services. We see some important limitations in this research, including the following:

- This is correlational research, which means an association does not necessarily mean that one thing causes the other thing. This has been the biggest criticism of this research, particularly by the medical community.
- Without further interviews, it is impossible to determine whether or not those with ACEs actually healed the adverse experiences they had as a child. Naturally, if they did, the long-term effects would likely be diminished. It would be interesting to find out through further interviews of the subjects in these studies whether or not they did seek counseling or in other ways attempted to heal the wounds from adverse childhood experiences.
- The 10 original questions focused mostly on experiences of childhood abuse. Little can be determined from the study's questions about the long-term effects of neglect, which we find is more impactful than the long-term effects of abuse.
- This was self-report and isn't the most reliable method for collecting these data. It suggests that the results may be underreported.
- Our clinical research indicates that developmental traumas are caused by neglect rather than abuse. Please utilize the several tools we developed to assess the long-term effects of neglect.

Even though there are limitations to these studies, they are having a significant impact on the awareness of the general public about the long-term effects on physical health of childhood adverse experiences. This impact is similar to the impact that second-hand smoke research findings had on the general public in the stop smoking campaign. Most of that research was correlational, but it influenced public opinion and led to the U. S. government declaring that smoking was harmful to your health.

The Road Scholar Program. Whether you are a solo traveler or a couple, the Road Scholars is for passionate lifelong learners, usually over the age of 50. If travel to other countries is on your 'bucket list," then Road Scholars, formerly known as Elderhostel, **will** provide you with an in-depth learning experience about destinations, subjects and ideas that intrigue elders! Their programs are all-inclusive. From expert-led lectures and field trips to lodgings, most meals, gratuities, and group transportation—they handle all the details and all the costs incurred during our programs, including those you might not anticipate. On their International trips, they take care of your airfare, too. They have negotiated special fares and routings that work best — on premium economy and business class fares, too. For contact information, here is the link: https://www.roadscholar.org/practical-information/how-it-works/.

College for Seniors. People are living longer than ever before, and doing so in better health. So what can you do when you retire and want to keep your mind sharp or need to gain additional skills to stay competitive at work? For many, the answer is to go back to school. At the same time, schools want their classrooms to be full of engaged students, regardless of age. In the interest of continuing education, many colleges and universities offer reduced or free college tuition to senior citizens (typically, adults 60 and up, although the rules vary).

In fact, we found at least one college or university in every state with a College for Seniors Program! While some institutions only allow senior students to audit classes, many offer the chance to earn credits toward a degree at a reduced — or completely waived — tuition rate. Does your state have a continuing education you can use in your golden years? Actually, options exist in every state. Find out what is available in your state check out at this site: https://www.thepennyhoarder.com/life/college/free-college-courses-for-senior-citizens/.

The Solari Report. Solari is a private company founded by Catherine Austin Fitts. I recommend them because they seem to provide useful information and services that elders might need. Their mission is to help you live a free and inspired life. This includes building wealth in ways that build real wealth in the wider economy. They believe that personal and family wealth is a critical ingredient of both individual freedom and community health and well-being. They publish *The Solari Report* which offers subscribers access to *private briefings via weekly audios with Catherine Austin Fitts* and her guests. Also, special reports focused on current financial and precious metals markets, geopolitical events as well as risk issues and opportunities impacting personal wealth, health and happiness.

The Solari Report provides up-to-date commentary on a wide range of current news and issues from the economy and the financial markets to geopolitics and health. In many communities there are groups of citizens that study and discuss the contents of *The Solari Report*. Subscribers to The Solari Report login to an expanded private website to post comments and questions. *Solari Updates* are free, weekly e-mail updates. https://home.solari.com/media-kit/

Bill Henderson's Cancer Free. Bill Henderson, who this book is dedicated to, has found over four hundred alternative cures for cancer. He has consulted with over 8,000 people with cancer. Before his death in 2016, he had a weekly online radio show where he interviewed experts in alternative medicine. You can go to: www.WebTalkRadio.net to get his archived interviews. He created *The Bill Henderson Protocol* which is an inexpensive yet potent cancer treatment. This protocol can be used by any cancer patient with any type of cancer. However, if the cancer is fast-spreading, has already spread significantly, or is a particularly dangerous type of cancer, a stronger protocol is recommended, such as the Cellect-Budwig, Cesium Chloride or High RF Frequency Protocol. His book, *Cancer Free*, is available at Amazon. He passed away in 2016 at the age of 90, but his work is being carried on by his wife, Terry. You can get her online newsletter by contacting her at http://www.Beating-Cancer-Gently.com

WHAT ARE SOME VISIONARY IDEAS THAT ADDRESS THE PROBLEM OF HOW TO BETTER HARVEST THE WISDOM OF OUR FATHERS AND GRANDFATHERS?

In this section I offer you some visionary ideas that address the problem of how we can do a better job of harvesting the wisdom of our fathers and grandfathers. All of these ideas are yet to be implemented or are in their early stages of being implemented. Some of these are my ideas and others come from the wise elder contributors to this book.

Listening Circles. For starters, here is an idea from wise elder contributor, **Raphael Peter Engel**: *"Create/Offer Listening Circle/Experiences where Elders and Millennials (the next generation) can come together in a pleasant setting and share, ask questions of each other, and experience the value of "being heard!" (possibly with a Talking Stick). The invitation could be made to any type of group, (assisted living, tech-based organizations, Blogs, the many online groups featuring an Elders and younger people Listening Circle, AARP, etc.)*

"Being able to speak in small, mixed groups, without the stigma of being ridiculed, made small etc. can allow wisdom to come to the surface. If these Circles have a clear Vision Statement and people know what they're coming to, magic can happen."

Dialogue Dinners with Wise Elder Participants. Following that is idea, here is one of my own: Create Dialogue Dinners where young people and elders can meet to discuss the current problems facing our country. The organization, *Food for Thought*, already organizes these kinds of events in Colorado Springs, CO that include a trained facilitator. Their groups are made up of 10-12 people and the discussion is guided by a set of ground rules that each group agrees to and they have a trained facilitator who remains neutral. Groups could be structured to include wise elders.

Neutral means that the facilitator does not share his or her opinions about the topics, personal information or experiences, but instead helps create a climate where participants feel comfortable sharing theirs. Groups meet for 4 additional gatherings and at the end of those sessions, each group can decide if they would like to continue on their own, without a trained facilitator. They might help you set up *Food for Thought* dinners that involve young people with elders to discuss the current problems that exist in your community. For more information about *Food For Thought* use this following link: https://foodforthoughtcs.org.

Community Conversations on Aging. *Food for Thought* in Colorado Springs, CO also hosts *Community Conversations.* These are one-time events focused on a particular topic that impacts Colorado Springs. One such event could focus on how we can better meet the needs of our growing elderly population. Their trained facilitators lead discussion groups as they all strive for the betterment of their community. Action items could be developed to follow-up this on-time event that could be presented to City Council or other groups who could implement the ideas. There also is an organization called *Public Agenda* that helps set up these events in your community. Public Agenda's model for Community Conversations encompasses several key principles, including:

- **Local Nonpartisan Sponsoring Coalition:** A coalition of local organizations and institutions sponsor and organize the Community Conversation.

- **Diverse Participants:** Participation that represents a cross section of the community—not just the *"usual suspects"*—to ensure that all groups and stakeholders are represented and heard from.
- **Dialogue in Small, Diverse Groups:** Small group discussions facilitated by well-trained and objective moderators and recorders who document the proceedings for effective follow-up.
- **The Power of Choicework:** Well-prepared discussion material designed to give people alternative ways of thinking about a complicated issue, or what Public Agenda refers to as *"Choicework."*
- **Forum Follow-Up:** Follow-up activity to connect the Community Conversation dialogue outcomes to ongoing or new action. Rather than lectures by experts, or gripe sessions by angry constituents, well-designed Community Conversations create a frank, productive problem-solving process in which diverse ideas are put on the table, diverse participants sit at the table, and people work to find common ground and solutions. Trained moderators from the community can help all participants contribute, while trained recorders capture the ideas and actions steps generated during the discussion.

Impacts and Outcomes. Community Conversations can have a concrete impact in various ways, from informing people about existing practices and government policies, to creating collaborations across existing community organizations and programs and to creating new citizen-led initiatives. If you are interested in helping to create a Community Conversation on how to better meet the needs of the elderly, here is the link: https://www.publicagenda. org/pages/community-conversations.

The Department of Aging. I believe we need a Cabinet level department in the federal government to help coordinate existing programs for the elderly and to develop new policies and programs designed to better meet the needs of our aging population. This agency would have a seat at the table with other federal level Cabinet departments to bring to the whole Cabinet ideas and proposals to improve the quality of life for our elderly population. This Department can also use tax money to help fund projects and programs for the elderly in local communities.

There are existing government agencies devoted to meeting the needs of the elderly. They include the Administration on Aging (AoA) within the Department of Health and Human Services. The AoA administers the Older Americans Act, which exclusively addresses the concerns of the 43 million

Americans age sixty and above. An example of the second type of agency is the Social Security Administration, which is charged with administering most titles of the Social Security Act. https://www.encyclopedia.com/social-sciences-and-law/law/law/social-security-act. Largely because of its old-age program for retired workers, most Social Security beneficiaries are elderly. These existing structures need to be elevated to a Cabinet level to coordinate policies and programs to better serve the needs of our increasingly aging population.

Wisdom Councils. The Wisdom Council or Civic Council offers a simple, inexpensive and rapid way to strengthen community members' self-organization and sense of responsibility. Councils could be established to address the needs of our elderly population and come up with specific recommendations to offer to local officials. A Wisdom Council is a one-time, randomly-selected group of 12-24 stakeholders who, through special facilitation, produce a consensus statement recommending possible solutions to better meet the need of our elderly population, which is made available to the larger population for further dialogue and action. Wisdom Councils have been held in Ashland, Oregon; Victoria, British Columbia; Port Townsend, Washington; and Asheville, North Carolina. For more information on starting a Wisdom Council in your area, use this link: http://www.tobe.net/about_us/our_story.html.

The Center for Wise Democracy. This organization offers a set of innovations by which *"we"* (a few of us) can facilitate *"all"* the people to come together as *"We the People."* This holistic strategy could be used to bring the wise elders to the table to:

- **Transform our global society**... It is possible to facilitate a transformation of global governance and economics, a way *"We the People"* can establish new institutions and solve the big issues ... e.g. poverty, terrorism, climate change, etc.
- **Transform American democracy**... It is possible to facilitate a rebirth of *"We the People"* to solve impossible-seeming national issues. (There have already been national-level experiments sponsored by the governments of Germany and Austria.) ... e.g. how to stop partisan battling, election reform, health care, money-in-politics, tax policy, etc.
- **Transform state-level governance**... It is possible to facilitate a new level of involvement and collaboration in solving state issues .... taxing, education, welfare, etc.

- **Transform local governance** (cities, communities)... It is possible to facilitate the people of your community to become more involved in resolving difficult public issues (see examples: https://www.wisedemocracy.org/examples.html)
- **Work with Organizations**... e.g. This same process is a breakthrough strategy for organizations as well, or any level of systems. (e.g. co-op: https://www.wisedemocracy.org/food-co-op.html, conferences: https://www.wisedemocracy.org/organizers-of-conferences.html, Swisscom IT: https://www.wisedemocracy.org/leaders-of-orgs.html)

If you are interested in participating in an existing group or starting one in your community, use the following link: https://www.wisedemocracy.org.

Wise Elders in the Classroom. Schools need to be encouraged to invite local wise elders to speak to their students. These wise elders would offer advice and answer questions about their lives and their accomplishments. Contact local school districts to determine how to implement this idea in your local schools. The George Lucas Foundation is spearheading such an idea. One such example that I have come across is the *Dear Wise Elders* project, which began in the New Brunswick Middle School in New Brunswick, NJ. The developer of the project, **David Eisenstein**, is a sixth-grade math teacher. He shared with other teachers -- and also with school and district administrators -- a vision that his school, designated as a priority school, could become a school of character, and in so doing, lift the students socially, emotionally, and academically.

In addition to participating in school-wide, social-emotional character development and culture and climate improvement initiatives generated by the school, David added his own innovation, the Dear Wise Elders project. Here is what David says about this project and his vision for its expansion. *"The Dear Wise Elders grew organically out of my work with older adults. I asked a group of seniors for help with a problem I had with my middle school classes. My students did not understand what was really worthy of respect.*

"The elders and I made a poster expressing all their ideas about respect, and I brought it to my classroom. The kids loved it, and we had a great discussion about respect that ended with the students writing letters thanking the elders and telling them stories about their own grandparents.

"I read these letters to the elders the following week. Many elders had tears in their eyes as we connected lives across the generations. These connections helped both groups. Our elders had found new people to talk with, and many

found new purpose in helping our children. At school, I found my students had more enthusiasm and enjoyed connecting with the elders. More than a few of my formerly blasé kids were eagerly participating in our morning lessons.

"To foster this work, I created the non-profit, Dear Wise Elders Foundation. Since the crux of the project is to connect the generations, it is a natural fit for the Internet. My plan is to have a safe space online where these connections can foster and grow.

"I am sure that all ages will benefit from participating, not just middle school. I have seen the impact with some children as young as six. So the foundation is actively seeking volunteers to help test the program with elementary school children. Educators can speak with program directors at local senior centers and assisted living facilities and ask them if they'd like their elders to participate. The workers in their facility can help the elders create the content and then give the content to the teachers whose classes are participating to use in their classrooms." You can contact David at http://www.dearwiseelders.org.

Create Wise Elders Speaker's Bureaus. As Wise elders in your community you can create a Speaker's Bureau that reaches out to offer to speak to any community or civic group. These speakers could be trained by a local Toastmaster's Club.

Colleges for Seniors. There are Colleges for Seniors programs in every state in the country. These are usually low cost or free classes taught by other seniors. Here is the link to locate a College for Seniors program in your state: https://www.thepennyhoarder.com/life/college/free-college-courses-for-senior-citizens/.

Legacy Classes at Local Colleges and Universities. Through the Continuing Education Departments, local colleges and universities could offer unique classes taught by a wise elder from the community. The teacher of the class could bring in other wise elders as guest speakers. There would be an attempt to reach out to the community agencies to send young people to this class. Other seniors could also attend and be inspired as a result of these classes to take action by volunteering as a mentor or engaging in some community project to promote intergenerational contacts.

Visiting the Elderly in Assisted Living or Nursing Homes. While this is already being done, there are a huge number of the elderly that never get a visitor. Churches and civic organizations in the community could be encouraged to participate on a regular basis. The main task of these visitors is to listen to the interesting stories of these people.

Wise Elder Self-Empowerment Circles. Wise elder contributor, **Aric Rohner**, suggested the following idea: *"The world is filled with many, many wise elders. One problem, as I see it, is that we do not feel empowered to take initiative. That could be for many reasons. For example, it could be societal pressure that devalues elders. Or it could be declining strength, energy, or faculties. With all due respect, these 'reasons' are simply handicaps, not fate. There are many younger people who face much worse and still empower themselves rather than waiting for others to empower them from the outside. The purpose of empowerment circles would be for elders to empower elders, providing community, collective purpose, and collective support around whatever we choose. This could be to improve our own lot or to serve others. Regardless of our individual skills and abilities, collectively we have massive resources."*

A Data Base of Elder Volunteers. Wise elder contributor, **Larry Lawn**, suggested that this data base would contain elders who are available as coaches or mentors for younger people who want to increase their self-awareness by learning different methods of self-discovery. This would attract people who are looking for deeper purpose or meaning at an early age and who want to pursue the question *"Who am I?"*

Wise Elder's Forum. Wise elder contributor, **Michael Harder**, created an online forum for the 18 contributors to this book and the readers of this book could continue to have a dialogue about the issues raised in this book.

Become A Nanoinfluencer. Wise elder contributor, **Gary Scott**, has some great suggestions on how wise elders can create and fulfill their *"nanopurpose."* He writes: *"You can use your wide experience to improve an existing movement or cause that you believe in and that's aligned with your purpose. A wise elder once influenced me greatly when he said 'we all need to have a purpose, not a goal.'" You first need to build a following using the process outlined below:*

1. *"**Create an important life purpose.** Wise Elders can use this process and fulfil their purpose instead of advertising a product. Choose a purpose that's important to you. This will help you create a passion that adds power to your purpose. For example, one meaningful movement today is the FIRE movement. (It stands for 'financial independence, retire early'). FIRE teaches financial responsibility. Examples of a nanopurpose beyond FIRE could be, 'retire early in good health and share what I learned with others' or 'retire early with well-educated kids and help others do the same' or 'retire early with strong spiritual values and find ways to share my values*

with others.' State your purpose and explain how it improves the benefits created by the movement, because it also allows a unique niche of followers to form. This allows a wise (or deeply experienced person) to be a nanoinfluencer.

2. **"Then, align yourself to organizations or people that you can assist, but can also spread the word about your influence.** *There are thousands of movements that can use the benefits of a more refined focus, so define your purpose then act on your passion. Choose a problem that can be eased or resolved with your influence. Ask yourself, 'how can I reach these people and build a following?' I learned a process for sharing advice in the 1970s. This routine has worked for me through numerous changes in communication technology and is still relevant in the modern world. The system is based on accumulating initial people with a problem (that influence can resolve).*

3. **"Next, build a list.** *I started by emailing each person on my list seven letters, one every two weeks apart. Each letter discussed a different problem they might have, how my influence might help and extended an invitation to come to group meetings.*

4. **"Finally, reach out and explain how your ideas might improve their life in some meaningful way.** *Today, instead of Wall Street Journal ads, I rely on key words from pathways like Facebook and Google and the viral impact of social media.*

The technology has changed greatly, but the four step routine is exactly the same.

- *Step #1: Have a well-defined purpose.*
- *Step #2: Align yourself with people and organizations that support your purpose.*
- *Step # 3: Build a list of contacts.*
- *Step #4: Reach out and explain the benefits to be gained from the influence offered.*

"Have a systematic way to stay in touch with those on your list, whether it's meetings, letters, emails, blogs, podcasts, tweets, Instagrams or any other modern communication that shares your thoughts and experiences on their problems and offers them solutions. Modern technology allows us to take an important purpose you believe in, make it better and then pass it along as nanoinfluencers."

Become Loyal to Your Inner Truth. Wise elder contributor, **Mark Joyous** shared his inspirational ideas, *"It seems my recent Birthday Candles have lit a long smoldering Fuse of Passion that Burns inside me to just finally let go & flow let it Rip = Ripple outward & reconnect with my deeper inner self & reconnect with others = Calling all Angels & Flying Hearts - Calling upward our Truest 'Higher Vibes Tribes' to see if we can't join hands & hearts & uplift each other to Dance into the Light - in Delightful Divine Dances that spiral us upward & onward to THRIVE & shed our light upon the trails we need to walk to fulfill our higher purposes & destinies...*

"It seems to me that the combination of our current currents of emotional energy and turbulent turmoil call for intuitive innate resonance, reasoning & knowledge - or WISDOM - beyond data & rational measurements: - (see News: today: Suicides being at a 50 Year Peak due to feelings of Hopelessness etc - by Mike Stobbe of the Associated Press) - it's not just the Trumpanzees but our systems of constant increase in stress & costs & speed & no time to digest or reflect & we're all guilty of US & THEM games - & all caught in whirlpools of past times...

"It seems to me that this combines with my own needs for launching my Higher Self toward whatever distant stars of destiny I am aiming my Astronaut Synergy Energy towards - I have to just drop anything that is not truly ME these days & follow the call of my Heart. As all my best Synergy Shamans say: "Become loyal to your innermost truth. Walk the path when all others abandon it. Follow the way of the Heart. Be Always Loyal.... to your Innermost Truth. Walk Life with loving kindness, powerful prayerful purpose, living beyond doubt-fear. Follow the Way... of your Heart.

"'I ask myself and all of you, 'What is your path?' You are in control of your Destiny. It's up to you to determine how events shape your outlook and your future. You may not control the winds, but you do set the sails. Still Crazy after all these years - (In a Good Way) - Still believing in Humanity's Uplift & Conscious Co-Evolutionary The leaps we must make to provide for a positive planet of 'THRIVE-ALL' = Are So FAR BEYOND mere 'Sustainability' or Spirituality - to a dimension of JOY that's often called Ecstatic Being - Nirvana or Heaven - All cultures have a term for it - just as all cultures have Golden Rules - but it involves us Living in the Light of our own Unique Gifts & Being Brave enough to listen to our own Hearts & have courageous conversations & 'Just do it!'"

Grand Friends. Wise elder contributor, **Lloyd Wright**, shares his idea that could involve wise elders. Lloyd writes, *"My idea is designed to help close the gap between those who have a lifetime contribution while living and those who* *are certain they have the answers, but are willing to listen. Years ago, our client at the television station, McDonalds, had an idea. They said, 'If we believe that it is important to deal directly with the family or rather the lack of family, it is vital to impact the youngest among us first.'*

"We saw violent crime on the up-swing in Colorado Springs, as we did in cities across America. We saw the crumbling of families from economic issues to a lack of a culture of simply 'not understanding how to be.' McDonalds believed that older people can make a difference to the children of broken families thereby influencing parents in those families.

They created a program called Grand Friends. I don't know if it even still exists, but it should and if it doesn't, wise elder men can restart it. Those of us who are retired or near retirement can give some time to this idea. Every single elementary and junior high teacher need helpers in the classroom. Teachers will bless us for the help and the children will bond and carry the lessons we can bring them, home every day.

"In my experience monitoring the program, I saw children's fascination by the stories and the mentoring. I watched as behavior literally changed in the classroom. A program like this has positive ramifications over a broad spectrum and should be recognized as a community effort from local government to business. I believe it can change an attitude, a mindset if you will, to realize the value of wise elder men and women."

Connecting Through Social Media. Wise Elder contributor, **Rafa Flores**, shared his ideas of how elders could connect with young people using social media. He wrote: *"Currently there are podcasts of many topics that are available on the 'web'. Is this where youth will find authentic wisdom? Face Book is filled with 'wise' platitudes. Is this where youth will find authentic wisdom? Do we design an app called 'Wise Elder' where a huge learned data base of one line platitudes is inputted by elders and the algorithm replies to a youth in an inter active way? www.cleverbot.com is one of those types of learning, talking computer algorithms that has been collecting phrases from the world wide web for 15 plus years. People who log on to this site, feel that they are talking to a real human while full well knowing that it is a computer program. The people who use this site know it is a computer and feel safer with the machine than a face to face encounter with a person. Society and our paradigms in action. This may be part of the solution to how we get there."*

Wise Elder Classes in Schools. Wise elder contributor, **Rafa Flores**, came up with an innovative idea to have wise elders actually teach a required course taught by 4-6 wise elders. He writes: *"As a part of the core curricula, all children throughout their educational experience should be required to attend wise elder classes. These classes would be taught by 4 to 6 pairs of elders who are unrelated to each other and are half male, half female. In these classes, children would be mentored, would be trained to seek wise elders whenever they need, and the paradigm shift in society regarding the value of elders would change."*

Now It is Your Turn. Do you have innovative ideas you would like to share with others? Well, we have created a way for you to start sharing your ideas. You can join the online Wise Elders Forums by doing either or both of the following things:

1. Go to Facebook and search for the private *"Wise Elder Forum."* You will need to request to join and then get instructions on what else you need to become part of this online group.
2. There is also a Google *"Wise Elder Forum."* You can search for it at https://groups.google.com/. After you have done that, you will have to request to become a member. After being accepted on the Forum, you can send emails to anyone else who has his/her email address listed as part of the forum at TheWiseElderForum@googlegroups.com or just log onto the Google group and read what is posted there. You can then join any of the ongoing conversations. These are ways that you can reach out to any of the wise elder contributors in this book and create an ongoing dialogue with them. If you found this book useful and perhaps inspiring, you need to continue getting more good information and contacts from the contributors and from other readers of the book.

NOTES

INTRODUCTION

1. Weinhold, B. (2015). *The Male Mother. The Missing Skill Set for Fathers.* Colorado Springs, CO: CICRCL Press.

2. Weinhold, B. (2016). *The Servant Leader: What the World Needs Now.* Colorado Springs, CO: CICRCL Press.

3. *The Male Mother* (2015) pp. 2-4.

4. Schawbel, D. Feb 3, 2017. *53 Of The Most Interesting Facts About Baby Boomers.* Retrieved from: http://danschawbel.com/blog/53-of-the-most-interesting-facts-about-baby-boomers/.

5. Pappas, C. (Jan. 29, 2016). *8 Important Characteristics Of Baby Boomers eLearning Professionals Should Know.* Retrieved from https://elearningindustry.com/8-important-characteristics-baby-boomers-elearning-professionals-know.

6. Menec, V. (August, 2012) *Why seniors matter-and how they contribute to our everyday lives.* Retrieved from https://evidencenetwork.ca/why-seniors-matter-and-how-they-contribute-to-our-everyday-lives-2/.

7. Fried, L. (Jun 1, 2014). Making aging positive. *The Atlantic.* Retrieved from https://www.theatlantic.com/health/archive/2014/06/valuing-the-elderly-improving-public-health/371245/.

8. Ibid.

9. Meade, M. (2018). What is an elder? *The Eldership Academy.* Retrieved from http://www.eldershipacademy.org/what-is-an-elder/

10. The idiot and the wise man. (2018). *Spiritual Short Stories.* Retrieved from https://www.spiritual-short-stories.com/an-idiot-and-a-wise-man-russian-story-by-osho/

CHAPTER ONE

11. Hou, J. (2010). *Healthy Longevity Techniques: East-West Anti-Aging Strategies.* Bloomington, IL: AuthorHouse.

12. Macisaac, T. (Sept. 21, 2014). Did ancient people really have lifespans longer then 200 years? *Epoch Times.* Retrieved from https://www.ancient-origins.net/human-origins/did-ancient-people-really-have-lifespans-longer-200-years-002093

13. Hou, (2010). ibid.

14. Macisaac, T. (Updated April 16, 2017). Did ancient people really have lifespans longer then 200 years? *Epoch Times*. Retrieved from https://www.theepochtimes.com/did-ancient-people-really-have-lifespans-longer-than-200-years_969966.html

15. Search for this reference: not coming up with it. Will continue to search for it.

16. Naman, M. (2018). 10 factors to consider before moving your parents in. *Caring. Com.* Retrieved from https://www.caring.com/articles/moving-in-aging-relative-or-parent/

17. No author. (Dec. 6, 2017). 7 cultures that celebrate and respect their elders. *The Huffington Post.* Retrieved from https://www.huffpost.com/entry/what-other-cultures-can-teach_n_483422

18. Maxime. (December 3, 2018). *458 Fascinating Wisdom Quotes From the Best Minds (Ever).* Retrieved from http://wisdomquotes.com/words-of-wisdom/

19. Linn, D. (1999). *Sacred Legacies: Healing Your Past and Creating a Positive Future,* New York, NY: Ballentine Books. Retrieved from https://innerself.com/content/personal/relationships/5656-becoming-a-wise-elder-by-denise-linn.html

20. Erikson's 8 stages of psychosocial development. *Lumen.* Retrieved from https://courses.lumenlearning.com/teachereducationx92x1/chapter/eriksons-stages-of-psychosocial-development/

CHAPTER TWO

21. Gottberg, K. Carl Jung and the art of aging well. Retrieved from *Huffington Post* https://www.huffingtonpost.com/author/kathy-gottberg 09/28/2015. Updated Dec 06, 2017.

22. Ibid.

23. Ibid.

24. Hillman, J. (2011). *Senex & Puer (Uniform Edition of the Writings of James Hillman, Book 3).* Zurich, Switzerland: Spring Publications.

25. Ibid.

26. Von Franz, M.L. (1978) The Process of Individuation. *C. G. Jung, Man and His Symbols,* London: Picador, p. 207-208.

27. Created by the author (2018).

28. LaBier, D. (2016). Attitude to Aging Impacts Everything About Aging. *Psychology Today.* Retrieved from https://www.psychologytoday.com/us/blog/the-new-resilience/201612/attitude-aging-impacts-everything-about-aging

29. Weinhold, B. (2017). *Twisted beliefs: Distorting the Lines Between Fantasy and Reality.* Colorado Springs, CO: CICRCL Press.

30. Ibid.

31. Ibid.

32. *The Wise Old Man.* Moral Stories. Retrieved from https://www.moralstories.org/the-wilse-old-man/

CHAPTER THREE

33. Fry, R, (May 24, 2016). For first time in modern era, living with parents edges out other living arrangements for 18,034 year-olds. *Pew Research Center*. Retrieved from http://www.pewsocialtrends.org/2016/05/24/for-first-time-in-modern-era-living-with-parents-edges-out-other-living-arrangements-for-18-to-34-year-olds/

34. Gaille, B. (2017). 23 statistics on grandparents raising grandchildren. Retrieved from https://brandongaille.com/21-statistics-on-grandparents-raising-grandchildren/

35. Old Wise Man (May 24, 2012). *Zendictive*. Retrieved from https://zendictive.wordpress.com/2012/05/26/old-wise-man/

CHAPTER FOUR

36. Campbell, J. (2008). *The Hero with a Thousand Faces: The Collected Works of Joseph Campbell*. Novato, CA: New World Library.

37. Harvey, A. (2000). *The Way of Passion: A Celebration of Rumi*. New York, Ny: Penguin. Putnam.

38. Arrian. A. (2007). *The Second Half of Life: Opening the Eight Gates of Wisdom*. Audio tape. Boulder, CO: Sounds True.

39. Pawula, S. (Nov. 23, 2017). *The True Meaning of Non-Attachment and How It Sets You Free*. Retrieved from https://www.alwayswellwithin.com/blog/2013/11/24/non-attachment

40. Moody, H. R., and Carroll, D. (1997) *The Five Stages of the Soul*. New York: Anchor Books, pp. 133–134).

CHAPTER FIVE

41. Levy, N. (July 11, 2017). *The Wisdom of Our Elders*. Retrieved from http://www.handmaker.org/about/blog/post/handmaker-blog/2017/07/11/the-wisdom-of-our-elders

42. *Words of Wisdom*. Retrieved from http://www.inhomecaresolutions.com/inhomecore/wp-content/uploads/2017/03/no.09-1.jpg

CHAPTER SIX

43. Lyon, L. (Sept 26, 2012). 26 steps that can lead to longevity. *U.S. News & World Report*. Retrieved from https://health.usnews.com/health-news/articles/2012/09/26/26-healthy-steps-that-can-lead-to-longevity

44. Bollinger, T. *How to Optimize Your Cells for Healthy Aging*. Retrieved from https://thetruthaboutcancer.com/healthy-aging/?mpweb=144-7466536-744164732

45. Weinhold, B. (2017). *The Servant Leader*. Colorado Springs, Co: CICRCL Press.

46. Felitti, V., Anda, R., et.al. (1998). Relationship of childhood abuse and household dysfunction to many of the leading causes of death in adults: The adverse child-

hood experiences (ACE) study. *American Journal of Preventative Medicine. 14* (4) pp. 245-258.

47. Gilbert, L. et.al. (2015). Childhood adversity and adult chronic disease: An update from states and the District of Columbia 2010. *American Journal of Preventative Medicine. 218* (3) pp. 345-349.

48. Brodie, W. (2001). *The Cancer Personality: Its Importance in Healing.* Retrieved from http://www.alternative-cancer-care.com/the-cancer-personality.html

CHAPTER SEVEN

49. Hoeller, S. (1989). *The Gnostic Jung and the Seven Sermons To The Dead.* Wheaton, IL: Quest Books.

50. Weinhold, B. & Weinhold, J. (2017). *How To Break Free of the Drama Triangle and Victim Consciousness.* Colorado Springs, CO: CICRCL Press.

51. Hillman, J. (1966). Betrayal: Lecture delivered October, 2, 1964. London, UK: *Guild for Pastoral Psychology.*

CHAPTER EIGHT

52. Robbins, L. (2015). *Gauging Aging: How Does the American Public Truly Perceive Older Age–And Older People?* American Society on Aging. Retrieved from https://www.asaging.org/blog/gauging-aging-how-does-american-public-truly-perceive-older-age-and-older-people

53. Berger, R. (2017) *Aging in America: Ageism and General Attitudes toward Growing Old and the Elderly.* Open Journal of Social Sciences, 5, 183-198. https://doi.org/10.4236/jss.2017.58015

54. Growing Old in America: Expectations vs. Reality. (2009). Taylor, P. Ed. *Pew Research Center.* Retrieved from http://www.pewsocialtrends.org/2009/06/29/growing-old-in-america-expectations-vs-reality/

55. Ibid.

56. Larsen, D. (Sept. 1, 2017). Ways to Honor Our Elders. *A Place For Mom.* Retrieved from https://www.aplaceformom.com/blog/8-22-16-ways-to-honor-our-elders/

57. Retrieved from https://www.aplaceformom.com/blog/5-13-14-reasons-to-learn-your-family-history/

CHAPTER NINE

58. Hollis, J. (2005). *Finding Meaning in the Second Half of Life: How to Finally, Really Grow Up.* New York, NY: Penguin Group.

59. Weinhold, B, (2917). *Freaked Out: How Hidden Developmental Traumas Can Disrupt Your Life and Relationships.* Colorado Springs, CO: CICRCL Press, pp. 41-44.

60. Diamond, J. (1989). *The Adrenaline Addict: Hooked on Danger and Excitement.* Willits, CA: Self- Published.

61. Feletti, V. & Anda, R. et al. (1998). Relationship of childhood abuse and household dysfunction to many of the leading causes of death in adults: The adverse childhood experiences (ACE) study. *Ma. J. Prev. Med.* 13(4). pp. 245–256.

62. Weinhold, B. & Weinhold, J. (2017a). *Breaking Free of The Drama Triangle and Victim Consciousness.* Colorado Springs, CO: CICRCL Press.

63. Weinhold, B, (2917). Freaked out: How hidden developmental traumas can disrupt your life and relationships. Colorado Springs, CO: CICRCL Press, pp.183-185.

64. Siegel, B. (1986). *Love, Medicine and Miracles.* New York: Harper and Row.

65. Weinhold, B. & Weinhold, J. (2017). *Betrayal and the Path of the Heart.* Colorado springs, CO: CICRCL Press

CHAPTER ELEVEN

66. Shilling, v. (March 18, 2017). 10 Ways to Respect Your Native Elders. *Indian Country Today.* Retrieved from https://newsmaven.io/indiancountrytoday/archive/10-ways-to-respect-your-native-elders-3h9-D7XKskGu3uUOGpAR7g/

67. How They Should They Be Treated (Sept 1, 2017). Retrieved from https://www.google.com/search?q=how+should+the+elderly+be+treated&sa=X&ved=2ahUKEwiOqMCY_e3eAhXn3YMKHdKDB7gQ1QIoB3oECAQQCA&biw=1252&bih=746

68. Rains M. and McClinn, K. (2013). What is your resiliency score? Retrieved from https://acestoohigh.com/got-your-ace-score/

69. Nakazawa, D. (Aug. 7, 2015). 7 Ways Childhood Adversity Can Change Your Brain. *Psychology Today.* Retrieved from https://www.psychologytoday.com/us/blog/the-last-best-cure/201508/7-ways-childhood-adversity-can-change-your-brain

Made in the USA
San Bernardino, CA
18 January 2019